Frankfurt

2nd Edition

by Darwin Porter & Danforth Prince

Here's what critics say about Frommer's:

"Amazingly easy to use. Very portable, very complete."

—*Booklist*

"Detailed, accurate, and easy-to-read information for all price ranges."

—*Glamour Magazine*

Wiley Publishing, Inc.

Published by:

WILEY PUBLISHING, INC.
111 River St.
Hoboken, NJ 07030

ISBN 0-7645-3912-4
ISSN 1534-9179

Editor: Billy Fox
Production Editor: Donna Wright
Photo Editor: Richard Fox
Cartographer: Elizabeth Puhl
Production by Wiley Indianapolis Composition Services

Front cover photo: View of City Hall with flowers in the foreground

For information on our other products and services or to obtain technical support, please contact our Customer Care Department within the U.S. at 800-762-2974, outside the U.S. at 317-572-3993 or fax 317-572-4002.

Wiley also publishes its books in a variety of electronic formats. Some content that appears in print may not be available in electronic formats.

Manufactured in the United States of America

5 4 3 2 1

Contents

List of Maps

ABOUT THE AUTHOR

Veteran travel writers **Darwin Porter** and **Danforth Prince** have written numerous best-selling Frommer's guides, notably to Germany, France, Italy, England, and Spain. Porter, who was bureau chief for the *Miami Herald* when he was 21, wrote the first Frommer's guide to Germany and has traveled extensively in the country. Prince, who began writing with Porter in 1982, worked for the Paris bureau of the *New York Times*.

AN INVITATION TO THE READER

In researching this book, we discovered many wonderful places—hotels, restaurants, shops, and more. We're sure you'll find others. Please tell us about them, so we can share the information with your fellow travelers in upcoming editions. If you were disappointed with a recommendation, we'd love to know that, too. Please write to:

Frommer's Portable Frankfurt, 2nd Edition
Wiley Publishing, Inc. • 111 River St. • Hoboken, NJ 07030

AN ADDITIONAL NOTE

Please be advised that travel information is subject to change at any time—and this is especially true of prices. We therefore suggest that you write or call ahead for confirmation when making your travel plans. The authors, editors, and publisher cannot be held responsible for the experiences of readers while traveling. Your safety is important to us, however, so we encourage you to stay alert and be aware of your surroundings. Keep a close eye on cameras, purses, and wallets, all favorite targets of thieves and pickpockets.

FROMMER'S STAR RATINGS, ICONS & ABBREVIATIONS

Every hotel, restaurant, and attraction listing in this guide has been ranked for quality, value, service, amenities, and special features using a **star-rating system.** In country, state, and regional guides, we also rate towns and regions to help you narrow down your choices and budget your time accordingly. Hotels and restaurants are rated on a scale of zero (recommended) to three stars (exceptional). Attractions, shopping, nightlife, towns, and regions are rated according to the following scale: zero stars (recommended), one star (highly recommended), two stars (very highly recommended), and three stars (must-see).

In addition to the star-rating system, we also use **seven feature icons** that point you to the great deals, in-the-know advice and unique experiences that separate travelers from tourists. Throughout the book, look for:

Finds	Special finds—those places only insiders know about
Fun Fact	Fun facts—details that make travelers more informed and their trips more fun
Kids	Best bets for kids—advice for the whole family
Moments	Special moments—those experiences that memories are made of
Overrated	Places or experiences not worth your time or money
Tips	Insider tips—some great ways to save time and money
Value	Great values—where to get the best deals

The following **abbreviations** are used for credit cards:

AE	American Express	DISC	Discover	V	Visa
DC	Diners Club	MC	MasterCard		

FROMMERS.COM

Now that you have the guidebook to a great trip, visit our website at **www.frommers.com** for travel information on more than 3,000 destinations. With features updated regularly, we give you instant access to the most current trip-planning information available. At Frommers.com, you'll also find the best prices on airfares, accommodations, and car rentals—and you can even book travel online through our travel booking partners. At Frommers.com, you'll also find the following:

- Online updates to our most popular guidebooks
- Vacation sweepstakes and contest giveaways
- Newsletter highlighting the hottest travel trends
- Online travel message boards with featured travel discussions

The Best of Frankfurt

The thriving industrial metropolis of Frankfurt, Germany's fifth-largest city and Goethe's hometown, may well be your first glimpse of Germany.

Most international flights land at Frankfurt's huge airport, and its massive 19th-century railway station is the busiest in Europe. Frankfurt is a heavily industrial city, with more than 2,450 factories operating around the *Furt* (ford) on the Main River, where the Frankish tribes once settled. As the home of the Bundesbank, Germany's central bank, Frankfurt is also the country's financial center. It's been a major banking city ever since the Rothschilds opened their first bank here in 1798. Frankfurt also has a leading stock exchange.

Frankfurt's international trade fairs in spring and autumn bring some 1.5 million visitors to the city and its Messe Frankfurt (fairgrounds), often causing a logjam at hotels. Fairs include the Motor Show, the Textile Fair, the Chemical Industries Fair, and the Cookery Fair. But the best known is the Frankfurt Book Fair, which draws some 5,500 publishers from nearly 100 countries and is the most important meeting place in the world for the acquisition and sale of book rights and translations.

If all roads used to lead to Rome, today they seem to converge on Frankfurt, making it the hub of a great network of European traffic routes. Frankfurt today is both a much visited business center and a tourist destination with a distinct personality.

1 Frommer's Favorite Frankfurt Experiences

- **Meeting Young Frankfurters at Chic Bars.** The young professionals of Frankfurt meet and mingle after work at some of Germany's hippest bars. Patronizing these places is the best way to sample the pulse of the city. Join the Versace crowd, for example, at Studio Bar and sip your cocktail against the bar's funky decor. This is a penthouse bar with a rooftop terrace. There are dozens of other similarly chic bars. See "Bars & Cafes" in chapter 9.

Germany

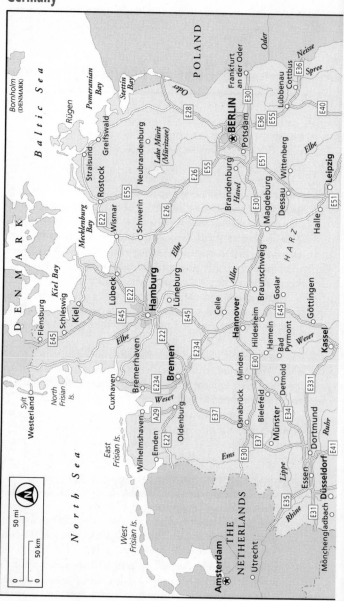

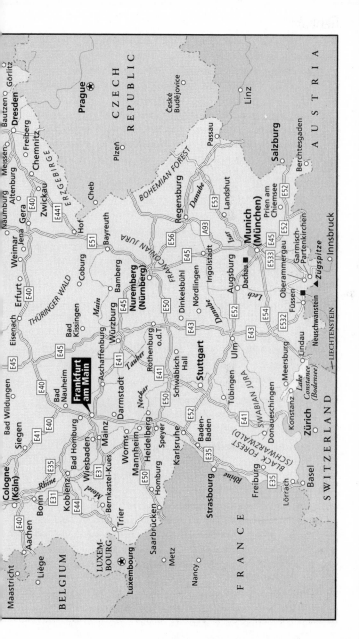

3

- **A Night in a Jazzkeller.** Frankfurt is Germany's jazz capital, mainly because of Der Jazzkeller. Established in the 1950s, it has hosted world-famous jazz performers like Frank Sinatra and Louis Armstrong. See "The Club & Music Scene" in chapter 9 for more details.

- **Strolling Among the Sheltering Palms.** Work off that pork knuckle lunch with a long walk through the Palmengarten. Numerous specimens of exotic flora vie for your attention, which easily strays to an ornamental pond surrounded by spinning mops of bright colors meant to evoke "dancing flowers." Rent a boat and go rowing on the small lake. See p. 118.

- **Taking in the View.** At the Main Tower Restaurant & Bar, you can truly sense why Frankfurt is called "Mainhattan," or Manhattan on the Main. As you head to the 53rd floor for a 360° panorama, you'll see a modern city of skyscrapers conjuring up visions of a Germanic Wall Street. The mighty metropolis is best viewed at night. See p. 73.

- **A Top Tipple of *Apfelwein*.** Don't think it's harmless cider: Frankfurt's apple wine is deceptively potent. You can sample it in such taverns as Zur Germania and Zum Gemalten Haus, south of the River Main in that little "town-within-a-town" of Sachsenhausen. It's typically downed with such dishes as *Rippchen mit Kraut* (smoked pork chop with sauerkraut). See "Sachsenhausen" in chapter 5.

2 Best Bets for Accommodations

See chapter 4 for full reviews of the following hotels.

- **Best Airport Hotel:** For those speedy takeoffs, **Frankfurt Sheraton Hotel,** Terminal 1 at the Flughafen (© **069/697-701**), puts you practically within boarding distance of your plane. A pedestrian bridge leads right into the terminal. Mercifully, the hotel is insulated from airport noise, and you're housed in great comfort, with everything designed to help you recover from jet lag. Business travelers will want to book into one of the so-called "Smart Rooms." See p. 63.

- **Best B&B:** Out in the Westend, **Hotel Liebig,** Liebigstrasse 45 (© **069/72-75-51**), is an upscale, intimate, and luxurious little inn decorated like the pages of a Laura Ashley catalogue. It's for the business or vacation traveler who seeks a more personalized atmosphere than that found at most of the Stadtmitte blockbuster hotels. See p. 59.

- **Best Boutique Star:** Billing itself as a "First Class Boutique Hotel," **Steigenberger Maxx Hotel Frankfurt City,** Lange Strasse 5–9 (✆ **069/21-930-0**), enjoys increasing favor among discerning travelers. Less expensive and minus the frills of the Steigenberger Frankfurter Hof, it caters to the no-nonsense traveler of today who wants top service and comfort, but not grandeur. See p. 55.

- **Best for Business Service:** Favored by business travelers from all over the world, **Arabella Sheraton Grand Hotel,** Konrad-Adenauer-Strasse 7 (✆ **800/325-3535** in the U.S. or 069/2-98-10), offers the best backup services for those conducting commerce in Frankfurt. In addition to its business center, each room comes with its own fax machine, dataport, and multilingual phone announcements. See p. 43.

- **Best Classic Hotel:** Known for elegance and style, **Hotel Hessischer Hof,** Friedrich-Ebert-Anlage 40 (✆ **800/223-6800** in the U.S. or 069/7-54-00), stands in a sea of commerce but elegantly removes itself, creating its own tasteful enclave within its interior. This is where you stay when you're negotiating that really big deal. Frankfurters will applaud your taste. See p. 46.

- **Best Historic Hotel:** Built in the late 19th century and still a city showcase, **Hotel National,** Baseler Strasse 50 (✆ **069/24-26-48-0**), was beautifully restored after Allied bombers delivered their payload. Still imbued with the aura of past glamour, the hotel has kept up-to-date and still attracts discerning visitors who prefer to avoid such over-commercialized "giants" as the Maritim. See p. 54.

- **Best Kept Secret:** One of the few hotels to escape wartime bombings, **Hotel Victoria,** Kaiserstrasse 59 (✆ **069/27306-0**), attracts savvy, in-the-know clients. All of its units are junior suites furnished with Italianate or Napoleonic furniture—grand comfort at competitive prices. See p. 54.

- **Best Lobby for Negotiating a Deal:** At the most famous, prestigious, and legendary hotel in Frankfurt, the **Steigenberger Frankfurter Hof,** Am Kaiserplatz (✆ **800/223-5652** in U.S. or 069/2-15-02), more big deals are made than perhaps anywhere else in Germany. At the book fair, for example, the lobby is awash with negotiations and contract signings. Established in 1872, the Frankfurter Hof still reigns supreme. See p. 50.

- **Best Location for the Fairgrounds:** One of the largest hotels in Germany, **Maritim Hotel Frankfurt,** Theodor-Heuss-Allee

(✆ **069/75-78-0**), an eight-story structure, is the only hotel in the city that provides direct access to the fairgrounds via a covered walkway. Exhibitors, salespeople, and buyers flock here. See p. 47.

- **Best Modern Hotel:** With its soaring 12-story atrium, the **Hilton Frankfurt,** Hochstrasse 4 (✆ **800/445-8667** in the U.S.), is firmly anchored in the 21st century. Since it opened in 1998, the hotel has won architectural awards for its theatrical design. Best are the executive units on the 11th and 12th floors. See p. 53.
- **Best Value:** One of the finest small hotels, **Mozart,** Parkstrasse 17 (✆ **069/55-08-31**), is a Westend winner, small and intimate and lying on the periphery of the Palmengarten. A polite, helpful staff welcomes you in style and treats you to comfort—all at a good price (at least by Frankfurt standards). See p. 61.
- **Best Weekend Escape:** If you're caught in Frankfurt for the weekend, nothing will restore your vitality more than the **Kempinski Hotel Gravenbruch Frankfurt,** at Neu Isenberg (✆ **06102/505-0**), set in a 14-hectare (36-acre) park on the city's outskirts. Built around the core of a 16th-century manor house, it is our favorite retreat. A man we encountered in the courtyard, shadowed by three Secret Service agents, agreed. It was Bill Clinton. See p. 62.

3 Best Bets for Dining

See chapter 5 for full reviews of the following restaurants.

- **Best Apple-Wine Tavern:** Nothing is more evocative of old Frankfurt than a meal at **Wagner's,** Schweizer Strasse 71 (✆ **069/61-25-65**), on the south bank of the Main. Charming and traditional, it's been serving *apfelwein* to diners since 1931, along with heaping platters of traditional German food such as schnitzels so large they overflow the plate. See p. 93.
- **Best French Cuisine:** Out in the Westend, **Erno's Bistro,** Liebigstrasse 15 (✆ **069/72-19-97**), is a chic rendezvous, and it remains one of the hottest dining tickets in Frankfurt. It uses only the freshest of ingredients, and serves food with a theatrical flair. The cuisine seems to improve year after year. See p. 84.
- **Best Hotel Restaurant:** Sheltered in Frankfurt's most prestigious hotel (the Steigenberger Frankfurter Hof), **Restaurant Français,** Am Kaiserplatz (✆ **069/2-15-02**), enjoys a grand

setting and delivers menu items that are composed of deluxe ingredients that are skillfully crafted in the kitchen and presented to admiring diners. See p. 67.

- **Best International Restaurant:** At the top of the heap among Frankfurt eateries, **Tiger Restaurant** (adjacent to the Tiger Palast theater), Heiligkreuzgasse 16–20 (✆ **069/92-00-22-50**), serves the best cuisine in Frankfurt. Ingredients are selected with loving care and fashioned into taste treats that please some of the world's most demanding palates. See p. 68.

- **Best for Making a Deal:** Attracting the literati, **Café im Literaturhaus,** Bockenheimer Landstrasse 102 (✆ **069/74-55-50**), is where you go to negotiate that book contract. It is, in fact, called "the largest literary marketplace in the world." Its international cuisine is good too. Even if you aren't looking to make a book deal, it's still a fine restaurant. See p. 88.

- **Best New Age Cuisine:** Nobody brings sunny Californian cuisine to Frankfurt better than **Pacific Colors,** in the lobby of the Hilton Hotel, Hochstrasse 4 (✆ **069/1338-000**). See p. 75.

- **Best Traditional Restaurant:** The age of Bismarck lives on at the **Weinhaus Brückenkeller,** Schützenstrasse 6 (✆ **069/29-80-07-0**), where strolling musicians entertain you as you partake of the refined German and international cuisine. Huge wooden barrels decorated with scenes from Goethe's *Faust* contribute to the atmosphere. See p. 70.

- **Best View:** From the 53rd floor of one of the tallest buildings in Frankfurt, **Main Tower Restaurant & Bar,** Neue Mainzer Strasse 52–58 (✆ **069/36-50-47-77**), dazzles not just with the panoramic scenery but also its excellent Continental cuisine, which is served to a diverse clientele from all over the world. See p. 73.

2

Planning Your Trip to Frankfurt

At the heart of the Continent and at the crossroads that linked the north of Europe with the Mediterranean, Frankfurt has always been fueled by trade and traffic. It still is today, after 12 centuries. In fact, even more people visit Frankfurt every year than live there. Its most famous historic resident, Goethe, would look with amazement at his native city playing host to the world in its latest reincarnation as "Bankfurt" or "Mainhattan" (Manhattan on the Main), as it is often called.

This chapter covers everything you need to know to make trip-planning a snap, from when to go to how to shop for the best airfare. Before you go, you might also want to scan what's out there at www.frankfurt-main.de.

1 Visitor Information

To get visitor information before leaving for Germany, you can contact the headquarters of the **German National Tourist Board** at Beethovenstrasse 69, 60325 Frankfurt am Main (✆ **069/974-640**). You'll also find a German National Tourist Office in **New York** at 122 E. 42nd St., 52nd Floor, New York, NY 10168-0072 (✆ **212/ 661-7200**); in **Toronto,** P.O. Box 65162, Toronto, ON M4K 3Z2 (✆ **877/315-6237**); and in **London** write to P.O. Box 2695, London W1A 3TN (✆ **020/7317-0908**). There are also tourist offices in about 20 other international cities, including Hong Kong, Johannesburg, Milan, Paris, and Sydney. You'll find the tourist board **online** at www.germany-tourism.de or you can **e-mail** the board at gntony@aol.com or germanto@idirect.com.

2 Entry Requirements & Customs

ENTRY REQUIREMENTS
Every U.S., Canadian, British, and Australian traveler entering Germany must hold a **valid passport.** You won't need a visa unless

you're staying longer than 3 months. Safeguard your passport in an inconspicuous, inaccessible place like a money belt. If you lose your passport, visit the nearest consulate of your native country as soon as possible for a replacement. It's always a good idea to keep a photocopy of your passport separate from the passport itself; the photocopy helps expedite replacement if your passport gets lost or stolen.

For an up-to-date country-by-country listing of passport requirements around the world, go to the "Foreign Entry Requirement" Web page of the U.S. State Department at **http://travel.state.gov/ foreignentryreqs.html**.

CUSTOMS
WHAT YOU CAN BRING INTO FRANKFURT
In general, items required for personal and professional use or consumption may be brought into Germany duty-free and without hassle. No duty is levied for a private car, as long as you report it. You can also bring in gifts duty-free up to a total value of 175€.

The following items are permitted into Germany duty-free from non-EU counties: 200 cigarettes, or 100 cigarillos, or 50 cigars, or 250 grams of smoking tobacco; 1 liter of liquor above 44 proof, or 2 liters of liquor less than 44 proof, or 2 liters of wine; 50 grams of perfume and 0.25 liters of eau de cologne; 500 grams of coffee; 100 grams of tea. From EU countries the duty-free limits are higher: 300 cigarettes; 1.5 liters of liquor above 44 proof, or 3 liters of liquor less than 44 proof, or 4 liters of wine; 75 grams of perfume and 0.375 liters of eau de cologne; 750 grams of coffee; 150 grams of tea. Duty-free allowances are authorized only when the items are carried in the traveler's personal baggage.

WHAT YOU CAN TAKE HOME FROM FRANKFURT
Returning **U.S. citizens** who have been away for at least 48 hours are allowed to bring back, once every 30 days, $800 worth of merchandise duty-free. You'll be charged a flat rate of 4% duty on the next $1,000 worth of purchases. Be sure to have your receipts handy. On mailed gifts, the duty-free limit is $100. With some exceptions, you cannot bring fresh fruits and vegetables into the United States. For specifics on what you can bring back, download the invaluable free pamphlet *Know Before You Go* online at **www. customs.gov**. (Click on "Travel" or "Publications," then "Know Before You Go.") Or contact the **U.S. Customs Service,** 1300 Pennsylvania Ave. NW, Washington, DC 20229 (© **877/287-8667**) and request the pamphlet.

For a clear summary of **Canadian** rules, write for the booklet *I Declare,* issued by the **Canada Customs and Revenue Agency** (© **800/461-9999** in Canada, or 204/983-3500; www.ccra-adrc. gc.ca). Canada allows its citizens a C$750 exemption, and you're allowed to bring back duty-free one carton of cigarettes, one can of tobacco, 40 imperial ounces of liquor, and 50 cigars. In addition, you're allowed to mail gifts to Canada valued at less than C$60 a day, provided they're unsolicited and don't contain alcohol or tobacco (write on the package "Unsolicited gift, under $60 value"). All valuables should be declared on the Y-38 form before departure from Canada, including serial numbers of valuables you already own, such as expensive foreign cameras. *Note:* The C$750 exemption can only be used once a year and only after an absence of 7 days.

Citizens of the U.K. who are **returning from a European Union (EU) country** will go through a separate Customs exit (called the "Blue Exit") especially for EU travelers. In essence, there is no limit on what you can bring back from an EU country, as long as the items are for personal use (this includes gifts), and you have already paid the necessary duty and tax. However, Customs law sets out guidance levels. If you bring in more than these levels, you may be asked to prove that the goods are for your own use. Guidance levels on goods bought in the EU for your own use are 800 cigarettes, 200 cigars, 1 kilogram of smoking tobacco, 10 liters of spirits, 90 liters of wine (of this not more than 60 liters can be sparkling wine), and 110 liters of beer.

The duty-free allowance in **Australia** is A$400 or, for those under 18, A$200. Citizens can bring in 250 cigarettes or 250 grams of loose tobacco, and 1,125 milliliters of alcohol. If you're returning with valuables you already own, such as foreign-made cameras, you should file form B263. A helpful brochure available from Australian consulates or Customs offices is *Know Before You Go.* For more information, call the **Australian Customs Service** at © **1300/363-263,** or log on to www.customs.gov.au.

The duty-free allowance for **New Zealand** is NZ$700. Citizens over 17 can bring in 200 cigarettes, 50 cigars, or 250 grams of tobacco (or a mixture of all three if their combined weight doesn't exceed 250g); plus 4.5 liters of wine and beer, or 1.125ml of liquor. New Zealand currency does not carry import or export restrictions. Fill out a certificate of export, listing the valuables you are taking out of the country; that way, you can bring them back without paying duty. Most questions are answered in a free pamphlet available at New Zealand consulates and Customs offices called *New Zealand Customs Guide for Travellers, Notice No. 4.* For more information, contact **New Zealand Customs,** The Customhouse, 17–21 Whitmore St., Box 2218, Wellington (ⓒ **04/473-6099** or 0800/428-786; www.customs.govt.nz).

3 Money

While this book includes listings of the best hotels, restaurants, and attractions in Frankfurt, our ultimate aim is to help you stretch your buying power—to show that you don't need to pay scalpers' prices for charm, top-grade comfort, and quality food. But be advised that Frankfurt can be a very expensive city, the equivalent of London and Paris.

Although prices are sky-high in Frankfurt, you generally get good value for your money. The inflation rate, unlike that of most of the world, has remained low. Hotels are usually clean and comfortable, and restaurants generally offer good cuisine and ample portions made with quality ingredients. Public transportation is fast and on time, and most service personnel treat you with respect.

In Germany many prices for children (generally defined as ages 6 to 17) are considerably lower than for adults. Children under 6 are often charged no admission or other fee. Always ask about discounts.

THE EURO

In 1999, the countries that chose to adopt the euro—Austria, Belgium, Finland, France, Germany, Ireland, Italy, Luxembourg, the Netherlands, Portugal, and Spain—officially locked their exchange rates together and switched most business transactions and computer and credit card banking over to the new single currency—which, after some ups and significant downs, currently seems level with the dollar ($1 = 1€). Greece joined the group in 2001. Several countries have opted out from switching over for the time being, including Britain, Denmark, and Sweden. Switzerland is not part of the EU.

ATMS

The easiest and best way to get cash away from home is from an ATM (automated teller machine). ATMs are found all over Frankfurt. The **Cirrus** (ⓒ 800/424-7787; www.mastercard.com) and **PLUS** (ⓒ 800/843-7587; www.visa.com) networks span the globe; look at the back of your bank card to see which network you're on, then call or check online for ATM locations at your destination. Be sure you know your personal identification number (PIN) before you leave home and be sure to find out your daily withdrawal limit before you depart. Also keep in mind that many banks impose a fee every time a card is used at a different bank's ATM, and that fee can be higher for international transactions (up to $5 or more) than for domestic ones (where they're rarely more than $1.50). On top of this, the bank from which you withdraw cash may charge its own fee. To compare banks' ATM fees within the U.S., use www.bankrate.com. For international withdrawal fees, ask your bank.

You can also get cash advances on your credit card at an ATM. Keep in mind that credit card companies try to protect themselves from theft by limiting the funds someone can withdraw outside their home country, so call your credit card company before you leave home.

TRAVELER'S CHECKS

Traveler's checks are something of an anachronism from the days before the ATM made cash accessible at any time. Traveler's checks used to be the only sound alternative to traveling with dangerously large amounts of cash. They were as reliable as currency, but, unlike cash, could be replaced if lost or stolen.

These days, traveler's checks are less necessary because most cities have 24-hour ATMs that allow you to withdraw small amounts of cash as needed. However, keep in mind that you will likely be charged an ATM withdrawal fee if the bank is not your own, so if you're withdrawing money every day, you might be better off with traveler's checks—provided that you don't mind showing identification every time you want to cash one.

You can get traveler's checks at almost any bank. **American Express** offers denominations of $20, $50, $100, $500, and (for cardholders only) $1,000. You'll pay a service charge ranging from 1% to 4%. You can also get American Express traveler's checks over the phone by calling ✆ **800/221-7282;** Amex gold and platinum cardholders who use this number are exempt from the 1% fee. AAA members can obtain checks without a fee at most AAA offices.

Visa offers traveler's checks at Citibank locations nationwide, as well as at several other banks. The service charge ranges between 1.5% and 2%; checks come in denominations of $20, $50, $100, $500, and $1,000. Call ✆ **800/732-1322** for information. **MasterCard** also offers traveler's checks. Call ✆ **800/223-9920** for a location near you.

Foreign currency traveler's checks are useful if you're traveling to one country, or to the euro zone; they're accepted at locations, such as bed-and-breakfasts, where dollar checks may not be

---

Tips **Dear Visa: I'm Off to Frankfurt!**

Some credit card companies recommend that you notify them of any impending trip abroad so that they don't become suspicious and block your charges when the card is used numerous times in a foreign destination. Even if you don't call your credit card company in advance, you can always dial the card's toll-free emergency number if a charge is refused—a good reason to carry the phone number with you. But perhaps the most important lesson here is to carry more than one card with you on your trip; a card might not work for any number of reasons, so having a backup is the smart way to go.

---

accepted, and they minimize the amount of math you have to do at your destination. **American Express** offers checks in Australian dollars, Canadian dollars, British pounds, euros, and Japanese yen. **Visa** checks come in Australian, Canadian, British, and euro versions; **MasterCard** offers those four plus yen and South African rands.

If you choose to carry traveler's checks, be sure to keep a record of their serial numbers separate from your checks in the event that they are stolen or lost. You'll get a refund faster if you know the numbers.

CREDIT CARDS

Credit cards are a safe way to carry money, they provide a convenient record of all your expenses, and they generally offer good exchange rates. You can also withdraw cash advances from your credit cards at banks or ATMs, provided you know your PIN. If you've forgotten yours, or didn't even know you had one, call the number on the back of your credit card and ask the bank to send it to you. It usually takes 5 to 7 business days, though some banks will provide the number over the phone if you tell them your mother's maiden name or some other personal information. Your credit card company will likely charge a commission (1% or 2%) on every foreign purchase you make, but don't sweat this small stuff: For most purchases, you'll still get the best deal with credit cards when you factor in things like ATM fees and higher traveler's check exchange rates.

MasterCard and Visa are commonly accepted at most establishments in the world. American Express is number three. Diners Club, disappearing in many establishments, is still widely accepted in Frankfurt.

What Things Cost in Frankfurt	**Euros/US$**
Taxi from airport to Stadtmitte	25.00
Underground transit, one-way, within central Frankfurt	1.65
Underground from Stadtmitte to Frankfurt's suburbs	3.20
Local telephone call	.15
Lunch for one at Main Tower Restaurant (moderate)	24.00
Lunch for one at Bull + Bear (inexpensive)	12.00
Dinner for one, without wine, at Weinhaus Brückenkeller (expensive)	56.00
Dinner for one, without wine, at Charlot (moderate)	40.00
Dinner for one, without wine, at Indian Curry House (inexpensive)	16.00
Double room at Le Meridien Parkhotel (very expensive)	345.00
Double room at Best Western Scala (moderate)	120.00
Double room at Hotel Consul (inexpensive)	77.00
Half a liter of beer	2.00–3.00
Coca Cola in a restaurant	2.00–3.00
Cup of coffee	2.00–3.00
Glass of wine	4.00–7.00
Roll of color film, 36 exposures	5.00
Admission to Goethe Haus	5.00
Movie ticket	5.00–8.00
Tickets to Alte Opera	35.00–72.00

4 When to Go

CLIMATE

Frankfurt has a temperate, changeable climate. Winters are generally cool and wet, though temperatures often dip below freezing and it sometimes snows. Summers are pleasant and rarely blazingly hot; however, for this reason Frankfurt establishments often lack air-conditioning. Many visitors find fall and late spring to be the best times to come to the city.

Frankfurt's Average Daytime Temperature & Rainfall (Inches)

	Jan	Feb	Mar	Apr	May	June	July	Aug	Sept	Oct	Nov	Dec
°F	34	36	42	49	57	63	66	66	58	50	41	35
°C	1	2	6	9	14	17	19	19	14	10	5	2
Rainfall	6.5	5.1	5.6	5.7	5.9	5.5	5.0	5.1	4.2	4.8	6.5	6.0

HOLIDAYS

Public holidays are January 1 (New Year's Day), Easter (Good Friday and Easter Monday), May 1 (Labor Day), Ascension Day (10 days before Pentecost/Whitsunday, the 7th Sunday after Easter), Whitmonday (day after Pentecost/Whitsunday), October 3 (Day of German Unity), November 17 (Day of Prayer and Repentance), and December 25 to 26 (Christmas). In addition, the following holidays are observed in some German states: January 6 (Epiphany), Corpus Christi (10 days after Pentecost), August 15 (Assumption), and November 1 (All Saints' Day).

FRANKFURT CALENDAR OF EVENTS

The German National Tourist board (GNTB) publishes a free calendar of forth-coming events in Germany three times a year, in April, October, and January; the first two are half-yearly calendars and the latter is a yearly preview. They each give the dates of trade fairs and exhibitions, theatrical and musical per-formances, local and folk festivals, sporting events, conferences, and con-gresses throughout Germany, including Frankfurt. Specific dates given below are for 2004.

February

Frankfurt International Spring Fair. This is one of the principal consumer-goods trade fairs of Europe, and its origins go back centuries. For information, contact the **Messe Frankfurt Gubh** (© **069/7-57-50;** fax 069/75-75-64-33; 770/984-8023 in the U.S.). February 20 to 24.

Fasching. Carnival festivals take place throughout Germany, reaching their peak on the Tuesday (Mardi Gras) before Ash Wednesday (Feb 24).

April

Spring Dippemess. Traditional folk fair with high-tech rides and the traditional *Dippemarkt* (pottery market) at Ratsweg Square, center of the festival (© **069/2123-8990**). April 1 to 30.

Online Traveler's Toolbox

Veteran travelers usually carry some essential items to make their trips easier. Following is a selection of online tools to bookmark and use.

- **Visa ATM Locator** (www.visa.com), for locations of PLUS ATMs worldwide, or **MasterCard ATM Locator** (www. mastercard.com), for locations of Cirrus ATMs worldwide.
- **Foreign Languages for Travelers** (www.travlang.com). Learn basic terms in more than 70 languages and click on any underlined phrase to hear what it sounds like.
- **Intellicast** (www.intellicast.com) and **Weather.com** (www.weather.com). Give weather forecasts for cities around the world.
- **Mapquest** (www.mapquest.com). This best of the mapping sites lets you choose a specific address or destination, and in seconds, it will return a map and detailed directions.
- **Universal Currency Converter** (www.xe.com/ucc). See what your dollar or pound is worth in more than 100 other countries.

May

International May Festival, Wiesbaden. This city near Frankfurt hosts a premier cultural event—a series of artistic celebrations lasting one month. For information, contact the **Wiesbaden Tourist Office,** Rheinstrasse 15 (© **0611/1-72-97-80**).

June

Waldchestag. Frankfurt's National Festival takes place in the *Stadtwald,* the city forest. Rides, food fairs, and various forms of entertainment are featured (© **069/2123-8990**). Early June.

August

Museum Embankment Festival. This is a spectacular cultural and art festival, attracting both patrons and sightseers from around the globe. The banks of the Main are turned into a gigantic stage set for a multitude of artistic performances, highlighted by a wide range of music and special exhibitions at the major museums. Late August.

September

Fall Dippemess. This traditional folk fair with high-tech rides takes place at Ratsweg, the festival square. It centers around the *Dippemarkt* (© **069/2123-8990**). Early September.

October

Frankfurt Book Fair. A major international event for publishers, book dealers, agents, and authors. Contact the **Frankfurt Tourist Office** at © **069/21-23-8990** or www.frankfurt-book-fair.com. Mid-October.

November/December

Christmas Market. These take place all over Germany, but especially at Frankfurt, where locals and visitors buy their holiday presents from a wide array of merchants. The most active markets are found at Römerberg, Paulsplatz, Liebfrauenberg, Neue Kräme, Fahtor, and Mainkai. November 9 to December 19.

5 Travel Insurance

Frankfurt is not viewed as a risky destination, but the prudent traveler may want the extra protection of insurance in case of unforeseen disaster.

Check your existing insurance policies and credit card coverage before you buy travel insurance. You may already be covered for lost luggage, cancelled tickets, or medical expenses. The cost of travel insurance varies widely, depending on the cost and length of your trip, your age, health, and the type of trip you're taking.

TRIP-CANCELLATION INSURANCE   Trip-cancellation insurance helps you get your money back if you have to back out of a trip, if you have to go home early, or if your travel supplier goes bankrupt. Allowed reasons for cancellation can range from sickness to natural disasters to the State Department declaring your destination unsafe for travel. (Insurers usually won't cover vague fears, though, as many travelers discovered when they tried to cancel their trips in Oct 2001 because they were wary of flying.) In this unstable world, trip-cancellation insurance is a good buy if you're getting tickets well in advance—who knows what the state of the world, or of your airline, will be in 9 months? Insurance policy details vary, so read the fine print—and especially make sure that your airline or cruise line is on the list of carriers covered in case of bankruptcy.

For information, contact one of the following insurers: **Access America** (© 866/807-3982; www.accessamerica.com), **Travel**

Tips **Quick ID**

Tie a colorful ribbon or piece of yarn around your luggage handle, or slap a distinctive sticker on the side of your bag. This makes it less likely that someone will mistakenly appropriate it. And if your luggage gets lost, it will be easier to find.

Guard International (℅ 800/243-3174; www.travelguard.com), **Travel Insured International** (℅ 800/243-3174; www.travel insured.com), and **Travelex Insurance Services** (℅ 888/457-4602; www.travelex-insurance.com).

MEDICAL INSURANCE With the exception of certain HMOs and Medicare/Medicaid, your medical insurance should cover medical treatment—even hospital care—overseas. However, most out-of-country hospitals make you pay your bills up front, and send you a refund after you've returned home and filed the necessary paperwork. And in a worst-case scenario, there's the high cost of emergency evacuation. If you require additional medical insurance, try **MEDEX International** (℅ 800/MEDEX00 or 410/453-6300; www.medex assist.com) or **Travel Assistance International** (℅ **800/821-2828;** www.travelassistance.com; for general information on services, call the company's Worldwide Assistance Services, Inc., at ℅ **800/777-8710**).

LOST-LUGGAGE INSURANCE On international flights (including U.S. portions of international trips), baggage is limited to approximately $9.05 per pound, up to approximately $635 per checked bag. If you plan to check items more valuable than the standard liability, see if your valuables are covered by your homeowner's policy, get baggage insurance as part of your comprehensive travel-insurance package, or buy Travel Guard's "BagTrak" product. Don't buy insurance at the airport, as it's usually overpriced. Be sure to take any valuables or irreplaceable items with you in your carry-on luggage, as many valuables (including books, money, and electronics) aren't covered by airline policies.

If your luggage is lost, immediately file a lost-luggage claim at the airport, detailing the luggage contents. For most airlines, you must report delayed, damaged, or lost baggage within 4 hours of arrival. The airlines are required to deliver luggage, once found, directly to your house or destination free of charge.

6 Health & Safety

STAYING HEALTHY

Frankfurt medical facilities are among the best in the world. If a medical emergency arises, your hotel staff can usually put you in touch with a reliable doctor. If not, contact the American embassy or a consulate; each one maintains a list of English-speaking doctors. Of course, in Frankfurt it is almost impossible to find a doctor who does not speak English. Medical and hospital services aren't free, so be sure that you have appropriate insurance coverage before you travel.

If you suffer from a chronic illness, consult your doctor before your departure. For conditions like epilepsy, diabetes, or heart problems, wear a **MedicAlert Foundation** emblem (℃ **800/825-3785** or 800/432-5378; www.medicalert.org), which will immediately alert doctors to your condition and give them access to your records through MedicAlert's 24-hour hot line. Membership is $35, plus a $20 annual fee.

Pack prescription medication in your carry-on luggage. Carry written prescriptions in generic, not brand-name, form, and dispense all prescription medications from their original labeled vials. Also bring along copies of your prescriptions in case you lose your pills or run out.

For more information, contact the **International Association for Medical Assistance to Travellers** (IAMAT; ℃ **716/754-4883** or 519/836-0102 in Canada; fax 519/836-3412; www.iamat.org). This organization offers tips on travel and health concerns in foreign countries, and lists many local English-speaking doctors.

STAYING SAFE

Violent crime is rare in Frankfurt, but can occur, especially around the rail station. Most incidents of street crime consist of theft of unattended items and pickpocketing. There have been a few reports of aggravated assault against U.S. citizens in higher-risk areas. American travelers are advised to take the same precautions against crime as they would in any American city.

The loss or theft abroad of a U.S. passport should be reported immediately to the local police and the nearest U.S. embassy or consulate. If you are the victim of a crime while overseas, in addition to reporting it to local police, you should contact the nearest U.S. embassy or consulate for assistance. The embassy/consulate staff can, for example, help you find appropriate medical care, contact family members or friends, and explain how funds can be transferred. Although the investigation and prosecution of the crime is solely the responsibility of local authorities, consular officers can help you to understand the local criminal justice process and to find an attorney if needed.

TRAVELERS WITH DISABILITIES

Most disabilities shouldn't stop anyone from traveling—there are more options and resources out there than ever before.

Germany is one of the better countries for travelers with disabilities, and Frankfurt itself has excellent facilities. The tourist office can issue permits for drivers to allow access to parking areas for those with disabilities.

Many travel agencies offer customized tours and itineraries for travelers with disabilities. **Flying Wheels Travel** (© 507/451-5005; www.flyingwheelstravel.com) offers escorted tours and cruises that emphasize sports and private tours in minivans with lifts. **Accessible Journeys** (© 800/846-4537 or 610/521-0339; www.disabilitytravel. com) caters specifically to slow walkers and wheelchair travelers and their families and friends.

Organizations that offer assistance to travelers with disabilities include the **Moss Rehab Hospital** (www.mossresourcenet.org), which provides a library of accessible-travel resources online; the **Society for Accessible Travel and Hospitality** (© 212/447-7284; www.sath.org; annual membership fees: $45 adults, $30 seniors and students), which offers a wealth of travel resources for all types of disabilities and informed recommendations on destinations, access guides, travel agents, tour operators, vehicle rentals, and companion services; and the **American Foundation for the Blind** (© 800/232-5463; www.afb.org), which provides information on traveling with Seeing Eye dogs.

For more information specifically targeted to travelers with disabilities, the community website **iCan** (www.icanonline.net/channels/travel/index.cfm) has destination guides and several regular columns on accessible travel.

GAY & LESBIAN TRAVELERS

Although Frankfurt is home to a burgeoning community of gays and lesbians, they tend to be less politicized and less aggressively visible than in cities like Berlin and Köln. Be alert to the city's self-image as a mercantile city that has catered to the fiscal (and sexual) needs of foreign visitors for about a thousand years. If sex-for-hire raises itself as an option, don't be shocked or even surprised. It's estimated that there are as many as 700 male prostitutes working the trade conventions. Most tend to congregate in the vicinity of Hauptbahnhof, and many are new immigrants from points farther east, including some of the former Soviet Republics or satellite states.

Hotel staffs long ago learned to cast a blind eye on the phenomenon of commercial gents entertaining guests in their quarters, and won't get involved unless needed. But if the idea of paid companionship appeals to you, be alert to the spread of STDs, and activate appropriate security measures first (such as, safeguard most of your cash and all of your valuables in your hotel safe before heading upstairs). But frankly, there are so many gay bars in Frankfurt, and such a plethora of ready, willing, and available gay men, that you'll probably find that paying isn't really necessary. Also, know that the rougher-looking the crowd in your gay bar of choice (as is the case in Frankfurt's most extroverted leather bar, the Stall), the less likely the chance that some of the other patrons will try to hustle you. In any case, if you're not interested, "just say no."

Before you go, consider picking up a copy of ***Frommer's Gay & Lesbian Europe.*** Although the guide is not Frankfurt-specific, it has full coverage of the true gay mecca of Germany, the capital city of Berlin. You might also want to pick up a handy little guide you can carry around in your pocket, ***Frommer's Portable Berlin.***

The **International Gay & Lesbian Travel Association (IGLTA)** (© **800/448-8550** or 954/776-2626; www.iglta.org) is the trade association for the gay and lesbian travel industry, and offers an online directory of gay- and lesbian-friendly travel businesses; go to their website and click on "Members."

TIPS FOR SENIORS

Don't be shy about asking for discounts, and always carry some kind of identification, such as a driver's license, that shows your date of birth. Many hotels and airlines offer special rates for seniors; ask when you make your reservations. Seniors often qualify for reduced admission to theaters, museums, and other attractions, and discounted fares on public transportation.

Travel Companion Exchange, P.O. Box 833, Amityville, NY 11701 (© **800/392-1256** or 631/454-0880; fax 631/454-0170; www.whytravelalone.com), helps travelers 45 and older find compatible companions through a personal voice-mail service. Contact them for more information.

A most helpful publication is ***101 Tips for the Mature Traveler,*** available from **Grand Circle Travel,** 347 Congress St., Suite 3A, Boston, MA 02210 (✆ **800/221-2610** or 617/350-7500; fax 617/346-6700; www.gct.com).

Grand Circle Travel is also one of the hundreds of travel agencies specializing in vacations for seniors, but many of these packages are of the tour-bus variety, with free trips thrown in for those who organize groups of 10 or more. Seniors seeking more independent travel should probably consult a regular travel agent. **SAGA International Holidays,** 222 Berkeley St., Boston, MA 02116 (✆ **800/343-0273;** www.sagaholidays.com), offers inclusive tours and cruises for those 50 and older. If you want something more than the average vacation or guided tour, try **Elderhostel,** 11 Avenue de Lafayette, Boston, MA 02111-1746 (✆ **877/426-8056** or 617/426-7788; fax 977/426-2354; www.elderhostel.org), or the University of New Hampshire's **Interhostel** (✆ **800/733-9753** or 603/862-1147; www.learn.unh.edu), both variations on the same theme: educational travel for seniors. On these escorted tours, the days are packed with seminars, lectures, and field trips, and all the sightseeing is led by academic experts. Elderhostel arranges study programs around the world for those ages 55 and over (and a spouse or companion of any age). Most courses last about 3 weeks and many include airfare, accommodations in student dormitories or modest inns, meals, and tuition. Write or call for a free catalog, which lists upcoming courses and destinations. Interhostel takes travelers 50 and over (with companions over 40), and offers 2- and 3-week trips, mostly international.

7 Getting There

BY PLANE

Flying time to Frankfurt is about 7½ hours from New York, 10 hours from Chicago, and 12 hours from Los Angeles. There are also nonstop flights from the U.S. to Munich and Düsseldorf (though not to Berlin).

Lufthansa (✆ **800/645-3880;** www.lufthansa-usa.com) operates the most frequent service and flies to the greatest number of Germany's airports. From North America, Lufthansa serves 16 gateway cities. In any season, there are more than 100 weekly flights from these cities to Germany. The largest of the gateways is the New York City area, where flights depart from both JFK and Newark airports. From JFK there are daily flights to Frankfurt. From Newark, there are daily flights to Frankfurt, Munich, and Düsseldorf. Lufthansa's other gateways include Atlanta, Boston, Chicago, Dallas/Fort Worth, Detroit, Houston, Los Angeles, Miami, Philadelphia, San Francisco, and Washington, D.C. Lufthansa also flies to Germany from Toronto, Vancouver, Calgary, and Mexico City. The airline has a 10% discount for seniors over 60; the reduction applies to a traveling companion as well.

Lufthansa has an alliance with **United Airlines** and **Air Canada** to provide seamless air service to Germany and other parts of the globe from North America. Dubbed **"Star Alliance,"** the union allows cross-airline benefits, including travel on one or all of these airlines on one ticket, and frequent-flier credit to the participating airline of your choice. The Star Alliance also includes Scandinavian Airlines System, Thai Airways International, and Varig.

American Airlines (℃ 800/443-7300; www.aa.com) flies non-stop to Frankfurt daily from Dallas/Fort Worth, Miami, and Chicago. From Frankfurt, Düsseldorf, and London, among others, American's flights connect easily with ongoing flights to many other German cities on Lufthansa or British Airways.

Continental Airlines (℃ 800/231-0856; www.flycontinental. com) offers daily nonstop service between Newark and Frankfurt and Düsseldorf. The airline maintains excellent connections between Newark and its hubs in Cleveland and Houston. Continental also offers discounts and other benefits to seniors 62 and over and to their traveling companions, regardless of age.

From JFK airport in New York, **Delta Airlines** (℃ 800/241-4141; www.delta.com) offers daily service to both Frankfurt and (via Brussels) Hamburg. Delta is especially strong in service to Germany from its home base in Atlanta, with two daily nonstops to Frankfurt and daily nonstops to Munich, as well as Hamburg and Stuttgart via Paris. Delta also offers frequent nonstops to Frankfurt from Cincinnati (one of its major Midwestern hubs).

If you fly one of **KLM's** (℃ 800/374-7747; www.klm.com) frequent nonstop flights into Amsterdam from New York's JFK and from Atlanta, you can include a stopover in Holland. From Amsterdam, many flights on both KLM and Lufthansa fly into all the major cities of Germany, especially Frankfurt. Flights to Frankfurt on **Northwest Airlines** (℃ 800/225-2525; www.nwa.com), KLM's partner, are available out of Boston and Washington, D.C.

United Airlines (℃ 800/241-6522; www.united.com) offers daily nonstops from Washington, D.C., and Chicago to Frankfurt.

Furthermore, because of the Star Alliance (see above), all German flights by Lufthansa or Air Canada are honored as part of a United ticket. If you're interested in taking advantage of the Star Alliance, be sure to notify the United ticket agent when you are booking or inquiring about your flight.

From London, **British Airways** (© 08457/733-377 in the U.K.; www.british-airways.com) and Lufthansa (© 0895/773-7747 in London; www.lufthansa.com) are the most convenient carriers to the major German cities, including Frankfurt, Düsseldorf, Köln, München, and Berlin. It also serves Bremen, Hannover, and Stuttgart. **British Midland** (© 0870/6070-555 in the U.K.; www.flybmi.com) has two daily flights to Köln, four daily to Frankfurt, and one daily to Dresden.

From Ireland, **Aer Lingus** (© 01/886-8888; www.aerlingus.com) flies between Dublin and Frankfurt and Düsseldorf; **Lufthansa** (© 01/844-5544; www.lufthansa.com) flies from Frankfurt to Dublin. From Australia, **Qantas** (© 008-112-121 in Australia; www.qantas.com.au) flies from both Melbourne and Sydney to Frankfurt via Asia. Lufthansa offers cheap fares in conjunction with Qantas.

BY TRAIN
Frankfurt's main rail station, the **Hauptbahnhof,** is the busiest in Europe, and the arrival point for some 1,600 trains per day carrying about 255,000 passengers. A train arrives from most major cities of Germany every hour until 8pm. Many other European cities also have direct rail links with Frankfurt. For travel information, ticket reservations, and seat information, call **Deutsche Bahn** (© 01805/194-195;** www.bahn.de). The cost is .50€ per minute.

British Rail runs four trains a day to Germany from Victoria Station in London, crossing the water by ferry or jetfoil. Two trains depart from London's Liverpool Street Station, via Harwich-Hook of Holland. Most trains change at Köln for other German destinations, such as Frankfurt. You can purchase tickets through British Rail travel centers in London (© 877/677-1066; www.britrail.com). See "Under the Channel," below, for information about the Eurostar service running between London and Brussels via the Channel Tunnel ("Chunnel").

Train journeys can be lengthy. If you go by jetfoil, Frankfurt is 10 hours away from London; by Dover-Ostend ferry, it's 13 hours; and via the Ramsgate-Ostend ferry, it's 14 hours.

From **Paris** several trains depart throughout the day for points east, fanning out across eastern France to virtually every part of

Germany, including Frankfurt. For railway information on the French rail lines anywhere in Europe, call ✆ **08-36-35-35-35**. Likewise, trains depart from throughout Austria, Italy, Holland, Denmark, and the Czech Republic for all points in Germany, interconnecting into one of the most efficient, and densely routed, rail networks in the world. For information and timetables prior to your departure, call **Rail Europe** at (✆ **800/848-7245;** www.rail europe.com).

BY CAR & FERRY

The A3 and A5 Autobahns intersect at Frankfurt. The A3 comes in from the Netherlands, Köln, and Bonn, and continues east and south to Würzburg, Nürnberg, and München. The A5 comes from the northeast (Hannover, Bad Hersfeld) and continues south to Heidelberg, Mannheim, and Basel (Switzerland). From the west, the A60 connects with the A66, which leads to Frankfurt and the inner city, hooking up with the A3. Road signs and directions are frequently posted.

If you want to bring your car over from England, you face a choice of ports, from which you'll continue driving to Germany. **P & O Ferries** (✆ **800/677-8585** for North American reservations, or 08705/20-20-20 in the U.K.; www.posl.com) has 30 to 35 ferryboat crossings a day, depending on the season, between Dover in England and Calais in northeastern France. The crossing can take as little as 1 hour and 15 minutes. Once in Calais, the drive to Köln in Germany takes about 3 hours; from there, you can make the final lap southeast to Frankfurt. Other options involve passage through the Netherlands from Harwich, in the east of England, to the Hook of Holland for a sea crossing of about 8 hours. You can also take your car via the **Chunnel** (see below.)

BY BUS (COACH)

Frankfurt has long-distance bus service to about 800 German and European cities. Buses depart from the south side of the Hauptbahnhof. For information, contact **Deutsche Touring,** Am Römerhof 17, 60426 Frankfurt am Main (✆ **069/79-03-50;** www. deutsche-touring.com). Buses on long-haul journeys are equipped with toilets and partially reclining seats. They stop for 60 minutes every 4 hours for rest and refreshment breaks.

UNDER THE CHANNEL

The $15 billion **Channel Tunnel** (or "Chunnel"), one of the great engineering feats of all time, is the first link between Britain and the

Flying for Less: Tips for Getting the Best Airfare

Passengers sharing the same airplane cabin rarely pay the same fare. Here are some ways to keep your airfare costs down:

- Passengers who can book their ticket **long in advance,** who can **stay over Saturday night,** or who **fly midweek** or **at less-trafficked hours** will pay a fraction of the full fare. If your schedule is flexible, say so, and ask if you can secure a cheaper fare by changing your flight plans.

- You can also save on airfares by keeping an eye out in local newspapers for **promotional specials** or **fare wars,** when airlines lower prices on their most popular routes. You rarely see fare wars offered for peak travel times, but if you can travel in the off-months, you may snag a bargain.

- Search **the Internet** for cheap fares.

- **Consolidators,** also known as bucket shops, are great sources for international tickets, although they usually can't beat the Internet on fares within North America. Start by looking in Sunday newspaper travel sections; U.S. travelers should focus on the *New York Times, Los Angeles Times,* and *Miami Herald.* For less-developed destinations, small travel agents who cater to immigrant communities in large cities often have the best deals. *Beware:* Bucket-shop tickets are usually nonrefundable or rigged with stiff cancellation penalties, often as high as 50% to 75% of the ticket price, and some put you on charter airlines with questionable safety records. Reliable

Continent since the Ice Age. The tunnel was built beneath the seabed through a layer of impermeable chalk marl and sealed with a reinforced concrete lining. The 50km (31-mile) journey between Great Britain and France takes 35 minutes, although actual time in the Chunnel is only 19 minutes. Once on the Continent, you can make a connection to Frankfurt fairly easily.

Rail Europe sells tickets on the **Eurostar** direct train service between London and Paris or Brussels (© **800/EUROSTAR** for information; www.eurostar.com). In the **United Kingdom,** make

GETTING THERE 27

consolidators are available worldwide and on the Net.
STA Travel (© 800/329-9537 in the U.S.; www.statravel.
com) is now the world's leader in student travel, thanks
to its purchase of Council Travel. STA also offers good
fares for travelers of all ages. **Flights.com** (© 800/TRAV-
800; www.flights.com) started in Europe and has excellent fares worldwide, but particularly to that continent. It
also has "local" websites in 12 countries. **FlyCheap**
(© 800/FLY-CHEAP; www.1800flycheap.com) is owned by
package-holiday megalith MyTravel and therefore has
especially good access to fares for sunny destinations. **Air
Tickets Direct** (© 800/778-3447; www.airticketsdirect.
com) is based in Montreal and leverages the currently
weak Canadian dollar for low fares; it'll also book trips to
places that U.S. travel agents won't touch, such as Cuba.
- Join **frequent-flier clubs.** Accrue enough miles, and you'll
be rewarded with free flights and elite status. It's free, and
you'll get the best choice of seats, faster response to
phone inquiries, and prompter service if your luggage is
stolen, your flight is canceled or delayed, or if you want to
change your seat. And you don't need to fly to build frequent-flier miles—**frequent-flier credit cards** can provide
thousands of miles for doing your everyday shopping.
- For many more tips about air travel, including a rundown
of the major frequent-flier credit cards, pick up a copy of
Frommer's Fly Safe, Fly Smart (Wiley Publishing, Inc.).

reservations for **Eurostar** at (© 0870/530-0003); and in the
United States at (© 800/848-7245).

The tunnel also accommodates passenger cars, charter buses,
taxis, and motorcycles from Folkestone, England, to Calais, France.
It operates 24 hours a day, 365 days a year, running every 15 minutes during peak travel times and at least once an hour at night.
Tickets may be purchased at the tollbooth. Contact **Le Shuttle**
(© 800/4-EURAIL in the U.S. and Canada or 0870/5353-535 in
England; www.eurotunnel.com).

Getting to Know Frankfurt

Frankfurt is a vast and sprawling city and can be confusing to the visitor. This chapter gives you the basic information you'll need to know once you're in Frankfurt, including an overview of the city's geography and systems of transportation. In addition, check out the "Fast Facts" section at the end of the chapter for details on everything from camera shops to local laundries.

1 Orientation

ARRIVING

Frankfurt's airport, **Flughafen Frankfurt/Main** (© 069/69-01; www.frankfurt-airport.de), lies 11km (7 miles) from the city center at the Frankfurter Kreuz, the intersection of two major expressways, A3 and A5. This airport, continental Europe's busiest, serves more than 240 destinations in about 110 countries worldwide, including many American cities. It's Germany's major international gateway. All important German airports can be reached via Frankfurt. Flying time from Frankfurt to Berlin and Hamburg is 70 minutes, and to München, 60 minutes.

At the **Airport Train Station** beneath Terminal 1, you can connect to German InterCity trains and S-Bahn commuter trains to Frankfurt and nearby cities. Terminal 2 is linked to Terminal 1 by a people-mover system, Sky Line, which provides quick transfers (the airport's standard connection time is 45 min. maximum).

Train information is available at the **German DB Travel Center** (© 01805/99-66-33). **S-Bahn** line S-8 between the airport and Frankfurt center runs every 10 minutes and deposits passengers at the main rail station in 11 to 15 minutes. A one-way ticket costs 5€; tickets should be purchased before boarding.

VISITOR INFORMATION

The **tourist office** has two locations: The Hauptbahnhof, opposite the main entrance of the train station (© 069/21-23-88-49; www. frankfurt-tourismus.de), open Monday through Friday from 8am to

9pm, Saturday and Sunday from 9am to 6pm. The one in Römer (© **069/21-23-87-08**) is open Monday through Friday from 8am to 5pm, Saturday and Sunday from 9am to 4pm, closing 1 hour later in the summer months. **Amerika Haus** is an American Cultural Institute at Staufenstrasse 1 (© **069/9-71-44-80**).

CITY LAYOUT

Most of the sights, nightlife, restaurants, and hotels lie in the **Stadtmitte,** or center of town. However, chances are you'll cross the River Main to visit the apple-wine taverns in the **Sachsenhausen** area. It is also possible that you'll seek out both restaurants and hotels in the increasingly fashionable **Westend** ("west end"). Most of the other areas of Frankfurt probably will not concern you unless you're hunting for intriguing restaurants in the **Nordend** ("north end") or even in the **Ostend** ("east end"). We've included a few of the best of these dining places outside the city center because transportation is so rapid. Often you can be where you want to go in no more than 20 minutes.

You can cover most of the heart of Frankfurt on foot. Nearly all the main sights, such as Goethe's house, lie within the boundaries of the old town walls, which today form a stretch of narrow parkland in almost a perfect half moon around the Altstadt (old city).

A good place to start exploring Frankfurt is at the **Römerberg,** or historical core of the city. This is actually the site where Charlemagne erected his fort. In medieval times, the Römerberg was the marketplace of Frankfurt.

Once one of the great old towns of Europe, the **Altstadt** was blasted off the planet in two horrendous air raids in 1944. Some of its buildings have been sympathetically reconstructed in the old style.

The most important building in the Stadtmitte is the red sandstone church of **St. Bartholomäus,** often called "the Dom," although it isn't a cathedral. It was the venue for the coronation of the Holy Roman Emperors even though it didn't have cathedral status.

Directly to the east of Römerplatz stands the glaring modern building, **Kultur-Schirn,** a cultural center where various exhibitions are held. It is a controversial, postmodern structure that meets with ridicule among Frankfurters who like their architecture traditional.

Goethehaus and **Goethe Museum** lie only a short walk north from the center of Altstadt. To the north of Goethe Museum is **Zeil,** Germany's Fifth Avenue and one of Europe's greatest shopping streets.

Another landmark of the Stadtmitte is **Hauptwache,** an 18th-century baroque building that lies at the junction of both the

Frankfurt Orientation

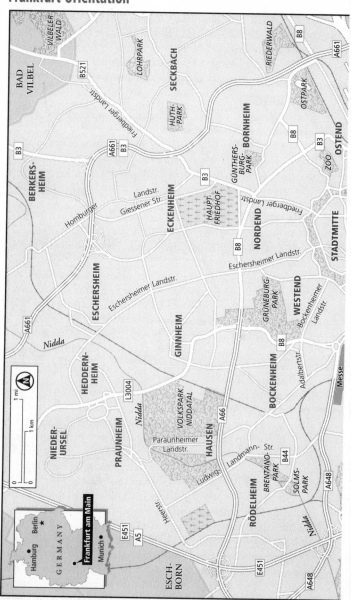

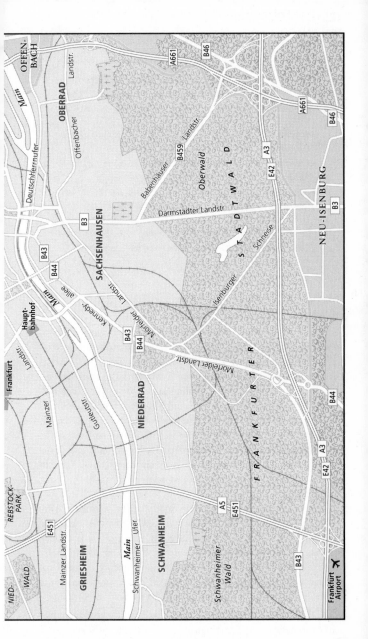

Did You Know?

- In 1944, Frankfurt celebrated its 1,200th anniversary.
- Locals sometimes call their town "Mainhattan" (Manhattan on the Main) or "Bankfurt," because of the hundreds of banks located here.
- Frankfurt has more cars per capita than any city in Germany.
- Frankfurt is the home of the oldest zoo, dating from 1858.
- Before the Nazis came into power, the second largest Jewish community in Germany lived in Frankfurt.
- Until the Third Reich took over, the Städel had the finest array of modern paintings in Germany. Some 500 masterpieces were removed and denounced as "degenerate."

U-Bahn and the S-Bahn lines. Northwest of the Hauptwache is the **Börse,** the stock exchange of Frankfurt.

The Hauptbahnhof, at the western edge of the center of town, opens onto a large street called **Am Hauptbahnhof.** As you walk out of the station, Düsseldorfer Strasse is on your left and Baselerstrasse is on your right, heading south toward the Main River. You have a choice of three streets heading east to the center of the **Altstadt:** Taunusstrasse, Kaiserstrasse, and Münchener Strasse. Münchener Strasse leads directly into **Theaterplatz,** with its opera house. Taunusstrasse goes to three of the major Altstadt squares in the southern part of the city: **Goetheplatz, Rathenauplatz,** and (most importantly) the **Hauptwache,** with its rail connections. You can find some of the best shops in this section of Frankfurt, along Kaiserstrasse.

The **Main River** flows slightly south of the Altstadt. Many bridges, including the **Alte Brücke** and the **Obermainbrücke,** cross this important waterway. On the south bank of the Main is a popular district, **Alt-Sachsenhausen,** which is the center of the applewine taverns (see chapter 5). For other major attractions, you'll have to branch out, heading east to the Frankfurt Zoo, or northwest to the Palmengarten (you can reach both easily by public transportation).

FINDING AN ADDRESS   During the rebuilding of Frankfurt after the devastating bombings of 1944, city planners adopted a consistent pattern of numbering the streets with all the even numbers on one side, and all the odd numbers on the opposite side. Unfortunately, there's little rhyme or reason to the point where the lowest numbers begin, but in many cases, they begin on the end that's closer to the city center, with numbers increasing the further away from Stadtmitte you go.

STREET MAPS   Arm yourself with a detailed street map, not the general overview that the tourist office hands out. Maps are sold at most bookstores and news kiosks. See "Bookstores" in "Fast Facts: Frankfurt," below.

FRANKFURT'S NEIGHBORHOODS IN BRIEF

Stadtmitte   The Altstadt, or inner core of Frankfurt, is centered around An der Hauptwache, a square on the right side of the Main River and Frankfurt's hub. Its centerpiece is the Hauptwache, a beautifully reconstructed building dating from 1730. South of the Hauptwache rises the beautiful Gothic Cathedral of St. Bartholomäus. You can cover most of the attractions of Stadtmitte on foot. It is the place to stay for convenience, as the greatest collection of hotels lies here—although other areas, such as the Westend, are starting to give Stadtmitte some competition.

Sachsenhausen   This district south of the Main River is where Frankfurters go to escape the commercialized inner core of the city. Even though it's been part of Frankfurt since 1318, Sachsenhausen still maintains some of the aura of a "town within a town." Sachsenhausen contains the apple-wine district and is filled with taverns where Frankfurters pig out and drink their beloved apple-wine. The street where most of the action occurs is Schweizer Strasse. The Sachsenhausen district is best approached by walking over Eiserner Steg, an iron footbridge over the Main. You can find most of the apple-wine taverns in the warren of narrow streets around the Affentorplatz.

Schaumainkai (Museumsufer)   Directly west of Sachsenhausen is the district of Schaumainkai, most often called "Museumsufer" as it is the site of the finest museums in Frankfurt. A total of seven museums all lie on the south bank of the Main between Eiserner Steg and Friedensbrücke. Two of the most important museums here are Liebieghaus and Museum für Kunsthandwerk.

Westend   The financial district of Frankfurt lies immediately to the northwest of Stadtmitte. Its power rose in the 19th century, and many members of Frankfurt's Jewish community, including the Rothschilds, lived here. In the 1960s this area was vastly developed, as old buildings gave way to modern office skyscrapers. The area is increasingly fashionable, and is the site of several hotels and restaurants. Its loveliest "green lung" is Grüneburg-park, a 19th-century park laid out in the English style. You can see joggers in Grüneburgpark throughout the day. On the north-eastern edge of the quarter lies the Botanischer Garten, one of the best places in Frankfurt to take a stroll.

Ostend   Many hotel concierges broadly hint that there's noth-ing to write about in the Ostend (east end) of Frankfurt. They refer to it as a neighborhood of *gastearbeiter* (guest workers) and brothels, with little of any particular interest for a tourist. But we think it's worth the trip here to sample the Greek cuisine at Platea Livingroom.

Nordend   This is a respectable middle-class neighborhood with lots of students. Many restaurants and bars are centered on or around the Bergerstrasse.

Gravenbruch   This is a verdant and leafy residential suburb, bisected with high-speed access roads. There are lots of trees and private homes out here. The main allure for visitors is the very large Kempinski Hotel Gravenbruch.

Rödelheim   This is a respectable upper-middle-class suburb. It's a fine place to live, but there's only one site of any interest to a visitor: the Italian restaurant Osteria Enoteca, which is worth the trip across town.

Heiligenstock   The main reason to go to this suburb of Frank-furt is to discover a dining secret known to savvy locals: Altes Zollhaus. Originally a tollhouse, this restaurant offers a rustic atmosphere and fine cuisine. It is especially popular with devotees of game who "flock" here in the autumn.

2 Getting Around
BY PUBLIC TRANSPORTATION
Frankfurt is linked by a network of fast, modern subways, trams, and buses, all of which are administered by the **RMV (Rhein-Main Verkehrsverbund),** Mannheimer Strasse 15 (© **069/27-30-70**). You can use all methods of public transport within their respective fare zones at a single price, which includes transfers between any of them. You can purchase tickets at the green, coin-operated auto-matic machines, labeled *Fahrscheine* ("tickets"), that are lined up adjacent to each of the points of departure. The machines accept all denominations of coins, and bills up to 25€, but be alert that any

change you receive is in coins, so try to use the smallest bills possible. A daily ticket, good for unlimited travel inside Frankfurt's central zone, costs 4.60€ for adults and 2.75€ for children. Zone charts and additional information, in six languages, are displayed on all the automatic machines. Except for bus travel (where you have the option of paying the driver directly for your passage), be sure to buy your ticket before you board any of the public transport conveyances of Frankfurt. If you're caught traveling without the proper ticket, you may be fined 40€.

If you want to simplify the ticket-buying process (and get a deal on museum admissions), consider the purchase of a **Frankfurter Tageskarte (Frankfurt Card)** from either of the city's tourist offices. These cards allow unlimited travel anywhere within the greater Frankfurt area, transport on the shuttle bus going to and from the airport, plus half-price admission to any of the city's museums. The cost is about 6€ for a 1-day card and 10€ for a 2-day card. For more information, contact the tourist office.

For more information about Frankfurt's public transportation system, call **RMV,** the city transport office (✆ **069/19449**).

BY TAXI

There's no surcharge for calling for a taxi; dial ✆ **069/54-50-11,** 069/23-00-33, or 069/25-00-01. Otherwise, you can get a cab either by standing at any of the city's hundreds of clearly designated taxi stands, or by hailing one with an illuminated dome light. Taxis charge by the trip and by the carload, without surcharge for pieces of luggage. Some are suitable for carrying up to six passengers, others for a maximum of four. Regardless of their size, the initial fee you pay for a Frankfurt taxi is 2€; additional kilometers cost 1.40€ to 1.50€ each, depending on the time of day. The most expensive rates are charged between the hours of 10pm and 6am; the least expensive are charged between 10am and 4pm.

BY RENTAL CAR

The big rental companies each maintain offices at the airport and at central locations throughout Frankfurt. The most reliable are **Avis,** whose downtown branch is inside the Hauptbahnhof (✆ **069/27-99-7010;** www.avis.de); and **Hertz,** whose offices are also in the Hauptbahnhof (✆ **069/23-04-84;** www.hertz.de), and on the Hanauer Landstrasse 117 (✆ **069/44-90-90**). Also recommended is **Europcar,** which maintains offices at the Hauptbahnhof (✆ **069/242/9810**) and downtown at Am Industriehof 3–5 (✆ **069/ 970-6410**).

CITY DRIVING   In Frankfurt driving presents fewer problems than in München or Berlin, where greater numbers of cars and barricades prevent you from turning when you need to. Frankfurt's biggest traffic headache usually involves rush-hour congestion, but without the labyrinthine nightmares you're likely to find in bigger, or older, cities. However, for sheer ease of moving around, we suggest that you use taxis or that you become familiar with the city's excellent public transport system.

Something to remember: City officials have synchronized many of the stoplights along the major boulevards and avenues of Frankfurt. That means that if you're driving on a long boulevard at a constant speed of 50km per hour (31 mph), you can hit most of the intersections en route with a green light. The Germans refer to this well-conceived system as the *Grüne Welle* (green wave), and many of them automatically adjust their driving rhythms to it. So remember, if you're driving on the city's outskirts, to try to maintain a constant speed of 50km per hour. For more information about Frankfurt's traffic patterns, traffic flows, and traffic rules, contact the ***Polizei Praesidium*** (Police Headquarters) at © **069/75-50-0.**

GASOLINE   *Benzine* (gasoline) is readily available throughout Frankfurt. The majority of modern vehicles were engineered to accept only *bleifrei* (unleaded), which is—for environmental reasons—the only kind that's offered in most gas stations. Most passenger cars work well with "normal" gasoline, which costs about 1.12€ per liter, or about 3.36€ per gallon (more than twice the going rate in the U.S.). Higher-octane varieties, identified as "super" or "super-plus," tally up to as much as 1.17€ per liter, or about 3.51€ per gallon—prices that many U.S. residents consider lethal. Consequently, be prepared to spend as much as 50€ to 55€ to fill up the gas tank of an average-size rental car, either in Frankfurt or anywhere else in Germany.

PARKING   Parking on the streets of Stadtmitte Frankfurt can be trying and expensive, so consequently, many commuters simply opt to park in any of the city's many garages. Two of the biggest and most central include **Parkhaus am Kaiserplatz,** am Kaiserplatz (© **069/215-666**); and—within a very short walk of the railway station—**Parkhaus Hauptbahnhof,** Wilhelm-Leuschner Strasse 1 (© **069/271-36-890**). In both garages, 24 hours of parking costs about 20€.

BY BICYCLE

Some office workers commute to their jobs by bicycle every day, but they tend to have nerves of steel, an intimate familiarity with the traffic patterns of the city, and well-developed glutes and thighs. Recreational cyclists usually stick to the well-marked bicycle trails that flank the edges of the Main. Wide, broad, and relatively flat, they extend northward to the industrialized suburb of Höchst, and southward for about 80km (50 miles) to the scenic town of Aschaffenburg. (En route, you'll cycle through a folkloric village called Salegenstatt.) Bike routes in and around Frankfurt are marked with a blue and white sign showing a cyclist.

You can haul your bike onto the buses, U-Bahns, or S-Bahns of Frankfurt without charge, although during periods of extreme congestion (some routes during rush hour), the conductor might ask you to wait for the next bus or subway because of the crush of commuters.

You can rent a bike for 10€ per day from **Radschlag GmbH,** Hallgarten Strasse 56 (② **069/45-20-64;** www.radschlag.de); Tram 12 to Rothschildallee or U-Bahn 4 to Höhenstrasse.

ON FOOT

For walkers, the most interesting streets of Frankfurt are those within its medieval and commercial core, the district known as Stadtmitte, where venerable churches and monuments such as Goethe's birthplace coexist with some of the tallest buildings in Germany. After you wander around the Römer (City Hall) district, visiting historic churches, you might consider a promenade along either verdant bank of the Main as an interlude from city congestion. Each of the two riverbanks is lined with about a half-dozen museums, many of which we recommend. Overall, few other cities in Germany offer as unusual (some say schizophrenic) an insight into the cheek-by-jowl existence of Germany's medieval past with its present-day role as an economic powerhouse.

You can cover most of the inner-core of the city on foot, as nearly everything lies within a 20- to 30-minute walk. However, if you're venturing farther afield, such as into Nordend or Westend, you can rely on the efficient public transportation.

 FAST FACTS: Frankfurt

American Express Centrally located at Kaiserstrasse 10 (② **069/ 2193-8860;** U-Bahn/S-Bahn: Hauptwache), the American Express offices are open Monday through Friday from 9:30am to 6pm, Saturday from 10am to 1pm.

Bookstores The best English-language bookstore is **British Bookshop,** Börsenstrasse 17 (*©* **069/28-04-92;** U-Bahn/S-Bahn: Hauptwache). It's open Monday through Friday from 9:30am to 7pm and Saturday from 9:30am to 4pm. Many English-language (as well as French, Italian, and Spanish) editions are also for sale at **Sussmann's Presse und Buch,** Zeil 127 (*©* **069/ 1-31-07-51;** U-Bahn/S-Bahn: Hauptwache), open Monday through Wednesday and Friday from 9am to 7pm, Thursday from 9am to 8pm, and Saturday from 9am to 4pm.

Business Hours Most **banks** are open Monday through Friday from 9am to either 1 or 3pm. Most other **businesses and stores** are open Monday through Friday from 9 or 10am to either 6 or 6:30pm and on Saturday from 9am to 2pm. On *langer Samstag,* the first Saturday of the month, shops stay open until 4 or 6pm. Some stores close late on Thursdays (usually 8:30pm).

Consulates The **U.S. Consulate** is at Siesmayerstrasse 21, 60323 Frankfurt (*©* **069/7-53-50),** and the **British Consulate** is at Bockenheimer Landstrasse 42, 60323 Frankfurt (*©* **069/1-70-00-20).**

Currency Exchange Go to the Hauptbahnhof's **Reise-Bank AG** kiosk (*©* **069/24-27-85-91** or 069/24-27-85-92), which is open daily from 7:30am to 9pm. The same bank maintains two separate branches within the Frankfurt airport. The smaller branch (*©* **069/69-07-20-71)** is open daily from 7am to 7pm; the larger (*©* **069/69-03-50-61)** is open daily from 6am to 11pm.

Dentist For an English-speaking dentist, call *©* **069/19292** to arrange an appointment.

Doctor For an English-speaking doctor, call *©* **069/19292** to arrange an appointment.

Drug Laws Penalties for illegal drug possession in Germany are severe. You could go to jail or be deported immediately.

Drugstores For information about pharmacies open near you, call *©* **069/19292.** Otherwise you can go to Kissel-Apotheke, Mörfelder Landstrasse 235 (*©* **069/63-11-522).**

Electricity The voltage in Germany is 220 AC (50 cycles). A transformer and a plug that fits the German socket will be needed for U.S. appliances. Many leading hotels will supply these.

Emergencies Dial (© **110** for the police; (© **112** for a fire, first aid, or ambulance; (© **069/1-92-92** for emergency medical service; and (© **069/660-72-71** for emergency dental service.

Eyeglasses The best range of contact lenses, sunglasses, glasses, and sports glasses is found at **Abele Optik,** Schiller-strasse 4 ((© **069/29-67-59**). The shop also does frame and lens repairs. Open Monday through Friday from 10am to 7pm, Saturday 9:30am to 4pm.

Internet Access Head for **CyberRyder,** Tongegasse 31 ((© **069/ 913-96-754;** info@cyberyder.de), open Monday through Thursday from 9am to 11pm, Friday and Saturday from 9am to 1am, and Sunday from 2 to 11pm.

Laundry Try **SB Wasch Center,** Grosse Seestrasse 46 ((© **069/ 70-74-618;** U-Bahn: Leipziger Strasse), which is open daily from 6:30am to 10pm.

Liquor Laws As in many European countries, drinking laws in Frankfurt are flexible, enforced only if a problem develops. Officially, you must be 18 to consume any kind of alcoholic beverage, but bars and cafes rarely request proof of age. Drinking and driving, however, is treated as a very serious offense.

Luggage Storage/Lockers Lockers can be rented and luggage stored at the Hauptbahnhof.

Mail General delivery—mark it POSTE RESTANTE—can be used in any major town or city in Germany. You can pick up your mail upon presentation of a valid identity card or passport. Street mailboxes are painted yellow. It costs 1.50€ ($1.35) for the first 5 grams (about ⅕ oz.) to send an airmail letter to the United States or Canada, and 1€ (90¢) for postcards. To mail a package, go to one of the larger post offices, preferably the main branch in the area. All letters to the U.K. cost .55€ (50¢). See also the "Post Office" entry below.

Photo Supplies Frankfurt is one of the best-equipped cities in Europe for photographers. Go to **Foto Firle,** Leipzieger Strasse 18 ((© **069/77-77-4343;** U-Bahn: Leipzieger Strasse), which offers the city's most comprehensive range of photo supplies. Open Monday through Friday from 9:15am to 6:30pm, Saturday from 9:15am to 1:30pm.

Police Throughout the country, dial (© **110** for emergencies.

Post Office There's a post office at the Hauptbahnhof 60036 Frankfurt (© 069/9751-1004), open Monday through Friday from 6:30am to 9pm, Saturday from 8am to 6pm, and Sunday and holidays from 11am to 6pm.

Restrooms There are many decent public facilities in central Frankfurt, especially in the Altstadt. A restroom is called a *Toilette* and is often labeled wc, with either F (for *Frauen*, women) or H (for *Herren*, men).

Safety Frankfurt is a relatively safe city, but you should still stay alert at all times. Stay out of the area around the Hauptbahnhof at night, as muggings are frequent.

Taxes As a member of the European Union, Germany imposes a tax on most goods and services known as a **value-added tax (VAT)**, or in German, *Mehrwertsteuer*. Nearly everything is taxed at 15%, including vital necessities such as gas and luxury items such as jewelry. VAT is included in the prices of restaurants and hotels. Note that goods for sale, such as cameras, also have the 15% tax already factored into the price; but the listed prices of services, such as getting a mechanic to fix your car, don't include VAT, so an extra 15% will be tacked on to the bill. Stores that display a "Tax Free" sticker will issue you a Tax-Free Shopping Check at the time of purchase. When leaving the country, have your check stamped by the German Customs Service as your proof of legal export. You can then get a cash refund at one of the Tax-Free Shopping Service offices in the major airports and many train stations, and even at some of the bigger ferry terminals. Otherwise, you must send the checks to Tax-Free Shopping Service, Mengstrasse 19, 23552 Lübeck, Germany. If you want the payment to be credited to your bank card or your bank account, mention this. There is no airport departure tax in Germany.

Taxis See "Getting Around," earlier in this chapter.

Telegrams/Telex/Fax You can send all of these at the **post office** at the Hauptbahnhof (© 069/9751-1004). See above for hours.

Telephone The country code for Germany is 49. To call Germany from the United States, dial the international access code, which is 011, then 49, then the city code, then the regular phone number. *Note:* The phone numbers listed in this book are to be used within Germany; when calling from abroad, you omit the initial 0 in the city code.

You can place local and long-distance calls from all post offices and coin-operated public telephone booths. The unit charge is .25€. More than half the phones in Germany require an advance-payment telephone card from **Telekom**, the German telephone company. Post offices and newsstands sell phone cards; they cost 5€ to 50€. Rates are measured in units rather than minutes. The farther the distance you are calling, the more units you consume. For example, a 5-minute call to the United States costs 41 units. Telephone calls made through hotel switchboards can double, triple, or even quadruple the regular charge. Therefore, try to make your calls outside your hotel at a pay phone or post office. Post offices can also send faxes for you.

German phone numbers are not standard and come in various formats. In some places, numbers have as few as three digits. In cities, one building's number may have five digits whereas the phone next door might have nine digits. Germans also often hyphenate their numbers differently. But since all the area codes are the same, these various configurations should have little affect on your phone usage once you get used to the fact that numbers are inconsistent and vary from place to place.

To call the U.S. from Germany, dial 01 followed by the country code (1 for the States), then the area code, and then the number. Alternatively, you can dial the various telecommunication companies in the States for cheaper rates. From Germany, the access number for **AT&T** is ℭ **01300010**; for **MCI**, ℭ **0800-888-8000**; and for **Sprint**, ℭ **0800/888-0013**. You can use **USA Direct** with all telephone cards and collect calls; the number from Germany is ℭ **01-30-00-10**. You can use **Canada Direct** with Bell telephone cards and collect calls. The Canada Direct number from Germany is ℭ **01-30-00-14**.

Time Germany operates on Central European time (CET), which means that the country is 6 hours ahead of Eastern Time (ET) in the United States and 1 hour ahead of Greenwich mean time. Summer daylight savings time begins in Germany in April and ends in September—there's a slight difference in the dates from year to year—so there may be a period in early spring and in the fall when there's a 7-hour difference between U.S. ET and CET. Always check if you're traveling during these periods, especially if you need to catch a plane.

Tipping If a restaurant bill says *Bedienung,* that means a service charge has already been added, so just round up to the nearest euro. If not, add 10% to 15%. Round up to the nearest euro for taxis. Bellhops get 1€ per bag, as does the doorman at your hotel, restaurant, or nightclub. Room cleaning staffs get small tips in Germany, as do concierges who perform some special favors such as obtaining hard-to-get theater or opera tickets. Tip hairdressers or barbers 5% to 10%.

Water The tap water in Frankfurt, as in all German cities, is safe to drink. However, most Frankfurters prefer to ask for bottled water, either carbonated or noncarbonated.

4

Where to Stay

Frankfurt is notorious for room shortages during busy trade fairs. If you have the bad luck to arrive when one of them is scheduled, you might find all the central hotels fully booked. To find an available room, head to one of the tourist offices. Either branch will charge you 3€ to 5€ for a room-finding service.

Even without the fairs, Frankfurt is one of the world's great commercial hubs, so businesspeople pour into the city at all times of the year. Hotels, for the most part, are expensive. However, you can sometimes negotiate a rate decrease on weekends when the business clients aren't predominant. Hotels also tend to be booked well in advance, so it's important to make reservations.

Most hotels won't quote prices charged at *Messen* (trade fairs) until they see how the market is going. There are more than two dozen of these fairs a year, including the famous Frankfurt Book Fair. Sometimes publishers and editors reserve the same room as much as 2 years in advance.

Nearly all the major hotels in the city center are convenient to the train station, the business district, and the fairgrounds. Of course, you can take a taxi, but walking time is often no more than 20 minutes to where you're going.

If you want lower prices, head for one of the small inns or pensions in the outlying district. All of them are linked by efficient public transportation that will get you into the city in about 20 minutes. And if you didn't reserve a room during the *Messen,* you'll have to head for the boondocks anyway since chances are all the inner-city hotels will be booked.

1 Stadtmitte (the Inner City)

VERY EXPENSIVE

Arabella Sheraton Grand Hotel ⨕   This hotel in the heart of the shopping district is one of the most modern and glamorous in Frankfurt, though it's not as stylish as either the Steigenberger Frankfurter Hof or the Hessischer Hof. It is, however, a cut above the Maritim out by the fairgrounds. This 10-story building is designed in an international, big-city style, and is a favorite of business travelers who enjoy the in-room fax phones, dataports, and multilingual phone announcements. In its guest rooms, the Arabella escapes from the chain curse, presenting accommodations that range in style from Italian modern to Art Deco, with some "fantasy-themed" suites. The marble bathrooms have heated floors. The hotel has an atrium lobby.

The hotel's restaurants are some of the most popular in the city with business travelers and are heavily booked during the trade fairs.

The hotel operates both a Japanese and a Thai restaurant. There's also a rustic German restaurant offering regional specialties, as well as a bar and a cafe. For a review of the hotel's main restaurant, Peninsula, see p. 70.

Konrad-Adenauer-Strasse 7, 60313 Frankfurt am Main. ℂ **800/325-3535** in the U.S. and Canada, or 069/2-98-10. Fax 069/2-98-18-10. www.arabellasheraton.com. 378 units. 345€–365€ double; from 675€ suite. AE, DC, MC, V. Parking 21€. U-Bahn: Konstablerwache. **Amenities:** 3 restaurants; 2 bars; indoor pool; health club; gym; solarium; business services; 24-hr. room service; laundry/dry cleaning. *In room:* A/C, TV, minibar, hair dryer, trouser press.

Frankfurt Marriott ⓖ   This is Europe's biggest Marriott, and, with 44 floors, the tallest hotel in Europe. It's on the same comfort level as its major competitors, the Inter-Continental, Hilton, and Maritim, although we've found those properties to be better run with more helpful staffs. The black, white, and glass-fronted tower (built in 1973) that contains the hotel has only banks and corporate offices on the lower 26 floors. Hotel rooms are on the upper floors, a design that guarantees you sweeping views over the surrounding cityscape from any bedroom. Although it isn't directly connected to the fairgrounds, it's only about a 5-minute walk away. Don't expect intimacy or even a sense that the overworked staff particularly understands what's going on within this blockbuster. There's a bureaucratic feel to many of the exchanges you're likely to have with the reception staff, and enormous confusion about rates. Despite that, if you nail down your arrival dates and the tariffs you'll pay, you can have a comfortable stay. The marble-floored lobby functions as a kind of clearinghouse, shuttling guests through reception on their way to their rooms high in the sky, or to any of the hotel's three restaurants. The most unusual restaurant is a much-publicized, and somewhat noisy, sports bar called Champion's. Bedrooms are tastefully conservative, contemporary-looking, and comfortable,

Stadtmitte Accommodations

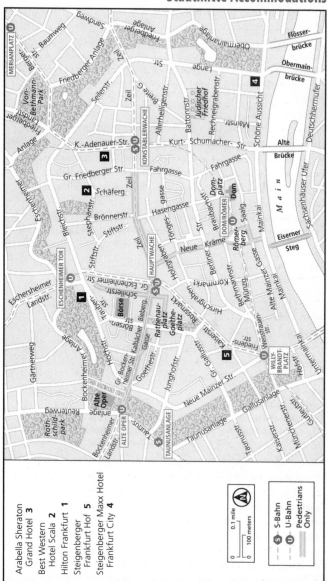

Arabella Sheraton
Grand Hotel **3**

Best Western
Hotel Scala **2**

Hilton Frankfurt **1**

Steigenberger
Frankfurt Hof **5**

Steigenberger Maxx Hotel
Frankfurt City **4**

S S-Bahn
U U-Bahn
Pedestrians
Only

0   0.1 mile
0   100 meters

with recently renovated bathrooms, deep upholstery, and a bland international decor.

Hamburger Allee 2–10, 60486 Frankfurt am Main. (𝄢) **800/228-9290** in the U.S., or 069/79-55-0. Fax 069/79-55-2341. www.marriott.com. 588 units. 155€ double; 194€ executive-floor double; from 333€ suite. AE, DC, MC, V. Parking 22€. U-Bahn: Messe Frankfurt. **Amenities:** 3 restaurants (including Tex-Mex and Japanese); sports bar; fitness center; sauna; whirlpool; secretarial service; 24-hr. room service; babysitting. *In room:* A/C, TV, minibar, hair dryer, safe, trouser press.

Hotel Hessischer Hof 𝄢𝄢𝄢 Frankfurt doesn't get much better than this. Only the Steigenberger Frankfurter Hof knocks it from the top rank of hotels in the city. A private and traditional place with an elegant atmosphere, this boxy, nine-story hotel has luxe style and amenities all the way. The hotel is located opposite the trade-fair building. The relatively modest postwar exterior doesn't prepare you for the spacious and glamorous interior. Many of the bedrooms are furnished with antiques. The bathrooms are equipped with perfumed soap and other thoughtful little extras such as luxurious bathrobes and tub-and-shower combos. In the older part of the building, accommodations are traditionally furnished, with antiques, chandeliers strung from high ceilings, and 19th-century lithographs. Compared to rooms in this section, the Frankfurter Hof and Meridien have more-elegant units. But in the newer *Nordflügel* (north wing), the bedrooms outrank even the stiffest Frankfurt competitors. The hotel staff follows the old European custom of having guests leave their shoes outside the bedroom door at night, to be returned shined the next morning.

Friedrich-Ebert-Anlage 40, 60325 Frankfurt am Main. (𝄢) **800/223-6800** in the U.S. and Canada, or 069/75-40-00. Fax 069/75-40-29-24. www.hessischer-hof.de. 117 units. 400€ double; from 625€ suite. Children under 13 stay free in parent's room. AE, DC, MC, V. Parking 16€. S-Bahn: Platz der Republik. **Amenities:** Restaurant; bar; fitness equipment; 24-hr. room service; babysitting; laundry/dry cleaning. *In room:* A/C, TV, minibar, hair dryer, safe.

Hotel Inter-Continental Frankfurt 𝄢𝄢𝄢 This hotel doesn't get the praise it deserves, but it's a cut above most of the other modern hotels that compete with it, including the Marriott and Hilton. It occupies a pair of tall buildings—20 and 21 floors, respectively—set across the street from one another, a short walk south of the railway station and the red-light district. Both buildings have separate reception areas (although you can register in either for accommodations in both buildings), lots of beige marble and mahogany or walnut paneling, a uniformed and highly competent staff, and a sense of cosmopolitan sophistication. The more plush, and more expensive, rooms lie in the *Mainflügel* (main wing) building. Each has deep upholstery, heavy curtains, and impeccable good taste. Somewhat less glamorous and slightly smaller rooms are across the street, in what's referred to as the *Stadtflügel* (city wing).

Wilhelm-Leuschner Strasse 43, 60329 Frankfurt am Main. © **800/327-0200** in the U.S., or 069/2605-0. Fax 069/252467. www.interconti.com. 770 units. 210€–365€ double; 510€–625€ suite. Extra bed 30€. Rates include breakfast. AE, DC, MC, V. Parking 22€. U-Bahn: Hauptbahnhof. **Amenities:** 2 restaurants; bar; piano bar; nightclub; Frankfurt's largest hotel swimming pool; fitness center; sauna; whirlpool; solarium; business center; 24-hr. room service. *In room:* A/C, TV, minibar, hair dryer, safe.

Le Meridien Parkhotel *Kids*

We prefer this hotel over its bigger, more impersonal competitors, the Frankfurt Inter-Continental and the Frankfurt Marriott Hotel. Le Meridien Parkhotel provides its guests—who mainly come from the world of commerce—with warmth, personal attention, and convenience: You can walk over to the fairgrounds in a few minutes. The hotel opens onto a verdant, parklike square. It has two sections: an ornately decorated, recently renovated 1905 palace, and a sleek but duller 1970s boxy wing. In the older part, rooms have a luxurious atmosphere and are individually designed. We prefer the older, more traditional rooms in the palace, although they are more expensive than those in the annex. Palace accommodations are smaller, however. The annex gives you high ceilings, and the rooms are larger with built-in furnishings. Each unit comes with combo tubs and showers, robes, and deluxe vanity items. For families who travel upscale, this is a traditional favorite because of its gracious welcome and helpful staff. All rooms and suites are in the five-star category.

Wiesenhüttenplatz 28–38 (near the Hauptbahnhof), 60329 Frankfurt am Main. © **800/225-5843** in the U.S. and Canada, or 069/2-69-70. Fax 069/2-69-78-84. www.lemeridien-frankfurt.com. 296 units. 345€–415€ double; 495€–595€ suite. AE, DC, MC, V. Parking 20€. S-Bahn: 8. **Amenities:** Restaurant; bar; sauna; solarium; spa; business center; limited room service; babysitting; laundry/dry cleaning. *In room:* A/C, TV, minibar, hair dryer.

Maritim Hotel Frankfurt

This is the one of the largest hotels in Germany, with a layout that almost defines it as a small town within a city. Set behind a curved, mostly glass eight-story facade, it's the only hotel in Frankfurt with direct access, via a covered walkway, to the trade fairgrounds. As such, its self-anointed goal involves servicing the needs of exhibitors, salespeople, and buyers who pour in and out of its low-ceilinged, marble-sheathed lobby on frantic business trips. Expect well-orchestrated but somewhat

Frankfurt Accommodations

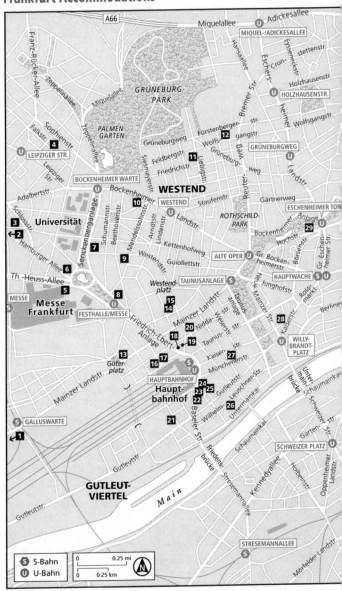

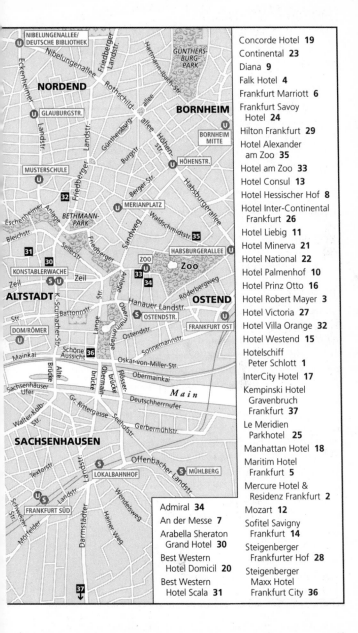

anonymous comforts at this Bauhaus-industrial behemoth, and a location that requires a bit of a hike, or a taxi ride, to more scenic and historic neighborhoods of Frankfurt. Bedrooms may be neutral, but they are more stylish than those at the Marriott across the street. Each very comfortable unit comes with a writing desk. Bathrooms are well equipped, from deluxe toiletries to combo shower and tub. This is commercialized Germany at its most unapologetic, but considering the many facilities at your fingertips, plus the proximity to the Fairgrounds, the convenience of a stay here is worth it.

Theodor-Heuss-Allee 3, 60486 Frankfurt am Main. ℭ 069/75-78-0. Fax 069/75-78-10-00 www.maritim-hotels.de. 543 units. 270€–315€ double; 370€–510€ suite. AE, DC, MC, V. Parking 22€. U-Bahn: Messe Frankfurt. **Amenities:** 2 restaurants; 2 bars; pool; fitness club; sauna; massage; solarium; 24-hr. room service. *In room:* A/C, TV, minibar, hair dryer, safe.

Steigenberger Frankfurter Hof 𝕽𝕽𝕽   This is the most famous, most prestigious, and most legendary hotel in Frankfurt, with service and a historic setting that's unmatched anywhere else in town, even by its nearest competitor, Arabella Sheraton. Although less highly rated, the only hotel in Frankfurt that really matches it (though not in dining) is our favorite, the Hessischer Hof. The highly visible five-story flagship of one of Germany's most elegant hotel chains, it was established in 1872 behind a landmark stone facade that's very prominent and grand. Its rooms are hotly contested by visiting dignitaries, especially during the Frankfurt Book Fair. At that time, the entire building is taken over by book signings, book deals, and book drama, with negotiations and contract signings in hallways, stairwells, and throughout the hotel. Guests as prominent as the former king of Greece have been denied a room during the book fair. Public areas are discreet and plush; bedrooms have high ceilings, are flooded with sun, and are gracefully furnished. All have built-in safes and some of the largest and most up-to-date full bathrooms in Frankfurt. Some of the more traditional rooms have valuable antiques, but those in the Bethmann Wing have a 1970s aura with bland blond wood furnishings. Even the lithographs hanging in the upstairs corridors reek of deeply entrenched 19th-century virtues at this much-renovated but charmingly traditional hotel. Its art collection, including Gobelin tapestries, French antiques, and 18th-century portraits, is noteworthy.

Am Kaiserplatz, 60311 Frankfurt am Main. ℭ **800/223-5652** in the U.S. and Canada, or 069/2-15-02. Fax 069/215-900. www.steigenberger.com. 332 units. Mon–Thurs 405€–455€ double, Fri–Sun 150€–170€ double. Weekday rates do not include breakfast; weekend prices do include breakfast. 515€–1,095€ suites

(Kids) Family-Friendly Hotels

Admiral (p. 58)   This family favorite near the zoo has rooms that are simply furnished but comfortable—and the price is right.

Kempinski Hotel Gravenbruch Frankfurt (p. 62)   Right outside Frankfurt, this hotel lies in a 15-hectare (36-acre) park. Families can go for walks along its jogging trail, and kids 12 and under stay free in their parent's room.

Le Meridien Parkhotel (p. 47)   Children under 16 stay free in their parent's room at this pricey chain hotel located across from a city park.

weeklong, without breakfast. AE, DC, MC, V. Parking 20€. U-Bahn: Willy-Brandt-Platz. **Amenities:** 2 restaurants (see chapter 5); bar; health club; sauna; solarium; business center; 24-hr. room service; babysitting; valet/laundry. *In room:* A/C, TV, minibar, hair dryer, safe.

EXPENSIVE

An der Messe ⓖ   This quiet charmer is the choice of seasoned and discriminating visitors to Frankfurt. It's just a 5-minute walk from the university, the Hauptbahnhof, the banking district, and the fairgrounds. The staff does much to make guests feel comfortable. Rooms are large and stylishly furnished; many have an Asian motif. The bathrooms are luxurious and have tub-and-shower combos. A half-dozen singles are rented, but they're hard to come by unless you reserve well in advance.

Westendstrasse 104, 60325 Frankfurt am Main. ⓒ **800/221-6509** in the U.S., or 069/74-79-79. Fax 069/74-83-49. 45 units. 123€–149€ double. Rates include breakfast. AE, DC, MC, V. Underground garage parking 11€. Tram: 16 or 19. **Amenities:** Breakfast dining room; babysitting; laundry/dry cleaning. *In room:* TV, minibar, hair dryer.

Best Western Hotel Domicil ⓖ (Value)   Rooms at this hotel are more compact than at some of its nearby competitors, but they're well organized, well scrubbed, and attractively furnished with wood-veneer furniture, some of it built into the wall. Bathrooms are genuinely tiny, with showers ringed with plastic curtains and absolutely no extra space for primping. But to its advantage, it's considered relatively affordable for the neighborhood, and as such, it attracts a regular repeat clientele who feel lucky to secure rooms during the height of the trade fairs. It lies a 3-minute walk northeast from the railway station, behind an angular and boxy-looking facade that's ochre-colored and trimmed in stone. The lobby is one of the most attractive in the district—modern, glistening, and partially sheathed in polished granite.

Karlstrasse 14, 60329 Frankfurt am Main. © **800/528-1234** in the U.S., or 069/27-11-10. Fax 069/25-32-66 www.domicil-frankfurt.bestwestern.de. 68 units. 138€ double. Rates include breakfast. AE, DC, MC, V. U-Bahn: Hauptbahnhof. **Amenities:** Breakfast buffet. *In room:* TV, minibar, hair dryer.

Concorde Hotel 𝄐   Set less than a block from the railway station, in a much-renovated stately looking building, this hotel offers rooms that are affordable whenever there's no trade fair, and (for Frankfurt) acceptably priced when fairs are in progress. Not as appealing as either the Steigenberger InterCity Hotel or the Manhattan Hotel, it nonetheless is chockablock full during many weeks of the business calendar. Rooms are compact and not particularly distinguished, with color schemes of beige and soft grays and tiled shower-only bathrooms whose size is equivalent to a medium-size closet. The largest and most sought-after rooms are any whose last digit is "6." (Such as 16, 26, 36, 46, and so on.)

Karlstrasse 9, 60329 Frankfurt am Main. © **069/24-24-22-0.** Fax 069/24-24-22-88. www.hotelconcorde.de. 45 units (with shower only). 105€ double. Rates include breakfast. AE, DC, MC, V. Parking 15€. U-Bahn: Hauptbahnhof. **Amenities:** Bar; office center. *In room:* TV, minibar.

Frankfurt Savoy Hotel 𝄐   A 10-story corner blockbuster, this hotel is a winning choice in spite of an undesirable location across from the train depot and on the doorstep to the red-light district. The hotel used to be called Scandic Crown, and most of its rooms still evoke Scandinavia, with built-in furnishings. Bedrooms are narrow but comfortable nonetheless. Go for one of the accommodations in the 14-series block of rooms, as they are more spacious and more inviting. Avoid the units in the 15-series because of their "clipped architectural corners." There is much to make you want to hang out here, including the penthouse health club, the pool, and possibly the only "micro-eatery" in Frankfurt with only eight choice tables (reservations are imperative). Bathrooms are well equipped with combo tubs and showers.

Wiesenhüttenstrasse 42 (near the Hauptbahnhof), 60329 Frankfurt am Main. (© **069/27-39-60.** Fax 069/27-39-67-95. www.savoyhotel.de. 144 units. 170€ double. Rates include buffet breakfast. AE, DC, MC, V. Parking in nearby multistory car park 17€. U-Bahn/S-Bahn: Hauptbahnhof. **Amenities:** Restaurant; pool; health club; sauna; solarium; room service 6am–midnight; laundry/dry cleaning. *In room:* TV, minibar, hair dryer, trouser press.

Hilton Frankfurt 🏨🏨

Every European city boasts a spectacularly modern hotel dripping with a sense of postmodern architectural daring and imagination. In Frankfurt, that hotel is the Hilton, whose soaring 12-story atrium and vast expanses of glass have won architectural awards since it opened late in 1998. The Inter-Continental knocks it off its pedestal, but the Hilton is better than Maritim and Marriott. Come here for a sense of design-related theatricality, a cooperative and well-trained staff, and very comfortable bedrooms, each with a definite sense of hipster style and whimsy. They come in different degrees of luxury and view, with varying prices, depending on amenities, size, and panorama. Classic rooms overlook the hotel's central atrium and are the least expensive. Park rooms are the same size and overlook the world outside. Deluxe rooms are somewhat bigger, with very comfortable furnishings and small-scale niceties. Executive rooms, positioned on the 11th and 12th floors, have the best accessories, and provide access to a private concierge and a private bar with complimentary drinks and snacks.

Hochstrasse 4. 60313 Frankfurt am Main. ✆ 800/445-8667 in the U.S., or 069/1338-000. Fax 069/1338-1338. 343 units. 364€ double; from 615€ suite. AE, DC, MC, V. Parking 20€. U-Bahn: Eschenheimer Tor. **Amenities:** Restaurant; 2 bars; pool; health club; 24-hr. room service; babysitting; laundry/dry cleaning. *In room:* A/C, TV, minibar, hair dryer, safe.

Hotel Minerva 🏨

Opened in 2000, in a location just southwest of the railway station, this is one of the newest and most modern-looking hotels in Frankfurt. Its glass and granite facade rises in distinct contrast to the older, dingier buildings that flank it on either side. Inside, you'll find seven stories with carpets and plain walls, attractively glossy wood-grained furniture, more space than you might have expected, and tiled bathrooms with tub and shower that are large enough to really let you move around. Rooms overlooking the back of the hotel are a bit quieter than those facing the street. Overall, it's a highly appealing choice, equivalent in many ways to its nearby neighbors, the Manhattan and the Steigenberger Inter-City Hotel.

Stuttgarter Strasse 31. 60329 Frankfurt am Main. ✆ 069/256-176-00. Fax 069/256-17-601. www.hotelminerva.de. 50 units. 75€–80€ double; 200€ suite. Rates include breakfast. AE, DC, MC, V. Parking 5€. U-Bahn: Hauptbahnhof. **Amenities:** Breakfast room. *In room:* A/C, TV, minibar, hair dryer, safe.

Hotel National 🏵🏵 Within this neighborhood near the railway station, very few other hotels retain as distinct an impression of their 19th-century grandeur. It was originally built late in the 1800s as a city showcase, and carefully restored after its wartime damage into something that's genuinely charming, friendly, European, and well managed. Bedrooms and the tiled bathrooms with tub and shower are larger, and have higher ceilings, than most of its competitors, and are outfitted with furnishings (a few of which are antique) that are cozy and very comfortable, if not cutting-edge. Artwork in the rooms includes reproductions of paintings by such favorites as Degas.

Baseler Strasse 50, 60329 Frankfurt am Main. © 069/24-26-48-0. Fax 069/23-44-60. www.hotelnational.de. 70 units. Mon–Thurs 90€–125€ double, Fri–Sun 72€–95€ double. Extra bed 35€. Rates include breakfast. AE, DC, MC, V. Parking 15€. U-Bahn: Hauptbahnhof. **Amenities:** Restaurant; bar. *In room:* TV, minibar, safe.

Hotel Victoria 🏵 Set within a 5-minute walk east from the railway station, this hotel is contained within a stately looking 1893 building that was one of the few in the neighborhood to escape wartime bombings. The junior suites in this hotel are genuinely elegant, with Italianate (or Napoleonic) furniture and lots of style. Conventional doubles are clean, well organized, and comfortable, but without the style of the suites. Some units comes with a well-maintained bathroom with a shower and tub.

Kaiserstrasse 59, 60329 Frankfurt am Main. © 069/27306-0. Fax 069/27306-100. www.hotelbook.com/static/welcome_21614.html. 75 units. 95€ double; 110€ suite. Extra beds 20€. Rates include breakfast. AE, DC, MC, V. Parking 15€. U-Bahn: Hauptbahnhof. **Amenities:** Standup cafe. *In room:* A/C, TV, minibar, safe.

Manhattan Hotel 🏵 This is one of the most desirable hotels near Frankfurt's railway station, offering rooms that are priced about the same as those at the also-recommended Concorde, but with larger sizes and more-appealing furniture. Renovated into its present sleek and urban-inspired format in 1997, with a tongue-in-cheek resemblance to the Gotham City imagined in the Batman comic books of long ago, it celebrates the similarities of Manhattan, USA, and "Mainhattan"-am-Main (a nickname for Frankfurt). Bedrooms are blue, black, and white, with tiled shower-only bathrooms and a bit more *lebensraum* (living space) than you might expect. They only serve breakfast, but dozens of restaurants lie within a short walk.

Düsseldorfer Strasse 10, 60329 Frankfurt am Main. © 069/26-95-97-0. Fax 069/26-95-97-777. www.manhattan-hotel.com. 60 units (with shower only). 130€ double. Rates include breakfast. AE, DC, MC, V. Parking 15€. U-Bahn: Hauptbahnhof. **Amenities:** Lobby-level cocktail bar. *In room:* TV, minibar, safe.

Mercure Hotel & Residenz Frankfurt ⟨꘎⟩   This hotel is much bigger than it appears, thanks to the fact that its units are evenly distributed between two buildings—one with four floors, the other with five—set diagonally across a quiet intersection from one another. Its location is unusually suburban-looking and verdant, despite the fact that it's only a 10-minute walk to the northern edge of the fairgrounds. Each of the accommodations contains a tiny kitchen that management unlocks only for clients who opt to move in for a month or more. Such courtesies are not extended to conventional, short-term hotel guests. You get clean, well-organized bedrooms with conventional contemporary furniture and tiled bathrooms with a tub and shower, an informed reception staff, and a businesslike environment that's ideal for anyone attending a trade fair.

Voltastrasse 29, 60486 Frankfurt am Main. ⟨Ⓒ⟩ **069/7-92-60.** Fax 069/79-26-16-06. H1204@accor-hotels.com. 424 units. Mon–Thurs 179€–197€ double, Fri–Sun 98€ double. Mon–Thurs 256€ suite, Fri–Sun 190€ suite. AE, DC, MC, V. Parking 7€. U-Bahn: Westbahnhof. **Amenities:** Breakfast room. *In room:* A/C, TV, minibar, safe.

Sofitel Savigny Frankfurt ⟨꘎⟩   The architecture and design of the lobby are a lot less dramatic than those of other comparably priced hotels in Frankfurt, including An der Messe, but its bedrooms are stylish, comfortable, and—for the most part—recently renovated, with conservatively contemporary color schemes of royal blue and cream. The hotel was built in the 1950s, then expanded 15 years later. Today, it consists of two interconnected and much-renovated buildings of five and six floors respectively, both within a 5-minute walk northwest of the fairgrounds. The marble and wood-sheathed lobby melds directly into a bar/buffet area that can get very busy, creating the impression that the party might be spilling over into reception, which can make check-in somewhat more animated.

Savignystrasse 14, 60325 Frankfurt am Main. ⟨Ⓒ⟩ **069/753-30.** Fax 069/753-31-75. www.sofitel.com. 155 units. 281€ double; 396€ suite. AE, DC, MC, V. Parking 17€–20€. U-Bahn: Messe Frankfurt or Hauptbahnhof. **Amenities:** Restaurant; bar; nearby health club; 24-hr. room service. *In room:* A/C, TV, minibar.

Steigenberger Maxx Hotel Frankfurt City ⟨꘎⟩   Defining itself as a "First Class Boutique Hotel," and managed by one of Germany's most prestigious hotel chains, this is the newest four-star hotel in Frankfurt. It's part of the nationwide Steigenberger association but doesn't provide as many of the frills as the five-star hotels within this chain. But its rates are less expensive, making it attractive to business travelers who don't particularly care about unnecessary frills. Bed-rooms are conservatively furnished, masculine looking, and unpretentious, with lots of rattan, a writing desk, and much comfort. About a third overlook the Frankfurt skyline; most of the others open onto the River Main. Each comes with a small but neatly tiled bathroom with tub and shower.

Lange Strasse 5–9, 60311 Frankfurt am Main. ℂ **069/21-930-0.** Fax 069/21-930-599. www.steigenberger.de. 149 units. 140€–180€ double; 199€–299€ suite. Rates include breakfast. AE, MC, V. Parking 10€. U-Bahn: Konstablerwache. **Amenities:** Restaurant (seafood and steakhouse); bar; fitness center; business center; room service 6:30am–midnight. *In room:* A/C, TV, minibar, hair dryer, safe.

MODERATE

Best Western Hotel Scala   Set behind a dull and angular facade, this simple hotel offers well-scrubbed, well-designed bedrooms that are a bit larger than the cramped lobby implies. Each has a mono-chromatic earth-toned color scheme, and enough small comforts to make most visitors feel content, if only for a night. Each accommodation has a small tiled bathroom with tub and shower, and some nonsmoking units are available. The neighborhood that contains this hotel has a higher percentage of gay bars and clubs than any other in Frankfurt, but despite that, many clients are businessmen who aren't particularly interested in the sexual brouhaha going on around them.

Schäfergasse 31, 60313 Frankfurt am Main. ℂ **800/528-1234** in the U.S., or 069/138-11-10. Fax 069/28-42-34. www.scala.bestwestern.de. 40 units. Mon–Thurs 120€ double, Fri–Sun 85€ double. Rates include breakfast. AE, DC, MC, V. Parking 3€. U-Bahn: Konstablerwache. **Amenities:** Breakfast room. *In room:* TV, minibar.

Continental   The choice of many businesspeople, this hotel is a leader among middle-bracket hotels near the Hauptbahnhof. Founded in 1889, it enjoyed its heyday in the Belle Epoque era. The rooms are modern and comfortable, though the 30 rooms that have shower-only bathrooms are small. Around the corner are lively bars, but serenity prevails inside. The windows have been soundproofed to keep out traffic noise.

Baseler Strasse 56, 60329 Frankfurt. ℂ **069/23-03-41.** Fax 069/23-29-14. www.hotelcontifrankfurt.de. 83 units (30 with shower only; 53 with bathtub only). 130€ double. Rates include buffet breakfast. AE, DC, MC, V. Parking 15€. U-Bahn/S-Bahn: Hauptbahnhof. **Amenities:** Restaurant. *In room:* TV.

Hotel Prinz Otto   Other than the fact that it has a brick neoclassi-cal facade that's a lot more historic looking than those of its neighbors, there's very little that's particularly distinctive about this small-scale and completely unpretentious hotel. However, rooms tend to be fully booked during trade fairs because they are clean and relatively inexpensive. Each unit comes with a very small tiled bathroom with a shower stall. Accommodations are scattered over the four floors of this once private home and there is no elevator.

Ottostrasse 5, 60329 Frankfurt am Main. © 069/25-30-30. Fax 069/25-26-04. www.hotel-prinz-otto.de. 23 units. 65€ double; 80€ triple. Rates include breakfast. AE, DC, MC, V. Parking 12€. U-Bahn: Hauptbahnhof. **Amenities:** Breakfast room. *In room:* TV.

Hotel Villa Orange ⓐ *Finds*   This hotel resulted from the radical renovation, in 2000, of a century-old building with lots of architectural character. A team of architects and decorators with taste and talent created a conservative and very elegant decor that combines lots of natural hardwoods into the kind of cozy nest where a business or leisure traveler will feel eminently comfortable. Bathrooms contain shower/tub combinations, and come in color schemes of either hypermodern black and white, or rustic country schemes of blue. Overall, the hotel is comfortable, intimate, very tasteful, and well mannered—a fine alternative to one of the mega-hotels.

Hebelstrasse 1, 60318 Frankfurt. © 069/40584-0. Fax 069/40584-100. www.villa-orange.de. 38 units. Mon–Thurs 140€–150€ double, Fri–Sun 98€–120€ double. Rates include breakfast. AE, DC, MC, V. U-Bahn: Musterschule or Merienplatz. **Amenities:** Bar; concierge; babysitting; laundry/dry cleaning; pressing. *In room:* A/C, TV, minibar.

InterCity Hotel ⓐ *Value*   This is one of the best of the modern hotels near the railway station, and features a carefully designed layout that resulted from collaboration with the usually much more upscale Steigenberger Group. You'll find it immediately to the north side of the railway station, behind an antique 19th-century facade that opens into a much-renovated granite-sheathed lobby. Rooms are outfitted with blue and various pastel color schemes, and contain blond wood furniture, carpeting, and a sense of businesslike calm. A working desk with a modem for laptop connections and a minibar are built into opposite corners of the room. Each room is soundproofed against outside noises, although those facing away from the railway station are quietest of all. Bathrooms are compact and efficient, lined with white tiles and containing tubs with showers. The quality of the rooms and the comfort level at this hotel are uniformly high, albeit without the many extra niceties and services that many Europeans traditionally associate with Steigenberger. But in light of prices that are much lower than at more elegant Steigenberger-managed hotels, such as the Frankfurter Hof, no one seems to care.

Poststrasse 8, 60329 Frankfurt am Main. ✆ **069/273910.** Fax 069/27391-999. www.intercityhotel.de. 384 units. 72€–135€ double; 287€–385€ suite. Rates include breakfast. AE, DC, MC, V. Parking 12€. U-Bahn: Hauptbahnhof. **Amenities:** Restaurant; *stube* (beer bar); laundry/dry cleaning. *In room:* A/C, TV, minibar, hair dryer, safe.

INEXPENSIVE

Admiral *(Kids)* This hotel is a favorite with families, who like its location near the zoo, a short haul from the center of Frankfurt. The rooms are plainly but comfortably furnished, with a natural-wood, Scandinavian-style decor. The bathrooms are small but adequate, each with a shower stall. The hotel serves only breakfast.

Hölderlinstrasse 25, 60136 Frankfurt. ✆ **069/44-80-21.** Fax 069/43-94-02. www. hoteladmiral.de. 48 units. 82€ double. Rates include breakfast. DC, MC, V. Parking 6€. U-Bahn: Zoologischer Garten (Zoo). **Amenities:** Breakfast room. *In room:* TV, minibar.

Hotel am Zoo This modern hotel is bland on the outside but welcoming on the inside. The rooms are well maintained, with simple but comfortable modern furnishings; most contain minibars and TVs. Each of the accommodations comes with a small, tiled, shower-and-tub bathroom. The street-level breakfast room is the hotel's most charming feature, with linen-covered tables and stained-glass windows. Trams stop across the street.

Alfred-Brehm-Platz 6 (across from the zoo entrance), 60316 Frankfurt. ✆ **069/94-99-30.** Fax 069/94-99-31-99. www.hotel-am-zoo.com. 85 units. 106€ double. Rates include continental breakfast. AE, DC, MC, V. Parking behind the hotel 5€. Tram: 11, 14, or 16. **Amenities:** Restaurant; bar; laundry/dry cleaning. *In room:* TV, minibar, hair dryer, safe.

Hotel Consul This is a simple and cost-effective hotel with absolutely no architectural pretensions and a mostly Israeli staff who work hard to help newcomers to Frankfurt navigate the rituals of the trade fairs. Bedrooms are equivalent to the simple, contemporary lodgings you might have lived in during your student years, with acceptable-size bathrooms with showers and durable, cheerful-looking furniture. Rooms are always very clean. This is definitely a cosmopolitan and international place—many members of the staff speak numerous languages (some speak as many as five). If the hotel is fully booked (a likely possibility during important trade fairs), a member of the staff will direct you to the 33-room **Hotel Topas** (Niddastrasse 88, D-60329; ✆ **069/23-72-28;** same e-mail as the Hotel Consul), where rates, accommodations, and quality of staff are equivalent. The Topas lies 3 blocks to the northwest, in a position that's even closer to the railway station.

Mainzer Landstrasse 118, 60327 Frankfurt am Main. 🕻 **069/97-57-00-0.** Fax 069/ 97-57-00-36. 22 units. Mon–Thurs 77€ double, Fri–Sun 65€ double. Rates include breakfast. AE, DC, MC, V. U-Bahn: Hauptbahnhof; Tram 12. **Amenities:** Breakfast room. *In room:* TV, minibar.

Hotelschiff Peter Schlott ⭐ *Finds*   This 1950s riverboat, now permanently moored at the Frankfurt suburb of Höchst, has some of the smallest but most evocative hotel rooms in the area. The style evokes life at sea: Everything is tiny and cramped; mattresses are a bit thin. But the unusual nature of the accommodations help soften any disagreeability, and the waters of the Main lap soothingly beneath your portholes. You have to exercise caution on this ship's narrow and steep staircases. If you have enormous amounts of luggage, consider a stay in a more conventional hotel.

Mainberg, 65929 Frankfurt. 🕻 **069/300-4643.** Fax 069/307-671. www.hotel-schiff-schlott.de. 19 units (all with wash basins, 10 with showers, none with toilets). 60€ double without shower; 80€ double with shower. Rates include breakfast. AE, DC, MC, V. S-Bahn: Höchst. **Amenities:** Restaurant. *In room:* No phone.

2 Westend

EXPENSIVE

Falk Hotel   Behind a bleak exterior is a good little hotel. It's located on a small, quiet side street in the center of the city, near the fairgrounds, the main railway station, and the university. This hotel is bright and modern, but has enough traditional touches to lend warmth and coziness. The small, uncluttered guest rooms are spotlessly maintained, each with a tidily kept shower-only bathroom. For most of the year, the hotels are priced at the lower end of the scale, except during fairs.

Falkstrasse 38A, 60487 Frankfurt. 🕻 **069/70-80-94.** Fax 069/70-80-17. www. hotel-falk.de. 29 units (with shower only). 129€ double. Rates include buffet breakfast. AE, DC, MC, V. Parking 8€. U-Bahn: Leipziger Strasse. **Amenities:** Breakfast room. *In room:* TV, minibar.

Hotel Liebig ⭐ *Finds*   The aura within this upscale B&B is small-scale, intimate, and luxurious, with a decor that might have been lifted directly from the pages of a Laura Ashley (or a Versace) catalogue. As such, it presents a welcome change for business travelers looking for something more personalized, and less anonymous, than what's available at one of the blockbuster hotels closer to the fairgrounds. The town house that contains it was built in 1905, and retains its ornate maroon sandstone facade, its curving interior staircase, and proportions that hint at its origins as an upscale private home. The full bathrooms are handsomely decorated and spotlessly maintained.

Liebigstrasse 45, 60323 Frankfurt am Main. © **069/72-75-51.** Fax 069/72-75-55.www.liebig.de. 20 units. 128€–152€ double. Breakfast 12€ extra. AE, MC, V. Parking 12€. U-Bahn: Westend. **Amenities:** Breakfast room; garden. In room: TV, minibar.

Hotel Palmenhof ⭑   This five-story Art Nouveau building is a short walk from the Botanical Gardens. Some of the original architectural features have been preserved, and the 1890s reddish sandstone facade is quite grand. It stands across from the Café im Literaturhaus, a wining and dining spot where authors are seduced during book fairs. The interior has such architectural features as skylights beaming light down onto Belle Epoque furnishings. Rooms are somewhat fussy but are well kept and often contain high ceilings. Each comes with a well-maintained private bathroom with tub and shower.

Bockenheimer Landstrasse 89–91, 60325 Frankfurt. © **069/753-0060.** Fax 069/753-00666. www.palmenhof.com. 46 units. Mon–Thurs 140€–160€ double, 225€ suite; Fri–Sun 65€ double, 155€ suite. AE, DC, MC, V. Free parking. U-Bahn: Westend. **Amenities:** Laundry/dry cleaning. In room: TV, minibar, hair dryer.

Hotel Robert Mayer ⭑ *Finds*   This is one of the most artfully decorated hotels in town. It's within walking distance of Frankfurt's trade-fair complex. Though the building dates from 1905, the rooms date from 1994, when the manager hired 11 lesser-known artists to each impose his or her vision on one of the bedrooms. You might find a thought-provoking jumble of furniture inspired by Frank Lloyd Wright, or an anonymous Milanese postmodernist set adjacent to pop art. Creature comforts, however, remain high. There's no restaurant on the premises, but many dining options lie within a short walk.

Robert-Mayer-Strasse 44, 60486 Frankfurt. © **069/970910.** Fax 069/97091010. www.art-hotel-robert-mayer.de. 11 units. 129€ double. Rates include breakfast. AE, DC, MC, V. U-Bahn: Bockenheimer Warte. In room: TV.

Hotel Westend ⭑   This small-scale hotel, which was built in the late 19th century, is a winner, thanks to its courtly staff and its carefully polished roster of French and German antiques. Bedrooms are small with tidy bathrooms, each with a shower stall and tub. There's no restaurant on the premises, but few of the clients, many of whom seem involved in some kind of media, seem to mind; dozens of dining options lie within a short walk. The location is a 5-minute walk from the fairgrounds.

Westendstrasse 15, 60325 Frankfurt. © 069/746-702. Fax 069/745-396. www.
westend.com. 20 units. Mon–Thurs 130€ double, Fri–Sun 110€ double; 220€ double during trade fairs. Rates include breakfast. AE, MC, V. Free parking. U-Bahn:
Hauptbahnhof. **Amenities:** Breakfast room; garden. *In room:* TV, minibar.

INEXPENSIVE

Diana *(Value)*   Spotless and homey, the Diana is a bargain. It's a copy
of a private villa, with a drawing room and an intimate breakfast
salon. It's located in the Westend district on a pleasant residential
street. The small bedrooms are rather lackluster, but comfortable
and clean, each with a neat little bathroom with a shower stall.

Westendstrasse 83, 60325 Frankfurt. © 069/74-70-07. Fax 069/74-70-79. 26
units. 90€ double; 220€ triple. Rates include continental breakfast. AE, DC, MC, V.
Parking 5€. U-Bahn: Westend. Bus: 17. **Amenities:** Breakfast room. *In room:* TV.

Mozart *(Value)*   Perhaps the best small hotel in Frankfurt, the
Mozart stands on the periphery of the Palmengarten, right off the
busy Fürstenbergerstrasse. Everything inside—walls, furniture,
linens—is white or pink. Rooms are small but comfortable, each
with a neat shower-only bathroom. The breakfast room, with its
crystal chandeliers and Louis XV–style chairs, could pass for an
18th-century salon. The staff is polite and helpful.

Parkstrasse 17 (near the Alte Oper), 60322 Frankfurt am Main. © 069/55-08-31.
Fax 069/1568061. 35 units (with shower only). 125€ double; during trade fairs
150€ double. Rates include buffet breakfast. AE, DC, MC, V. Closed Dec 24–Jan 1. U-
Bahn: Holzhausenstrasse. Bus: 36. **Amenities:** Breakfast room. *In room:* TV, minibar.

3 Ostend (East End)

EXPENSIVE

Hotel Alexander am Zoo   Built in 1994 in a glistening, all-
white design, a very short walk north of the zoo, this is one of the
most appealing small hotels in the East End. Guests appreciate its
very quiet setting far removed from the bustle of the city center.
Rooms contain wood and wood-veneer furniture, very modern tile-
sheathed bathrooms, and a sense of streamlined but very comfortable
efficiency. Under separate management, and attached to the hotel, is
a highly promising newcomer, Restaurant Lavalle, a Mediterranean
restaurant whose decor evokes a prosperous farmhouse in Tuscany.

Waldschmidtstrasse 59–61, 60316 Frankfurt am Main. © 069/94-96-00. Fax 069/
94-96-07-20. www.alexanderamzoo.com. 59 units. Mon–Thurs 145€–170€ double, Fri–Sun 85–125€ double. Rates include breakfast. AE, DC, MC, V. Parking 12€.
U-Bahn: Habsburger Allee. **Amenities:** Restaurant; bar; sauna; Turkish bath; limited room service; business services; babysitting; laundry/dry cleaning. *In room:* TV,
hair dryer, minibar, iron/board.

4 Gravenbruch

VERY EXPENSIVE

Kempinski Hotel Gravenbruch Frankfurt ✮✮✮ *(Kids)* No other hotel in Frankfurt manages to combine urban glamour with manor-house charm as effectively as this one. Set within a 15-hectare (36-acre) park, with sweeping views over ponds and woodlands, it's distinctly different from the giant hotels of Frankfurt's commercial core, few of which seem as artfully relaxed or as genuinely elegant as this one. Although its core is a 16th-century manor house, only the building's original facade and an antique stable block remain unchanged from their original construction. What greets you today is a rambling, elongated labyrinth of well-proportioned wings and hidden courtyards, some designed like miniature Japanese gardens with splashing fountains and exotic horticulture.

Public areas are richly upholstered and accessorized with hectares of marble, polished hardwoods, and a lobby fireplace that blazes merrily throughout the winter. Views from the bedrooms over lawns and woodlands inspire a sense of Zen-like calm that have soothed the spirits of recent visitors such as Bill Clinton, Madeleine Albright, and showbiz icon Brigitte Nielsen. Bedrooms are large—and in the case of the suites, very large—with more space than in equivalently priced accommodations in the city center. Room decors are uniformly tasteful, each evoking what you might expect within a conservative but cultivated private home, each with solid, comfortable furnishings. The newest rooms, completed in 2000, are a bit more imaginative, outfitted like an upscale bachelor's apartment with cherry, teak, aluminum, and earth-toned velvet. Regardless of their individual differences, each contains a plug-in phone jack for a computer modem.

Graf zu Ysenburg und Budingen Platz 1, D-63263 Frankfurt. © 06102/505-0. Fax 06102/505-900. www.kempinski-frankfurt.com. 285 units. 170€–250€ double; from 210€ suite. Weekend rates 166€ double; from 290€ suite. Children under 12 stay free in parent's room. AE, DC, MC, V. Parking 11€. Free shuttle transfers between the hotel, the airport, and downtown Frankfurt on request every day 10am–2pm. **Amenities:** 2 restaurants; bar; winter garden; beer garden; live jazz; indoor and outdoor (heated) pools; sauna; solarium; business center; hair dresser; "beauty farm"; 24-hr. room service; massage. *In room:* A/C, TV, minibar, hair dryer, safe.

5 Airport Hotels

EXPENSIVE

Frankfurt Sheraton Hotel ⊕   This hotel is closer to the airport than the Steigenberger (see below), and is actually linked to Terminal 1 by a pedestrian bridge. This is one of the leading airport hotels of Germany. Insulated from jet noise, it is usually filled with red-eyed guests catching up on their sleep. The hotel is prepared to receive patrons from virtually anywhere, selling them "survival kits" that include razors, T-shirts, slippers, and toothbrushes. Even the meals are designed to help alleviate jet lag. This is a large nine-story structure shaped like the letter **S**. The main lobby is so busy you may take it for the airport terminal itself. Bedrooms are midsize to large, and are furnished in a sleek, modern style with full tub-and-shower bathrooms. The so-called "Smart Rooms" are the best, designed for the business traveler, with faxes, dataports, big desks—the works.

Terminal 1, 60549 Frankfurt Flughafen. ℂ **069/697-701.** Fax 069/69-77-22-09. www.sheraton.com/frankfurt. 1,006 units. 180€–345€ double; from 495€ suite. AE, DC, MC, V. **Amenities:** 2 restaurants; 2 bars; indoor pool; gym; sauna. *In room:* A/C, TV, minibar, hair dryer, safe.

Steigenberger Airport Hotel ⊕   If you'd like to escape the actual airport itself, this deluxe choice is relatively convenient, reached by a free shuttle that runs to and from the airport every 15 minutes. It's been massively renovated, reopening in 2003 with its room count considerably increased. On a more attractive site than the Frankfurt Sheraton, the Steigenberger lies in a forested area cut through with jogging trails. Most rooms open onto views of the forest, and each is spacious, attractively decorated, and loaded with amenities. Some of the more recently decorated accommodations have the bright look of a German resort. Each comes with a full bathroom with big tubs for long soaks after flights. One habitué who claims he checks in at least once a month, calls this his "crash pad" (perhaps not the best choice of words for describing an airport hotel).

Unterschweinstiege 16, 60549 Flughafen Frankfurt. ℂ **069/697-50.** Fax 069/69-75-25–05. www.steigenberger.de. 572 units. 230€–355€ double; from 410€ suite. AE, DC, MC, V. **Amenities:** Restaurant; buffet Fri 6–11pm, Sat 11am–3pm; cafe; piano bar; 24-hr. room service; babysitting; laundry/dry cleaning. *In room:* A/C, TV, minibar, hair dryer.

5

Where to Dine

Almost overnight, without much of the world being aware, the city of Frankfurt became one of Europe's great dining capitals. Everybody knows it for its banking and business, but serious gourmets also descend on the city, which offers one of Europe's most varied choices of cuisines. It still doesn't have the eclectic mixture of New York (which has virtually every cuisine served on earth), but Frankfurt is getting there.

For years, visitors to the famous Frankfurt Book Fair always went home saying, "You can't get a decent meal in Frankfurt." That wasn't ever *really* true, and it's gross libel today.

Still fighting to overcome a terrible culinary reputation, Frankfurt has moved forward, ranking up there with Berlin and München as a dining mecca.

Bistros have popped up in all districts, some serving such good food that patrons come from across town to sample the wares. Many of these bistros—and we've recommended the best of them—are cutting-edge.

Today three out of four restaurants opening in Frankfurt are not German. The city is becoming ever more diverse, in the way New York is. Newly arrived immigrants from the far corners of the earth are breathing life into Frankfurt's dining scene by opening restaurants and introducing their native cuisines to the city.

Today "fusion" is the word. Many restaurants mix cuisines such as American and Continental, French and Italian, German and Asian. The Japanese and Thai chefs are making the strongest showing among the foreign eateries.

Of course, Frankfurt lent its name to a sausage, which the Americans turned into "hot dog." And you can still get old-fashioned fare like steamed pork ribs with heaping portions of sauerkraut. This type of food is served mainly in the apple-wine taverns along the south bank.

1 Restaurants by Cuisine

ALSATIAN

Bistrot 77 🍴 (Sachsen-
   hausen, $$$, p. 90)

AMERICAN

Chicago Meatpackers
   (Stadtmitte, $, p. 79)
Surf 'nd Turf Steakhouse 🍴
   (Westend, $$$, p. 88)

AUSTRALIAN

Yours Australian Restaurant
   and Bar 🍴 (Stadtmitte, $,
   p. 83)

AUSTRIAN

Café Laumer 🍴 (Westend,
   $, p. 90)
Edelweiss 🍴 (Sachsenhausen,
   $, p. 92)

CAJUN

King Creole 🍴 (Nordend,
   $$, p. 97)

CALIFORNIAN

Pacific Colors 🍴 (Stadtmitte,
   $$, p. 75)

CONTINENTAL

Bistro Rosa 🍴 (Westend, $$,
   p. 89)
Charlot (Stadtmitte, $$,
   p. 72)
Exil 🍴 (Nordend, $$, p. 96)
Gargantua 🍴🍴🍴 (Westend,
   $$$$, p. 84)
Grössenwahn 🍴 (Nordend,
   $$, p. 97)
Oscar's 🍴 (Stadtmitte, $$,
   p. 74)

Platea Livingroom 🍴
   (Ostend, $$$, p. 95)
Plaza 🍴 (Stadtmitte, $$,
   p. 76)
Villa Merton 🍴🍴🍴
   (Westend, $$$$, p. 85)

EUROPEAN

Main Tower Restaurant &
   Bar 🍴 (Stadtmitte, $$,
   p. 73)

FRENCH

Avocado Bistro 🍴🍴🍴
   (Stadtmitte, $$$, p. 68)
Bistro Rosa 🍴 (Westend,
   $$$, p. 89)
Bistrot 77 🍴 (Sachsen-
   hausen, $$$, p. 90)
Brasserie (Stadtmitte, $$,
   p. 71)
Erno's Bistro 🍴🍴🍴
   (Westend, $$$$, p. 84)
Jasper's 🍴 (Sachsenhausen,
   $$, p. 91)
Knoblauch 🍴 (Westend, $$,
   p. 89)
Restaurant Français 🍴🍴🍴
   (Stadtmitte, $$$$, p. 67)

GERMAN

Altes Zollhaus (Heiligen-
   stock, $$, p. 100)
Brasserie (Stadtmitte, $$,
   p. 71)
Café Laumer 🍴 (Westend,
   $, p. 90)
Frau Schmidt (Sachsen-
   hausen, $, p. 92)
Haus Wertheym (Stadtmitte,
   $, p. 79)

Maingau Stuben ⓡ (Sachsenhausen, $$, p. 91)

Paradies (Stadtmitte, $$, p. 75)

Römer Bembel (Stadtmitte, $, p. 81)

Steinernes Haus (Stadtmitte, $, p. 82)

Wagner's ⓡ (Sachsenhausen, $, p. 93)

Weinhaus Brückenkeller ⓡ (Stadtmitte, $$$, p. 70)

Zum Bitburger (Stadtmitte, $, p. 83)

Zum Grauen Bock (Sachsenhausen, $, p. 94)

Zum Schwarzen Stern ⓡ (Stadtmitte, $$$, p. 71)

Zur Germania ⓡ (Sachsenhausen, $, p. 95)

GREEK

Exedra ⓡ (Stadtmitte $$, p. 72)

Nibelungenschaenke (Nordend, $$, p. 98)

Platea Livingroom ⓡ (Ostend, $$$, p. 95)

HESSIAN

Haus Wertheym (Stadtmitte, $, p. 79)

Historix (Stadtmitte, $, p. 80)

Maingau Stuben ⓡ (Sachsenhausen, $$, p. 91)

Solberfässje ⓡ (Stadtmitte, $, p. 82)

Zum Gemalten Haus (Sachsenhausen, $, p. 94)

Zum Grauen Bock (Sachsenhausen, $, p. 94)

INDIAN

Indian Curry House (Stadtmitte, $, p. 80)

INTERNATIONAL

Altes Zollhaus (Heiligenstock, $$, p. 100)

Bull + Bear (Stadtmitte, $, p. 78)

Café im Literaturhaus ⓡ (Westend, $$$, p. 88)

Central Park (Stadtmitte, $, p. 78)

Harvey's ⓡ (Nordend, $, p. 99)

Holbein's ⓡ (Sachsenhausen, $, p. 92)

Knoblauch (Westend, $$, p. 89)

Mövenpick am Opernplatz (Stadtmitte, $, p. 81)

Paradies (Stadtmitte, $$, p. 75)

Real Kantine (Stadtmitte, $, p. 81)

Stars & Starlets (Stadtmitte, $$, p. 77)

Tiger Restaurant/Palastbar & Tigerbistrot ⓡⓡⓡ (Stadtmitte, $$$$, p. 68)

Villa Merton ⓡⓡⓡ (Westend, $$$$, p. 85)

Weinhaus Brückenkeller ⓡ (Stadtmitte, $$$, p. 70)

ITALIAN

Gastronomie da Claudio ⓡ (Nordend, $$$, p. 96)

Osteria Divino & Cantina Divino (Stadtmitte, $$, p. 75)

Osteria Enoteca ⓡⓡⓡ (Rödelheim, $$$$, p. 100)

Ristorante Caruso ⍟ (Stadt-
mitte, $$, p. 76)

JAPANESE
Higematsu an der Börse
(Stadtmitte, $$, p. 73)
Mikuni (Stadtmitte, $$,
p. 74)

KURDISH
Tandure (Sachsenhausen, $,
p. 93)

MACEDONIAN
Exedra ⍟ (Stadtmitte, $$,
p. 72)

MEDITERRANEAN
Avocado Bistro ⍟⍟⍟
(Stadtmitte, $$$, p. 68)
Peninsula ⍟ (Stadtmitte,
$$$, p. 70)

SEAFOOD
Fisch-Brenner ⍟ (Nordend,
$, p. 98)
Surf 'nd Turf Steakhouse ⍟
(Westend, $$$, p. 88)

SWISS
Mövenpick am Opernplatz
(Stadtmitte, $, p. 81)

THAI
Tamnak Thai (Stadtmitte,
$$, p.77)

TURKISH
Tandure (Sachsenhausen, $,
p. 93)

VEGETARIAN
Wolkenbruch (Nordend, $,
p. 99)

2 Stadtmitte (the Inner City)
VERY EXPENSIVE
Restaurant Français ⍟⍟⍟ FRENCH   This restaurant is very stylish and very conscious of maintaining the top-notch standards that you might expect of an upscale hotel restaurant in Paris. It occupies a duet of stately looking rooms, outfitted in shades of imperial blue and gold, on the lobby level of Frankfurt's most prestigious hotel. Don't think you can go slumming if you drop in for a bite here. Jackets and ties are recommended for gentlemen. Menu items are cultivated, posh, and beautifully prepared and presented. The menu will have you salivating before you take a bite. The offerings fairly crackle with brilliant inventions such as goose liver terrine with an orange compote. Each day original soups are created, including, for example, cauliflower with nut butter. A delectable main course is the saddle of venison in an herb crepe with red cabbage and pear chutney. Another exciting main course is the grilled sea bass with two kinds of parsley and a ragout of mussels. What will the chef dazzle us with next? The maitre d' suggested saddle of suckling pig and pig's foot with stuffed vegetables, caramelized garlic, and a purple mustard sauce. We were indeed impressed.

In the Steigenberger Frankfurter Hof, Am Kaiserplatz. $\textcircled{C}$ **069/2-15-02.** Reservations required. Main courses 28€–34€. AE, DC, MC, V. Tues–Sat 6:30–11pm. U-Bahn: Willy-Brandt-Platz.

Tiger Restaurant/Palastbar & Tigerbistrot INTERNATIONAL This restaurant offers Frankfurt's finest dining. When Michelin first granted it a star in 2000, the city took notice. No one expected a restaurant associated with a cabaret to be as good as this. It's contained within a basement-level dining room that's immediately adjacent to a cabaret theater called Tigerpalast. Whimsical murals that might have been painted by a latter-day Jean Cocteau cover the walls of a dining room that has hosted Joan Collins, magicians Siegfried & Roy, lots of CEOs of local corporations, and most of the high-ranking ministers of the local government. Menu items are intensely cultivated and impeccably presented, as in the case of slices of sea bass resting under a spicy crust accompanied by sautéed pumpkin and mushroom foam, or the strudel of sole and scallops with spinach and a Noilly Prat sauce. The chef seems to perform culinary acrobatics in turning out such dishes as poached German beef with a potato risotto and fried artichokes in an herb sauce. Meals in the Palastbar & Tigerbistrot are less elaborate and cheaper, served under the vaulted brick ceiling of what was built as a warehouse about a century ago. Examples include vegetarian paella in saffron sauce; or breast of chicken stuffed with tomato, sage, and Parma ham, served with eggplant mousse and potato gnocchi.

Heiligkreuzgasse 16–20. $\textcircled{C}$ **069/92-00-22-50.** Reservations required. Main courses in Tiger Restaurant 25€–48€. Main courses in Palastbar & Tigerbistrot 20€–23€. Set-price menus in Palastbar & Tigerbistrot 36€–44€. AE, MC, V. Restaurant Tues–Sat 5–11pm. Palastbar & Tigerbistrot Tues–Sun 5pm–1am. U-Bahn: Konstablerwache.

EXPENSIVE

Avocado Bistro FRENCH/MEDITERRANEAN Chic, upscale, and soothing, this bistro has lots of fresh flowers, a turquoise and peach color scheme like you might expect in Florida, and an atmosphere that manages to be both grandly bourgeois and artsy at the same time. It's a suitable venue for either a seduction or a sales pitch; the kind of place where you frequently hear champagne corks popping. Menu items change with the seasons. Food selections on any given night are limited, but you're almost assured that every item is fresh and carefully chosen by the chef. Inventiveness and solid technique go hand in hand here. At our last meal we began with a confit of quail sprinkled with truffle oil, then moved

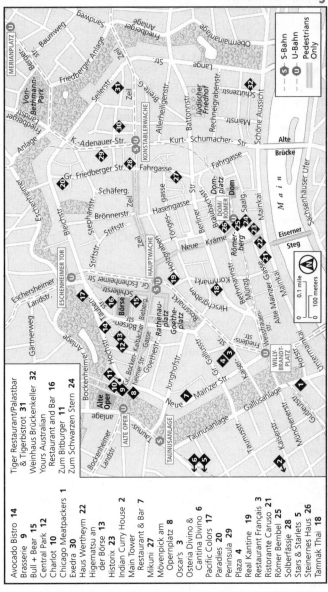

Avocado Bistro **14**
Brasserie **9**
Bull + Bear **15**
Central Park **12**
Charlot **10**
Chicago Meatpackers **1**
Exedra **30**
Haus Wertheym **22**
Higematsu an
der Börse **13**
Historix **23**
Indian Curry House **2**
Main Tower
Restaurant & Bar **7**
Mikuni **27**
Mövenpick am
Opernplatz **8**
Oscar's **3**
Osteria Divino &
Cantina Divino **6**
Pacific Colors **17**
Paradies **20**
Peninsula **29**
Plaza **4**
Real Kantine **19**
Restaurant Français **3**
Ristorante Caruso **21**
Römer Bembel **25**
Solbertfässje **28**
Stars & Starlets **5**
Steinernes Haus **26**
Tamnak Thai **18**

Tiger Restaurant/Palastbar
& Tigerbistrot **31**
Weinhaus Brückenkeller **32**
Yours Australian
Restaurant and Bar **16**
Zum Bitburger **11**
Zum Schwarzen Stern **24**

on to a saddle of turbot cooked in a saffron broth and filled with poached baby vegetables. The dish was made celestial with an accompanying champagne mousse. Another member of our party feasted on roasted saddle of rabbit served with plums in a coat of bacon on a mousse of beet roots, and filet of cod with apple and fig and red lentils. The desserts are divine—especially the chestnut mousse with chocolate truffles on rose pear *coulis*.

Hochstrasse 27. ℂ **069/292-867.** Reservations required. Set-price 3-course lunch 30€, 5-course dinner 57€. Main courses 24€–28€. AE, MC, V. Tues–Sat noon–2:30pm; Mon–Sat 6–11pm. U-Bahn: Opernplatz.

Peninsula ⟆ MEDITERRANEAN   One of Frankfurt's most stylish and elegant restaurants lies on the lobby level of the Arabella Sheraton Grand Hotel (see chapter 4). Mirrors and polished cherrywood adorn the dining room, which is a favorite of the city's industrial and financial moguls. The place is more intriguing at night; we find lunches here a bit dull. Although some German food critics rave about the place, we'd view it more as a convenience if you stay in the hotel. You eat well, but we wouldn't cross town to dine here, with all the more fascinating choices in Frankfurt. The chefs call their style *cuisine vitale,* stressing healthful and succulent preparations of artfully presented fresh ingredients. Examples include a liaison of salmon and John Dory filets with rice in chervil sauce, and a "composition of seafood" featuring several fish and shellfish, served with leaf spinach and two sauces. Some of the more recent dishes on the menu include grilled angler fish flavored with orange and chicory and served with roast potatoes; and roast cutlet of veal with tricolored beans and pan-fried potatoes. The dessert menu is appropriately elegant; a particular favorite is the Irish-coffee tart.

In the Arabella Sheraton Grand Hotel, Konrad-Adenauer-Strasse 7. ℂ **069/2-98-11-72.** Reservations recommended. Main courses 21€–26€. AE, DC, MC, V. Daily noon–2:30pm and 6–11:45pm. U-Bahn: Konstablerwache.

Weinhaus Brückenkeller ⟆ GERMAN/INTERNATIONAL Located in the heart of the Altstadt, this is one of Frankfurt's leading restaurants and a favorite spot of well-heeled North American visitors. Tables are candlelit, and strolling musicians encourage singing. Franconian carvings adorn the alcoves, and huge wooden barrels are decorated with scenes from Goethe's *Faust.* The food is light and subtle. A typical meal might begin with cream of sorrel soup, or more substantial roast goose liver with green beans, and perhaps a small salmon cake with caviar *crème.* The *tafelspitz* (boiled

beef) is the best in town. You might instead order filet of roast turbot with a white-wine cream sauce and a parsley risotto, or pink-
roasted saddle of lamb served with mashed potatoes flavored with
truffles and pimento. For a perfect finish, you might order a soufflé
of strawberries with vanilla sauce. The evening meal includes homemade sourdough bread. The wine cellar holds 285 selections of German wines, including the best from the Rhineland. Personal
attention and efficient service are hallmarks.

Schützenstrasse 6. **①** **069/29-80-07-0.** Reservations required. Main courses
28€–38€. AE, DC, MC, V. Daily 6pm–midnight. Closed Dec 20–Jan 8. U-Bahn: Konstablerwache.

Zum Schwarzen Stern ⑫ GERMAN   You'll likely be lured to
this place by its spectacular medieval facade, but the restaurant
inside is not as spectacular as the building itself. Still, it is warm and
inviting, and evocative of the Germany that existed before World
War I. Residents of Frankfurt often come here with nostalgic memories of their childhood. The kitchen produces the same hearty fare
it has for years, and does so exceedingly well. Frederick the Great
would surely have approved of the *tafelspitz* (boiled beef), which is
served with horseradish sauce. The filet of veal in a plum sauce flavored with Armagnac is prepared with meticulous care, as is the
goose breast flavored with aromatic cognac. The other dishes our
party enjoyed were a chile-flavored breast of chicken and a filet of
pork or beef with a creamy mushroom sauce. The mayor, we were
told, takes "only the most important journalists here when he shows
them Frankfurt."

Römerberg 6. **①** **069/29-19-79.** Reservations recommended. Main courses
12€–24€; 3-course set menu 36€; 4-course set menu 44€. AE, DC, MC, V. Daily
11:30am–11pm. U-Bahn/S-Bahn: Hauptwache.

MODERATE
Brasserie FRENCH/GERMAN   Slightly less expensive and less
formal than its cheek-by-jowl neighbor, the also-recommended
Charlot, this is a boisterous and convivial brasserie that can be a lot
of fun. There's a wood and brass-trimmed interior evocative of a setting you might expect to find in Paris, and during warm weather,
tables stretch onto the pavement, virtually within the shadow of
Frankfurt's stateliest building, the Old Opera House. The menu is
good but still a bit costly. You're paying for being at the very heart
of the old city. We were tempted by the marinated peppers with
fresh herb-laced cheese; it turned out to be a Mediterranean delight.

One member of our party opted for the seafood lasagna; the other fared better with the lobster salad with fresh green asparagus. A young couple dining nearby said neither of our dishes could match their choices—pike-perch with parsley-laced mashed potatoes and mustard sauce, and medallions of veal in a classic white-wine sauce. All four of us ended up enjoying a gratin of pineapple for dessert.

Opernplatz 8. 🅒 **069/91-39-86-34.** Reservations recommended. Main courses 11€–22€. AE, DC, MC, V. Daily 11am–midnight. U-Bahn: Alte Oper.

Charlot CONTINENTAL Few other restaurants evoke the Belle Epoque as effectively as this one. A bit grander and more formal than its also-recommended neighbor, Brasserie, it has an elaborate *Jugendstil* (Germany's answer to Art Nouveau) decor. The uniformed staff is mostly Italian and maneuvers effectively in the narrow spaces between tables. The restaurant offers a savory blend of cuisines from Italy, Germany, and France. Menu items change with the seasons, but might include carpaccio of tuna with herbs and fresh balsamic vinegar, pastas garnished with whatever seasonal vegetable is available at the time, braised filet of sole in the Provençal style, quail braised "in the Tuscan style," and roasted rack of lamb with black-peppercorn sauce. These dishes, more than those at any other cafe in central Frankfurt, evoke cafe dining, as do grilled sea bass with mustard sauce or veal cutlet in butter and sage. Everything is dependably good but not especially memorable. Tables expand onto the pavement in front during clement weather, offering a sweeping view over Frankfurt's stateliest buildings.

Opernplatz 10. 🅒 **069/28-70-07.** Reservations recommended. Main courses 20€–26€. AE, MC, V. Mon–Sat noon–3pm and 6pm–midnight; Sun 6pm–midnight. U-Bahn: Alte Oper.

Exedra 🅡 GREEK/MACEDONIAN Lots of local artists and administrators cite this as their favorite Greek restaurant in Frankfurt, and we agree. It lies behind a grand and ornate 19th-century facade, but once you're inside, you'll find a large and simply decorated *taverna* with big windows overlooking the street. Cuisine derives from northern Greece and several dishes merit special mention, especially the grilled lamb filet with feta cheese sauce and grilled sweet peppers. The cuisine is solid and reliable; we think you'll agree if you dig into the grilled octopus in oregano-flavored butter sauce. A local favorite is filet of lamb in a cheese sauce with grilled sweet peppers and home-fried potatoes. For something imaginative, try the leg of rabbit braised in shallots, cinnamon, and red wine. In the mornings and throughout the afternoon, the place functions as a neighborhood bar and cafe.

Heiligkreuzgasse 29. ☎ 069/28-73-97. Reservations recommended. Main courses 10€–19€. AE, DC, MC, V. Mon–Thurs 9am–1am; Fri 9am–2am; Sat 4pm–2am; Sun 4pm–1am. U-Bahn: Konstablerwache.

Higematsu an der Börse *(Finds* JAPANESE   Set beside a narrow alleyway that's difficult to find, just behind Frankfurt's stock exchange, this is the Japanese restaurant that many Japan-born residents of Frankfurt cite as their favorite. Look for this place on an alleyway within the triangle formed by the Grosse Bockenheimer Strasse, the Börsenstrasse, and the Hochstrasse. In some ways, it functions as the de facto home away from home for the hundreds of Japanese tourists and business travelers navigating their way through Frankfurt, a refuge from a metropolis that's tricky to understand, and a haven of supremely fresh sushi and sashimi. Expect a brightly lit and slightly claustrophobic warren of three pine-sheathed dining rooms, narrow stools pulled up to a lavish display of raw fish, and a no-nonsense, hysterically busy Asian staff that doesn't speak very much English or German. Don't expect bowing and scraping—this isn't the place for that kind of thing. The menu includes nearly every imaginable type of Japanese food, including our favorites: grilled eel with sushi rice, smoked salmon with salmon caviar, and chicken yakitori.

Meisengasse 11. ☎ 069/280-688. Reservations recommended for groups of 4 or more. Sushi 1.50€–4€ per piece; tempura 6€–7€ per portion; platters 13€–15€. AE, MC, V. Mon–Fri 11:30am–midnight; Sat–Sun 4pm–midnight. U-Bahn: Hauptwache.

Main Tower Restaurant & Bar ℛ EUROPEAN   Architecturally, this is the most unusual restaurant in Frankfurt, with a long line of diners who ascend every day for lunch, dinner, and afterwork cocktails. Set on the semicircular 53rd floor of one of the tallest buildings in Frankfurt, it offers a starkly postmodern environment of steel tables and minimalist chairs; the main aesthetic intrigue lies in views that extend for kilometers in all directions. The clientele is one of the most diverse in town, including grandmothers showing the view to their offspring, media hipsters affiliated with the building's TV stations, and newcomers trying to figure out the geography of Frankfurt. But the chefs don't try to get by on the view alone. Their cuisine is hardly the most imaginative in the city, but it is solid and reliable and prepared with fresh ingredients. Appetizers range from a smoked salmon with a pesto sauce to a carpaccio of beef with eggplant. Some of the best dishes here include tuna with spicy curried mashed potatoes, and filet of beef with a corn-flavored cream sauce and mushrooms, and Limousin lamb with sweetbread strudel.

In the Landesbank Hessen-Thüringen Building, Neue Mainzer Strasse 52–58. ⓒ **069/36-50-47-77.** Reservations recommended. Main courses 12€–28€. AE, DC, MC, V. Tues–Sun 5:30am–11pm (bar open until 1 or 2am). U-Bahn: Willy-Brandt-Platz.

Mikuni JAPANESE   It's obvious that this restaurant was originally designed as a Teutonic-looking German beer hall, a fact that you'll quickly surmise thanks to the *mitteleuropaische* (Middle European) paneling and accessories. But since new owners took over, there's also a handful of Japanese lanterns and paintings, and an all-Japanese staff who are far more fluent in German than in English. Service rituals and table settings are purely Japanese, and menu items focus on some of the best-tasting sushi, sashimi, tempura, miso soup, and teriyaki dishes in Frankfurt.

Fahrgasse 91–95. ⓒ **069/282-100.** Reservations recommended. Main courses 10€–34€; set-price menus 25€–30€. AE, MC, V. Mon–Sat noon–3pm and 6:30–10pm. U-Bahn: Konstablerwache.

Oscar's ⓐ CONTINENTAL   This is a bustling, hardworking replica of the kind of brasserie you might expect to find in France. Depending on the time of day, it adopts roles that include a morning cafe, a hard-drinking midafternoon and after-work bar, and a lunch and dinner environment that satisfies many of the office workers in the surrounding skyscrapers. This is the less expensive, and less formal, of the two restaurants within the Steigenberger Frankfurter Hof, one of Frankfurt's most prestigious hotels; as such, great amounts of attention are devoted to the food and service, despite the relatively reasonable prices. Menu items change every month, and are presented in ways both upscale and gourmet. Exceptional products are prepared with a finely honed technique, as exemplified by the penne pasta with arugula, tomatoes, and smoked mozzarella. Among the more appetizing selections are duck breast with arugula salad and sautéed lamb and Parma cheese. There's also a succulent, modernized version of lamb stew, or you can order grilled angler fish with potatoes. Dessert takes you to the tropics with a pineapple salad with a coconut and lime terrine.

In the Steigenberger Frankfurter Hof, Kaiserplatz. ⓒ **069/2-15-02.** Reservations recommended. Main courses 17€–20€. AE, DC, MC, V. Mon–Thurs 11am–midnight; Fri–Sat 11am–1am; Sun 5pm–midnight. U-Bahn: Willy-Brandt-Platz.

Osteria Divino & Cantina Divino ITALIAN   Simple, whole-some, and designed without too much regard for decor, this is a well-managed pair of unpretentious bistros that exist in stark contrast to the huge office buildings that rise nearby. They're managed by the very charming Olimpio Mautone, who sometimes plays medleys of Italian songs on his guitar as an accompaniment to dinners. The restaurants are set across the street from one another, each with the same hours and—except for very minor differences—roughly the same menu. Each contains simple wooden tables, a scattering of modern art, and a chattering, clattering sense of conviviality. Menu items are made from fresh ingredients, including the pastas, which are also made fresh daily. The best examples include tagliatelle with a tomato-based sauce that changes weekly, vegetable soup with fresh basil, and roasted guinea fowl with herbs. You are likely to be treated to braised arugula with strips of goose breast—a wonderful marriage of flavors—or a roulade of beef.

Zimmerweg 5–7. ℭ **069/72-13-08**. Reservations recommended. Main courses 8€–12€. No credit cards. Mon–Fri 11:30am–3pm and 6–midnight. U-Bahn: Hauptbahnhof.

Pacific Colors ℱ CALIFORNIAN   The most avant-garde hotel in Frankfurt, the Hilton, made special efforts to attract an avant-garde cuisine into this intensely dramatic lobby-level restaurant. It boasts a New Age design in (what else?) Pacific tones of sea green and blue, with big-windowed views over the trees and walkways of the Friedberger Anlage park. The food is what keeps gastronomes coming back—particularly those with a fondness for a Mediterranean-inspired cuisine that manages to be both airy and earthy. As conceived by culinary artist Andreas Mahl, the exact composition of the menu changes about every 3 months, but the best examples include a seafood medley: a trio of red snapper, white fish, and prawns served with spicy chile-laced noodles and a coriander syrup. The steak is also sumptuous: a filet mignon with an olive-and-potato tapenade.

In the lobby of the Hilton Hotel, Hochstrasse 4. ℭ **069/1338-000**. Reservations recommended. Main courses 17€–28€. AE, DC, MC, V. Daily noon–midnight. U-Bahn: Eschenheimer Tor.

Paradies GERMAN/INTERNATIONAL   This is a cozy German tavern, with half-timbered walls, exposed beams, and plenty of *gemütlichkeit* (roughly translated as a warm, cozy atmosphere with good company). The owner, Norman, caters to a mostly gay crowd, who usually consume aperitifs at the rustic-looking bar before chowing down at one of the cloth-covered tables. The menu includes traditionally prepared German dishes that change depending on the season and whatever is fresh at the time. The best examples include roasted haunch of venison served with gravy and almond-studded potato croquettes; a wide choice of schnitzels and sauerbratens; and roasted breast of goose with savory gravy. At Christmastime, a group of four can order an entire roasted goose, with all the trimmings, for 65€.

Alte Gasse 69. ⓒ 069/28-03-63. Reservations recommended on weekends. Main courses 10€–15€. MC, V. Daily 6pm–midnight (bar stays open until 1am). U-Bahn: Konstablerwache.

Plaza ⓡ CONTINENTAL The Plaza offers insight into the value some of Germany's large corporations place on the well-being of their employees. It was designed as a part of the street level of Frankfurt's most idiosyncratic skyscraper, the Commerz bank, by the Catalán designer Alfredo Arribas. Within a sun-flooded cocoon of laminated birch-veneer plywood, brushed aluminum, granite, and wraparound windows, you have a venue that functions as a cafe, a bar, or a full-fledged restaurant, depending on your schedule. "We have a goose today," the waiter whispered in our ear. And so he had. If we were expecting something German, we got Thai instead. It came as an appetizer: tender smoked breast of goose marinated in ginger and lemon grass and served on a bed of bean sprouts with a baked pickled plum. The soup was equally innovative—coconut with pumpernickel along with a fried banana dressed in bacon. Pastas are cooked al dente, and among the main courses we are especially fond of tuna and white marlin on a light crab foam with ginger carrots. Another exotic delight, evoking Morocco, is a lamb kebab on couscous with nuts, dates, and mints.

In the Commerzbank Building, Kaiserplatz. ⓒ 069/21-99-76-27. Reservations recommended for meals, not for drinks or snacks. 3-course business lunch 17€. Main courses 10€–16€. AE, MC, V. Mon–Fri 8am–10pm; Sun 11am–3pm. U-Bahn: Willy-Brandt-Platz.

Ristorante Caruso ⓡ NORTHERN ITALIAN This is one of the best bets for casual Italian dining in Frankfurt. This restaurant isn't particularly "decorated," featuring a much-used and not particularly imaginative ensemble of furniture that might have originally been installed sometime in the 1970s. However, the ambience that's created in this postwar ensemble of buildings just behind the Römer is warm and nurturing, with well-prepared food that's evocative of the mountainous region of northwestern Italy. For appetizers, the chef specializes in carpaccio, our favorite being one made with three types of fish. There's also a delectable carpaccio of herb-flavored raw salmon. All those soups from mamma's kitchen are here, including a truly excellent Italian minestrone. And then there's the pasta *fagiole*. The pastas reign supreme on the menu, with that old favorite *rigatoni ai quattro formaggi* (with four cheeses) winning new fans. Many of the pasta dishes are homemade, including ravioli served plain with butter and fresh sage. There's a special emphasis on a wood-fired grill, the aromas of beef, Italian sausage, and other meats perfuming the air. The filet steak with Gorgonzola is a specialty, and another rewarding dish is the mixed fish platter with monkfish, scampi, sole, and filet of turbot. The chef is also known for classic veal dishes including medallions in a lemon sauce.

Alte Mainzer Gasse 15. ℂ 069/2199-5754. Reservations recommended. Main courses 10€–16€. AE, MC, V. Sun–Fri noon–3pm and 6–11:30pm. U-Bahn: Römer.

Stars & Starlets INTERNATIONAL   Trade fairs in Frankfurt attract buyers and sellers from around the world. In light of this, the American-born designers of this place succeeded brilliantly at creating an environment so culturally neutral that virtually anyone, from anywhere, would be bemused and intrigued. The entrance lies at the bottom of what resembles a subway station in the shadow of the fairground's tallest tower, the red-sandstone skyscraper known as the *Messeturm*. Inside, you'll find a fantasy decor best described as a cross between *Alice in Wonderland* and *The Jetsons*. We're talking bright colors, sinuous lines, and cultural references that are very pop, very hip, and by now, intriguingly international. You can hang out at the sinuously curved bar for a high-octane cocktail, marveling at the varieties of people who'll be there with you. If your schedule segues into mealtime, expect steaks, salads, California wraps, fresh fish, and comfort food (after a day at the trade fairs, you'll probably need it) such as pastas. Know in advance that because of its location, this restaurant is likely to be mobbed during trade fairs, and much more sedate at other times.

At the foot of the Messeturm, Friedrich-Ebert-Anlage 49. ℂ 069/75-60-30-0. Main courses 14€–18€. 2-course set-price lunch 11€, 3-courses 13€. AE, DC, MC, V. Mon noon–3pm; Tues–Fri noon–11pm. U-Bahn: Messe Frankfurt.

Tamnak Thai THAI   This restaurant serves excellent Thai food that rivals and sometimes surpasses what you'd expect in grander, more expensive restaurants. Inside you'll find an all-teak environment that duplicates a riverside pavilion in Bangkok, a bamboo ceiling, lots of woodcarvings, and cuisine that can be as fiery or as muted as you request. The menu divides selections into chicken, pork, duck, prawn, fish, and vegetarian dishes. Curries, both red and green, are excellent, as are the dishes where the predominant flavors are lemon grass and ginger. Especially savory are king prawns with Thai curry and peanuts in coconut milk.

Berliner Strasse 64. ✆ **069/28-78-33**. Reservations recommended. Main courses 10€–17€. AE, DC, MC, V. Daily noon–3pm and 6pm–11pm. U-Bahn: Theaterplatz or Römer.

INEXPENSIVE

Bull + Bear INTERNATIONAL   The decor here might remind you of life inside a glass-sided cube, thanks to soaring ceilings and a glittery, metallic look that evokes the waiting room of an international airport. The room's focal point is a shimmering circular bar that's illuminated with pin lights and spotlights, like a high-tech version of a pagan temple. Many of the office workers in this intensely commercial neighborhood have been here at least once for lunch or dinner. Well-prepared menu items include club sandwiches, tortellini stuffed with ricotta and spinach, saddle of lamb with Provençal vegetables, and a wide selection of grilled Angus steaks. The clientele is as interesting as the food. Bull + Bear also serves as a singles bar and a late-night dance spot. In the basement, there's a dance floor that's usually mobbed, especially on Friday and Saturday, when it's the site of a well-attended after-work party. Dance to a live DJ playing house, techno, and trance music, which draws in a young, hip crowd. Cover charge is 8€. Drinks are reduced to 5€ each during happy hour, every day from 4:30 to 7pm.

Am Börsenplatz/Schillerstrasse 11. ✆ **069/133-887-33**. Reservations recommended for parties of 6 or more. Lunch salads, sandwiches, and platters 6€–8.50€; dinner main courses 13€–18€. AE, DC, MC, V. Mon–Thurs and Sun 10am–1am; Fri–Sat 10am–3am. U-Bahn/S-Bahn: Hauptwache.

Central Park INTERNATIONAL   Set close enough to the city's commercial core to be mobbed with after-work drinkers, this restaurant lies within an all-black, artfully lit cube, built almost entirely of metal and glass. On Saturday nights there is a live DJ playing dance music. Jutting incongruously into a commercial street in the town center, it provides a venue that's comfortable with both business and the arts, separating its rows of white-clothed tables from the bar and drinking stools with nylon strap dividers like those you see in airports. The overall effect is stylish, culturally neutral, and hip, an aura that's especially obvious as the cocktail hour segues into dinnertime.

Come here for virtually any cocktail known to humankind, although *mojitos* (a Cuban rum and lime cocktail) are especially in vogue. Menu items include burgers, pastas (including a *crespelle* filled with mushrooms in cream sauce); and platters such as a ragout of angler fish with a Thai curry sauce. There's also vegetarian risotto and tandoori chicken. The food is perfectly acceptable in every way, but most patrons here are on the see-and-be-seen circuit; it's great for people-watching.

Kaiserhofstrasse 12. © **069/91-39-61-46.** Reservations recommended. Pastas, sandwiches, and burgers 5€–11€. Platters 9.50€–23€. AE, DC, MC, V. Mon–Sat 11am–11:30pm. Bar open till 1am Mon–Wed, till 2am Thurs, and till 3am Fri–Sat. U-Bahn: Hauptwache.

Chicago Meatpackers *(Kids* AMERICAN Frankfurt celebrates the American experience with this mostly red and brown saloon, which is located behind an ornate 19th-century facade overlooking the backside of the Neues Opernhaus (New Opera House). A member of a chain that maintains other branches in Köln, Paris, London, and Düsseldorf, it offers a decor that evokes a cleaned-up version of the Chicago stockyards in 1948, with rough-textured planking, an amusing collection of old-fashioned Americana, and a well-rehearsed sense of internationalism. Despite the emphasis on Chicago and its meatpacking expertise, most of the beef served here is Argentinean. The steaks are tender, the ribs are zesty, the fried chicken is juicy, and everything is dished up in generous portions (there's very little fish, if any). Kids will love the burgers, which are the juiciest in town. Cocktails, which include such fanciful names as the "Beverly Hills," are priced at around 6.50€ to 7.50€, except during happy hour (5–7:30pm) and "The Blue Hour" (10:30–11:30pm), when they're reduced to around 4€.

Untermainanlage 8. © **069/23-16-59.** Main courses 7€–13€. AE, DC, MC, V. Mon–Thurs and Sun 11:30am–midnight; Fri–Sat 11:30am–1 or 2am. U-Bahn: Theaterplatz.

Haus Wertheym GERMAN/HESSIAN Few other restaurants evoke old Frankfurt as authentically as this half-timbered house that sits a half block from the Main, on a cobble-covered street near the Nikolaikirche. Originally built in 1479, then reconstructed in the same style after the 1944 bombings, it has a somewhat claustrophobic interior loaded with wood paneling and antique accessories, and cheerfully brusque waiters. Don't expect grand cuisine, or even any particular sense of internationalism; the aura here is that of a deeply entrenched monument featuring cuisine that hasn't changed very much in the past 50 years. Examples include pork schnitzels with french fries, pork schnitzels in green sauce, *frankfurter hacksteak* (chopped steak), and a fine version of *tafelspitz,* the boiled beef specialty beloved by the Austrians. Virtually everything here, unless you specify differently, is served with the restaurant's trademark green sauce and, in most cases, parsley potatoes.

Fahrtor 1. (C) **069/28-14-32.** Reservations recommended. Main courses 13€–22€. No credit cards. Daily 11am–11pm. U-Bahn: Römer.

Historix HESSIAN   This restaurant is positioned, almost like a museum exhibition to the age-old art of regional Hessian cooking, on the ground floor of Frankfurt's Historische Museum. As such, it attracts exhausted museum-goers looking for a respite from too much culture. But because of its low prices and well-prepared cuisine, it also attracts diners who might not have visited the museum in many years, if at all. There's a strong emphasis on maintaining a setting that looks historic and authentic to the age-old Hessian tradition of wine and apple-cider cellars, but the modern world is very much apparent through big, plate-glass windows that let in sunlight and a view of passersby in the old town outside. Expect a menu of purely traditional Hessian food, the kind that tastes fabulous with the tart and acidic flavor of hard cider. The best examples include pork schnitzels with green sauce, *tafelspitz, frankfurter hacksteak* (chopped steak), and roasted pork shank with green sauce. Most main courses are served with boiled and parsley-dotted potatoes. A half-liter (about a pint) of hard cider costs 3€.

In the Frankfurt Historische (Historic) Museum, Saalgasse 19, Altstadt. (C) **069/ 294-400.** Reservations recommended. Main courses 8€–11€. MC, V. Daily 11am–11pm. U-Bahn: Römerberg.

Indian Curry House *(Value* INDIAN   This is a well-scrubbed, cost-conscious eatery that's well known to the thousands of office workers who toil in the towers nearby. It features mass-produced versions of the varied cuisines of north and south India, which are displayed in bubbling containers on a glassed-in steam table near the entrance, immediately adjacent to a large bronze statue of a dancing Shiva bedecked with flowers. Don't expect fancy decor. You'll sit either in a cramped street-level room or at sturdy Formica-covered tables on a mezzanine upstairs. But the food is genuinely well prepared, so much so that it's delivered as takeaway to many nearby offices at lunch every day. Most dishes are accompanied with fragrant basmati rice.

Weserstrasse 17. ✆ 069/23-59-86. Reservations not accepted. Main courses 6€–9€. AE, DC, MC, V. Mon–Sat 11am–11pm. U-Bahn: Hauptbahnhof.

Mövenpick am Opernplatz *Kids* SWISS/INTERNATIONAL This busy member of a Swiss-owned restaurant chain is clean, efficient, and bustling, partly because of its location in the commercial heart of Frankfurt, and partly because of a well-maintained setting, good value, and reasonable prices. Within the busy premises you'll find three different areas: a simulation of an outdoor terrace, an informal spot with leather banquettes and the look of a French bistro, and an area that pays homage to the Art Deco heyday of Hollywood. Try the antipasto buffet, a lavish display containing salads, marinated fish and vegetables, guacamole, small tarts, and an herb-laden roster of competently prepared Italian dishes. There's also a large selection of salads and pastas, roast rib of Angus beef with horseradish cream sauce, scampi in bordelaise sauce, and more. Everything tastes good but is not exactly exciting. The reasonable prices and wide variety of choices make this a great place for families.
Opernplatz 2. ✆ 069/2-06-80. Reservations recommended. Main courses 10€–17€. AE, DC, MC, V. Mon–Sat 8am–11:30pm; Sun 11am–11:30pm. U-Bahn: Hausen.

Real Kantine INTERNATIONAL The staff here claims that you can tell what time it is by what the clients are wearing: Lunchtime and early evening draw an office crowd, usually wearing jackets and ties despite the counterculture appearance of a setting that's been described as a curvy blue-and-black glass box. Late night is a lot less conservative, especially when the upstairs singles bar (Studio) opens. Look for an especially active crowd every Wednesday, when the entire complex is mobbed with hard-drinking, hard-flirting workers from the local banks, who party here from just after work till around midnight. This cafe's curried chicken salad is known to most of the neighborhood as a meal-sized event that makes a worthy lunch. Other choices include a ragout of goose in mustard sauce, served with rigatoni and fresh tomatoes. The food is competent, even quite good at times, but it is the social scene that gets the raves.
Katharinenpforte 6. ✆ 069/29-20-34. Reservations recommended for groups of 4 or more. Main courses 9€–14€. No credit cards. Daily 10am–10:30pm. U-Bahn: Konstabler Hauptwache.

Römer Bembel *Value* GERMAN This is the cheapest and least pretentious of the three or four restaurants facing Frankfurt's Römer (town hall). The restaurant, named after a local cider jug that is traditionally salt-glazed in blue and gray, expands its interior during warm weather with tables that spill out onto the cobble-covered square in front. Despite the fact that this place was rebuilt from rubble in the wake of the city's 1944 bombings, you'll find a sense of *gemütlichkeit* (coziness) in the wood-paneled interior that absolutely reeks of old Germany. You practically expect to hear Greta Keller singing her World War II hit, *Lili Marleen* (which Marlene Dietrich changed into *Lili Marlene*) in the background. Don't come here for haute cuisine—this is old German cooking with a vengeance. But don't knock it; many visitors prefer such rib-sticking fare as filet of beef, and what meat eater doesn't like sauerbraten?

Römerberg 20–22. ✆ **069/28-83-83.** Reservations recommended. Main courses 8€–13€. AE, DC, MC, V. Daily 11am–midnight. U-Bahn: Römer.

Solberfässje ✪ *Finds* HESSIAN Cramped, old-fashioned, and gregarious, this restaurant is firmly committed to maintaining its role as the kind of beer bar and working-class restaurant that thrived in this neighborhood a century ago, when its clientele included mostly the horse cart drivers delivering supplies to homes and stores along the nearby Zeil. Food items focus on schnitzels, sauerbraten, roulades of beef, and the kinds of roasted knuckles and joints that dyed-in-the-wool beer lovers savor, and which have been associated with *bierkellers* (beer taverns) since anyone can remember. They include roasted shanks of lamb, veal, pork, beef, and turkey, each of which emerges savory and crackling from the ovens. There are also three versions of *eisbein* (pork knuckle): roasted, smoked or steamed. Rainer Sänger is the hardworking, English-speaking host. The restaurant's name, in Hessian dialect, refers to a medieval technique of preserving meat in barrels filled with salt.

Grosse Friedberger Strasse 8. ✆ **069/29-67-67.** Reservations recommended. Main courses 6€–13€. AE, DC, MC, V. Mon–Sat 10am–midnight. U-Bahn: Konstabler Hauptwache.

Steinernes Haus GERMAN The 500-year-old Steinernes Haus, in the historic heart of Frankfurt, was restored simply and unpretentiously after the war. Locals come here for the good German beer, along with hearty rib-sticking fare. Nouvelle here translates as anything that came after Bismarck. The daily main-dish specialty includes salad and potatoes. Other choices include a selection of sausages, beef filet, and such popular German dishes as *zigeunerhackbraten* (spicy meatloaf) and *frankfurter rippchen* (smoked pork). The best choice is a filet steak cooked on a hot plate right at your table.

Kids   Family-Friendly Restaurants

Chicago Meatpackers (p. 79)   Kids can satisfy American-style appetites at this chain restaurant. Burgers are the juiciest in town.

Holbein's (p. 92)   In the Städel Museum, Holbeins is known for its affordable prices and a menu wide ranging enough to please the various tastes of an extended family.

Mövenpick am Opernplatz (p. 81)   One of the best and most reasonably priced family dining rooms stands right in the heart of Frankfurt. It's a member of a Swiss chain known for its good value meals. There is an array of different dining venues here and a menu so wide-ranging it's almost guaranteed to please everybody in your family.

Zum Gemalten Haus (p. 94)   You can dine early at this apple-wine tavern, where children will discover some of the biggest and tastiest franks they've ever eaten.

Braubachstrasse 35 (around the corner from the Rathaus). ☎ **069/28-34-91.** Main courses 10€–24€; daily platters 7€–11€. MC, V. Daily 11am–1am. Tram: 11.

Yours Australian Restaurant and Bar ⚐ (Finds AUSTRALIAN This is one of the least highbrow restaurants in town, a folksy and extroverted setting. After several Australia-inspired drinks (one of the best is a Frozen Mango), you'll begin to get in the mood of Down Under. Amid replicas of hard-drinking kangaroos, and within a woodsy and virtually unbreakable setting that could survive a late-night drink fest with the rowdiest of rugby teams, you can order food that manages to be both juicy and exotic. The best examples include honey pepper-crusted chicken, grilled steaks (including versions crafted from emu, beef, and—yes—kangaroo), all kinds of burgers, salads, and sandwiches, and grilled skewers loaded with chunks of emu, kangaroo, and crocodile. Rack of Australian lamb or chicken Dijon are also worthwhile, if somewhat less exotic.

Entrances on Rahmhofstrasse 2 or in the Schillerpassage. ☎ **069/282-100.** Main courses 5€–17€. AE, DC, MC, V. Mon–Fri 11am–1am; Sat–Sun 9:30pm–midnight. U-Bahn: Hauptwache.

Zum Bitburger GERMAN This brewery-operated restaurant enjoys a long and proud tradition. Waiters somehow manage to slip through the crowds with mugs of beer and hearty platters of food.

The standard but well-prepared dishes include grilled rump steak, goulash, and sausages with red cabbage and home-fried potatoes. You can begin with the soup of the day, and there's always a fresh seasonal salad. You don't find too many German food critics here, but you do see a horde of hearty Frankfurters who enjoy robust fare like their mother made. The kitchen serves hot food until midnight.

Hochstrasse 54 (near the Alte Oper). ✆ **069/28-03-02.** Reservations required. Main courses 10€–21€. No credit cards. Mon–Sat 11am–1am. U-Bahn: Alte Oper.

3 The Westend

VERY EXPENSIVE

Erno's Bistro ★★★ FRENCH A chic midtown rendezvous, Erno's draws everybody from visiting film stars to bank executives. This cramped, claustrophobic place with an English-speaking staff offers fine service, plus a commendable cuisine that seems to improve year after year. Under its former chef and namesake, Erno Schmitt, this restaurant became the first in Frankfurt to earn a Michelin star. He's gone, but Valéry Mathis carries on in a grand tradition. Actually, we like this bistro better than before. Frankfurt foodies recommend the place for its great cuisine, people-watching, and sense of theatrical flair. The kitchen serves fish brought fresh by air from European waters. The chef offers both *cuisine moderne* and what is known as *cuisine formidable* ("awe-inspiring"). The most exciting (and expensive) appetizer is artichokes in puff pastry with sautéed potatoes and foie gras. For a main course, we'd suggest the pigeon with duck liver in a savory truffle sauce. Another excellent choice is filet of venison coated with truffles and served with a smooth and creamy savoy cabbage. A recent main course was a braised leg of rabbit so tender it fell off the bone. It was served on a bed of lentils and diced carrots infused with a soupçon of curry. The chef also regales you with rack of lamb with a ragout of white beans, and sea bass with beets and a truffle sabayon.

Liebigstrasse 15 (between the Alte Oper and the Palmengarten). ✆ **069/72-19-97.** Reservations required. Main courses 14€–38€; business menu (2 and 3 courses) 31€–41€; fixed-price menu 80€. AE, MC, V. Mon–Fri noon–2pm and 7–10pm. Closed mid-June to mid-July. U-Bahn: Westend.

Gargantua ★★★ CONTINENTAL One of the Westend's genuinely stylish restaurants evokes an upscale and somewhat snobbish 1920s-era bistro in Paris. Set on a verdant street corner with outdoor tables that are separated from the sidewalk with a wrought-iron fence, it's outfitted in tones of green and white, and named after the hearty gourmand that was created during the French Renaissance by Rabelais. The guiding force behind the cuisine here is a local food writer and columnist, Klaus Trebes, who with his wife, Monika, is usually directing the restaurant in a discreet, well-versed way that includes a sophisticated knowledge of German, Italian and Austrian wines. Patrons come here expecting a near-perfect dining experience, and that's what they get. Flavors, textures, and colors combine to delight in such dishes as a creamy soup with black sausage and Périgord truffles, or a zesty risotto with radicchio, squid, and spicy sausage. The chef is at his best when he's preparing sea bream with white beans, tomatoes, and olives with a bouillabaisse sauce, or oxtail in a black-truffle sauce. Deliciously aromatic in its *jus* is a duck breast in vinegar cherry sauce.

Liebigstrasse 47. ℂ **069/72-07-18.** Reservations required. Main courses 16€–29€. 6-course set-price dinner 65€, 4 courses 50€. AE, DC, MC, V. Mon–Fri noon–2:30pm and 6pm–1am; Sat 6pm–1am. U-Bahn: Westend.

Villa Merton ✦✦✦ CONTINENTAL/INTERNATIONAL Some of the most exquisite food in Frankfurt is served here; only Tiger is better. Dishes are filled with zesty flavors and a lot of creative imagination. The French neoclassical villa that contains this restaurant was built in 1925 by a wealthy metallurgist and industrialist, Richard Merton. Today, in an upscale neighborhood west of the Palmengarten, it's the headquarters of a private club that includes many of the diplomats and bankers of Frankfurt. On weekends it's reserved only for the use of its members. Monday through Friday, however, you can visit. Be warned in advance that this place does not resemble a conventional restaurant, and on some nights, especially Monday through Wednesday, it can appear somber and anything but cutting-edge. Lunchtime, however, attracts diplomats from the many nearby consulates, and can get very busy. The cuisine is superb, well worth the trek from central Frankfurt. Menu items change with the seasons. We went here with the mayor, who demanded that we try the cream of black salsify with truffles. We were so pleased, we told him when he retired as mayor he could hire out as a food critic. A new and delightful item is pigeon breast with a truffle-studded risotto. What a treat! The sea bass with smoked fish purée, artichokes, and fresh herbs is so superb we wanted to come back the next day and order it again. Another hit with discerning diners is rack of lamb with olive crumb and vegetable tart. In autumn, gourmets flock here for venison ragout with fresh chanterelles.

Frankfurt Dining

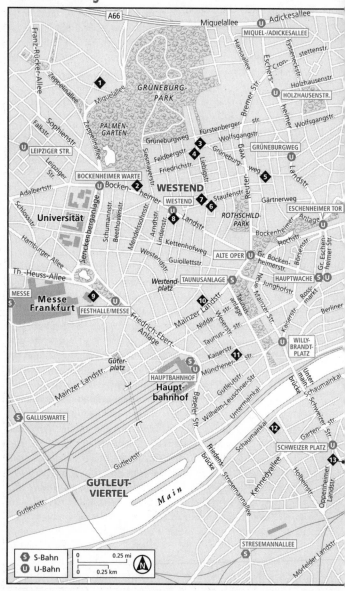

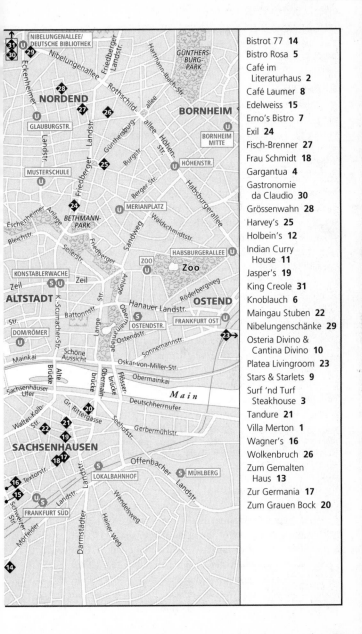

Am Leonhardsbrunn 16. ℭ **069/70-30-33.** Reservations required. Main courses 25€–30€; fixed-price lunch 28€; fixed-price 3-course dinner 52€, 4 courses 62€, and 5 courses 72€. AE, DC, MC, V. Mon–Fri 11am–3pm; Sat–Sun 6–10:30pm. U-Bahn: Leipziger Strasse or Bockenheimer Warte.

EXPENSIVE

Café im Literaturhaus Ɽ INTERNATIONAL   This is the literary focal point of Frankfurt, a city whose self-image is firmly entrenched as the site of the largest literary marketplace in the world. It's housed within what was built as a distinguished private villa in 1912, and which was acquired as the headquarters for a privately endowed literary organization in 1991. Today, it is the site of lectures and book signings by recognized critics, academics, and authors, many of whose works are available only in German. When lectures on Proust, Schiller, or Kafka are over, participants gravitate toward the in-house dining room, a high-ceilinged but sparsely furnished room that's patterned on the literary cafes of Vienna during the late 19th century. Don't expect to have free access to this building during the Frankfurt Book Fair as it is mobbed by some of Europe's biggest publishers. Most of the time, however, you'll be able to sit on one of the notoriously uncomfortable bentwood chairs, either in the spartan-looking inside or on the garden terrace, soaking up the auras of the literati. Sample dishes include risotto with Parmesan and vegetables, tagliatelle with a ragout of fish, ravioli with sage-flavored butter, Provençal-style fish soup, pork filet with apple-calvados sauce, and chicken tikka with eggplant salad. Although these dishes are quite tasty, the food seems a mere afterthought to all the business deals usually going on here.

Bockenheimer Landstrasse 102. ℭ **069/74-55-50.** Reservations recommended. Main courses 12€–20€. 3-course set-price menu 25€, 4 courses 36€. AE, MC, V. Sun–Fri noon–2:15pm and 6pm–midnight. U-Bahn: Westend.

Surf 'nd Turf Steakhouse Ɽ AMERICAN/SEAFOOD   From the name of this restaurant, you might expect a 1950s roadside American diner. No way. The aura here is fin de siècle. This was the home of Engelbert Humperdinck—not the Welsh singer, but the 19th-century composer of the opera *Hansel und Gretel.* The great writer Heinrich Hoffmann also resided in this building. Persons carrying old guidebooks show up here thinking the address is the Michelin-starred restaurant Humperdinck, but that's gone. While you still get a neoclassical atmosphere, it's now a venue for good-tasting steaks, zesty ribs, seafood combos, and some of the city's freshest fish. It remains to be seen whether this radical conversion of a Frankfurt monument to haute cuisine will find its footing.

Grüneburgweg 95 (near the Palmengarten). ℰ **069/722-122.** Reservations required. Main courses 20€–34€. AE, MC, V. Mon–Fri noon–3pm; Mon–Sat 6pm–midnight. Closed July 1–Aug 3. U-Bahn: Grüneburgweg.

MODERATE

Bistro Rosa ℱ CONTINENTAL/FRENCH   From the outside, the gingham curtains and brass rails of this place evoke a saloon. From the inside, the venue resembles a French bistro, complete with caricatures of pigs that bear vague resemblance to Toulouse-Lautrec, Goethe, and some of Germany's politicians, each of them satirically transmuted into more hoggish forms. Although pork occasionally appears on the menu, in the form of strips of filet of pork in a mustard-flavored cream sauce, for example, a more likely bet might include duck breast with orange sauce. You don't have to wait for the holiday season to enjoy those old-time German favorites, roast goose with red cabbage and chestnuts or roasted lamb in an herb-flavored crust. A dish unlikely to be found anywhere else is the breast of pheasant, a real delicacy, served with pineapple. Desserts include chocolate mousse or crème brûlée. In summer, a narrow terrace, separated from a parking lot by ivy-covered lattices, provides outdoor seating.

Grüneburgweg 25. ℰ **069/72-13-80.** Reservations recommended. Main courses 20€–24€. No credit cards. Mon–Sat 6pm–midnight. U-Bahn: Westend.

Knoblauch ℱ INTERNATIONAL/FRENCH   This is a less pretentious and less expensive version of the grander restaurant Erno's, which sits virtually across the street. Don't judge the place by its decor—it may remind you of a battered trucker's bar in central France, thanks to a rather artless collection of paintings and vertical-plank paneling that hasn't been upgraded since the 1960s. Cuisine, however, draws a loyal clientele back to the dining rooms for tastes of such seasonal dishes as wild greens with asparagus, salmon in herb sauce, quail in port wine sauce, stuffed breast of chicken with saffron sauce, and duck breast with honey sauce and vegetables. An uncompromising Teutonic staple that's almost constantly available (and was the preferred dish of Austrian emperor Franz Josef) is *tafelspitz*, a boiled beef main course served with horseradish. The restaurant contains room for only 10 tables, some of which might be occupied by families with young children.

Staufenstrasse 39. ℰ **069/72-28-28.** Reservations recommended. Main courses 9€–22€. No credit cards. Mon–Fri noon–2pm and 6:30pm–1am. U-Bahn: Westend.

INEXPENSIVE

Café Laumer ⚜ *Finds* GERMAN/AUSTRIAN   There are many cafes scattered throughout Frankfurt, but this one is proud of literary antecedents that are a bit deeper, broader, and more authentic than those that are cited by some of its competitors. No one will mind if you adopt this place as a cafe, but if you want full-fledged meals, they're available as well, but only until its regrettably early closing every day at 7pm. Menu items include crisp schnitzels, freshly made salads, grilled steaks with peppercorn sauce, roulades of beef or pork stuffed with herbs and bread crumbs, and when it's available, good-tasting fresh game and fish dishes. Framed honorariums on the walls of this place refer to its most historically famous client, a prominent scholar of Hegel and Marx, musicologist and philosopher Theodor Adorno (1903–69), who used to come here every day in the 1930s for coffee and conversation before moving on to professorships at Oxford and Princeton.

Bockenheimer Landstrasse 67. ✆ **069/727-912.** Reservations recommended for meals, not for drinks. Main courses 5€–12€. MC, V. Mon–Sat 7:30am–7pm; Sun 9am–7pm. U-Bahn: Westend.

4 Sachsenhausen

Alt-Sachsenhausen has been called the most quintessentially Frank-furtian neighborhood in the city, but now that the main street, Schweizer Strasse, is filled with bistros, cafes, and boutiques catering to tourists, some of the old character is gone. Nonetheless, it remains an interesting place, especially for its many apple-wine taverns.

EXPENSIVE

Bistrot 77 ⚜ FRENCH/ALSATIAN   This bistro remains chic after many years in business. German food critics still rave about it, and we always stop in at least once a year and find the cookery as fine as it ever was, which is saying a lot. The overall impression is one of light and glass, with a black-and-white tile floor and an airy latticework ceiling. In summer, tables are set on the terrace. Dominique and Guy Mosbach, two French citizens, have made a name for themselves with their contemporary cuisine, a frequently changing array of imaginatively prepared fish and meat dishes, along with intriguing appetizers and desserts. The chefs go to the market themselves, passing over what's dull until they find the freshest produce. Back in the kitchen, they handle these ingredients faultlessly and delicately season them, never overpowering natural flavors.

> (*Moments* **Getting Drunk on** *Apfelwein*
>
> In taverns throughout Frankfurt, you can drink local apple wine (similar to hard cider), which many locals enjoy and many foreigners consider a cousin to vinegar. Our verdict: It's an acquired taste. Tradition says that you won't like the apple wine until you've had three big steins. After that, what does taste matter? Our two favorite taverns are Wagner's (p. 93) and Zur Germania (p. 95).

Ziegelhüttenweg 1–3 (about 1km/¹/₂ mile from the city center), Frankfurt-Sachsenhausen. ℂ **069/61-40-40.** Reservations required. Main courses 22€–26€; fixed-price meals 25€; "menu surprise" 55€. AE, MC, V. Mon–Fri noon–2pm; Mon–Sat 7pm–midnight. Closed Dec 24–Jan 6. Bus: 62. Tram: 16.

MODERATE

Jasper's ℛ *Value* FRENCH   This stylish bistro, lined with mirrors and Art Nouveau accessories, evokes the French city of Lyon more than it does Frankfurt. A native Alsatian, Daniel Arlen is in charge of the menu, and each month he focuses on a different region of France, doing an exceedingly good job of presenting a medley of that section's regional dishes. His tomato-based fish soup is as good as some encountered on the French Riviera, and he prepares snails served with garlic sauce on a bed of spinach. His roast lamb is especially succulent, as is his roast goose in a traditional German style. His desserts are praiseworthy as well, and we approve of his decision to keep such stalwarts as chocolate mousse on the menu. Prices seem affordable for what you get.

Schifferstrasse 8 (near Affentorplatz), Sachsenhausen. ℂ **069/614-117.** Reservations recommended. Main courses 10€–19€; fixed-price menu 25€. AE, DC, MC, V. Mon–Sat 6pm–1am. Train: 16 or 17.

Maingau Stuben ℛ HESSIAN/GERMAN   One of the best-loved of the Sachsenhausen restaurants, this south-bank restaurant does a thriving business. Although food critics note a great variance in the cuisine at times, we have been richly rewarded on our visits. The menu isn't as old-fashioned as you might think by the traditional setting of subdued lighting and linen tablecloths. The chef does duck extremely well, and is also noted for his rack of venison served in a walnut crust. On a recent visit we enjoyed a saddle of rabbit wrapped around fresh green asparagus.

Schifferstrasse 38–40. ℂ **069/610-752.** Reservations recommended. Main courses 15€–22€. AE, MC. Tues–Sun noon–3pm; Tues–Sat 6–10pm. U-Bahn: Südbahnhof.

INEXPENSIVE

Edelweiss ✿ *Value* AUSTRIAN   This is the most visible and prominent Austrian restaurant in Frankfurt. At least some of its fans come here specifically for the reminders of their homeland to the east, including soccer stars in town from Austrian-based leagues, and many of the Austrian-born financiers who happen to be toiling away within the mega-conglomerates of the city's financial district. The setting is within a pair of well-scrubbed, wholesome-looking dining rooms that are paneled in light-grained hardwoods and lined with memorabilia that an Austrian would recognize immediately as a symbol of his or her homeland. Wines are equivalent to what you might expect at a *heurigen* (wine tavern) in the Vienna woods, and menu items read like the traditional, time-tested fare that might have appealed to the Habsburgs. Signature dishes include a delightful smoked breast of goose with salad greens and a paprika-flavored honey sauce; goulash soup; *tafelspitz* (boiled beef); Corinthian-style cheese noodles with burnt butter sauce, salad, and chives; Wiener schnitzels; and desserts that feature crepes with ice cream and chocolate sauce and a richly caloric custard known as *kaiserschmarr'n*.

Schweizer Strasse 96, Sachsenhausen. ✆ **061/61-96-96.** Reservations recommended. Main courses 10€–15€. AE, DC, MC, V. Mon–Fri 11:30am–midnight; Sat–Sun 5pm–midnight. U-Bahn: Schweizer Strasse.

Frau Schmidt GERMAN   There are lots of restaurants in Frankfurt serving traditional German food and apple wine, but this one is unusual in the degree to which it attracts sports fans. You'll enter it via a charming frescoed arcade depicting an idealized Teutonic life of long ago. Inside, you'll find well-scrubbed pinewood benches and tables, and a big TV screen broadcasting whatever sporting event (usually rugby or soccer) that most interests the die-hard fans of this place. Along with endless carafes of apple wine, patrons dig into the liver noodle soup and follow with a selection of wursts, including those delectable little white sausages evocative of Nürnberg. Main dishes, usually meat, often overflow the plate, especially the pork schnitzel. The roasted knuckle of pork with wine-marinated sauerkraut is a favorite of aging men who probably shouldn't be eating such a rich dish.

Textorstrasse 24. ✆ **069/62-13-13.** Reservations recommended. Main courses 7€–11€. No credit cards. Daily 11am–11pm. U-Bahn: Südbahnhof.

Holbein's ✿ *Kids* INTERNATIONAL   In stark contrast to the 19th-century architecture of the museum that rises around it, this restaurant occupies a soaring "glass box" that a team of designers added to what had been a U-shaped courtyard. Since its opening in 1999, it has become a restaurant destination that's sophisticated and stylish, as proven by the many clients who come here with absolutely no intention of visiting the museum afterward. On Saturday and Sunday it's particularly busy, thanks to extended families that sometimes drop in *en masse* for a communal meal. Menu items change with the season, but are likely to include such well-conceived choices as Asian-style pumpkin soup, American-style Caesar salad, tartar of salmon with a cucumber carpaccio, various forms of pike-perch, including a version with a dill sauce, surf and turf, and a zesty curried lamb.

In the Städel Museum, Holbeinstrasse 1. ℂ **069/660566-66.** Reservations recommended. Main courses 15€–25€. AE, DC, MC, V. Tues–Sun 10am–10:30pm. U-Bahn: Schweizer Platz.

Tandure TURKISH/KURDISH   Expect crowds of diners at this restaurant, which celebrates Turkish and Kurdish cuisine and sits behind an ornate 19th-century Teutonic facade. Part of its popularity derives from low prices and savory food that includes herbed yogurt with garlic and pickles; vegetarian kebabs and platters loaded with grilled eggplant and beans; succulent grilled versions of lamb cutlets; lamb sausages with onions; and eggplant stuffed with pine nuts, onions, and tomatoes. There's even an Anatolian pizza slathered with ground meat and herbs. A worthy beginning might be a heaping sample plate of the house's specialties, called *Tandus-platte,* with a savory selection of some of the restaurant's most asked-for specialties. The decor is rustic Anatolian, and includes weavings, carved wood, and copper pots.

Wallstrasse 10. ℂ **069/61-25-43.** Reservations recommended. Main courses 9€–22€. AE, MC, V. Daily 11am–3pm and 6pm–midnight. U-Bahn: Sachsenhausen.

Wagner's 🍴 GERMAN   This restaurant almost always factors into every Frankfurter's short list of charming and traditional apple-wine restaurants. It was established in 1931 in a labyrinth of half-paneled rooms, and other than upgrading the overworked kitchens, it hasn't changed very much since. Expect an environment that's gregarious, overcrowded, and smoky, and a clientele that's younger and more hip than those at such competitors as Zum Gemalten Haus. Chances are that you'll be seated elbow to elbow with strangers—who are usually indulgent with your lack of familiarity with the rituals here. Be warned in advance that production of large amounts of cigarette smoke is *de rigueur* here. Menu items are plunked down in front of you from a staff who literally has to elbow their way in and around the crowded tables. Meals tend to include schnitzels, *rippchen,* roasted knuckles of pork, and wursts, all of which usually taste wonderful with the local apple wine.

Schweizer Strasse 71. ℂ **069/61-25-65.** Reservations accepted only for groups of 10 or more. Main courses 7€–12€. MC, V. Daily 11am–1am. U-Bahn: Schweizer Platz.

Zum Gemalten Haus *(Kids* HESSIAN   Chances are you'll share a table here with other patrons—in the garden if the weather is fair. The kitchen provides ample portions of good Hessian cooking at this family-style dining room. You'll enter an elaborately frescoed room that's loaded with *gemütlichkeit* and local older patrons who seem to enjoy nursing a glass of apple wine or schnapps and reminiscing about yesteryear. This is about as authentic as an apple-wine tavern can get: claustrophobic, sun-flooded, sudsy, and covered with murals that, despite their sense of cornpone and kitsch, evoke a romanticized view of *Alte Hessen.* The menu is limited but savory. If you're in a group, try the "frankfurter platte," which usually includes liver paté, blood sausage, the chef's special frankfurter wurst, sauerkraut, and perhaps knockwurst with sauerkraut or potato salad. The *eisbein* (pork knuckle with mashed potatoes), washed down with apple wine, is the cook's specialty. If your kids are hot-dog fans, they can order the biggest, tastiest franks they've ever eaten. As you no doubt know by now, this cuisine is not for the faint of heart. No one's ever heard of mad cow disease around here or, if they have, they don't care. The apple wine is homemade.

Schweizer Strasse 67. ℂ **069/61-45-59.** Reservations recommended. Main courses 4€–12€. MC, V. Wed–Sun 10am–midnight. Tram: 16.

Zum Grauen Bock GERMAN/HESSIAN   Sometimes the communal singing here is so robust that it's necessary to slide back the roof on a summer night. An accordionist goes from table to table, involving everyone in the singing. Featured on the menu is *handkäse mit musik* (cheese with vinegar, oil, and onions), but you may want to leave the subtle pleasures of this dish to the locals. Instead, try a German specialty, *schweinshaxen,* the huge pork shank with sauerkraut and boiled potatoes. A good beginning is the liver dumpling soup or the goulash soup. As one local who shared a table with us said, "My wife and I come here to eat as Goethe did. We don't like slices of kiwi or mango on our meat."

Grosse Rittergasse 30–45. ✆ **069/61-80-26.** Reservations recommended. Main courses 6€–15€; 3-course fixed-price menu 14€–20€. AE, MC, V. Mon–Sat 5pm–1am. U-Bahn: Lokalbahnhof.

Zur Germania ✦ *(Finds)* GERMAN   It would be hard to get more local, or more authentic, than in this animated and earthy apple-wine house. The setting is a single room whose wood sheathing, brown paint, and battered benches and tables might remind you of a one-room schoolhouse. Very little about the place has changed since its founding in 1905. You'll sit elbow to elbow with fellow diners at long trestle tables, amid lots of cigarette smoke and conviviality. In summer, the venue expands onto an outdoor terrace. Menu items include a roster of sausages, as well as herb-enriched *rippchen mit kraut* (pork ribs with sauerkraut) and *handkäse mit musik,* a salty and rather pungent cheese with parsley and onions that invariably inspires you to order more drink. Other menu choices include pork filets with onions, grilled pork knuckle with potatoes, and lamb goulash.

Textorstrasse 16. ✆ **069/61-33-36.** Reservations recommended. Snacks 3€–15€. Main courses 14€–21€. No credit cards. Mon–Thurs 4pm–midnight; Fri–Sun 11pm–midnight. U-Bahn: Südbahnhof.

5 Ostend (East End)

EXPENSIVE

Platea Livingroom ✦ CONTINENTAL/GREEK   On busy nights, especially Thursday through Saturday, the numbers of people who manage to cram into this very hip restaurant and bar inspires awe (and envy) in virtually every other restaurateur in Frankfurt. It lies immediately adjacent to two of Frankfurt's most popular nightclubs (King Kamehameha and One Ninety East) within a secluded, brick-lined courtyard that's the headquarters of one of the city's most powerful labor unions. Expect a high-ceilinged, rigidly symmetrical rectangular room centered around a massive bar, white-clothed tables arranged on platforms around the perimeter, and an absolute crush of people crammed like sardines waiting for a table. Cuisine is Greek and redolent with eastern Mediterranean flavors. In this lively, casual atmosphere, you can sample a plate of mixed dips eaten with tasty bread fresh from the oven. The octopus salad is the only way to begin a proper meal in Greece, or so we were told, and it was perfectly marinated. Then it was on to tender lamb cutlets with aromatic seasonings, and the inevitable souvlaki. To continue in a solidly Greek vein, we sampled the tender roasted lamb, and one of us did even better with pike-perch filets with fresh spinach.

Hanauer Landstrasse 192. ℂ **069/480-026-60.** Reservations required. Lunch main courses 11€–15€; dinner main courses 14€–21€. AE, MC, V. Restaurant Mon–Wed 6–11pm; Thurs–Sat 6–11:30pm. Bar daily 11:30am–1am. Tram: 11 or 14.

6 Nordend (North End)

EXPENSIVE

Gastronomie da Claudio ⏣ ITALIAN   Few other restaurants in Frankfurt evoke the high-altitude Italian Dolomites as effectively, or as charmingly, as this one. It occupies the ground floor of an apartment building in a verdant residential neighborhood on the north side of town, on a quiet, well-heeled street. Claudio Bertozzi, originally from the Italian resort of Rimini, cites the origin of much of his cuisine as deriving from the gastronomic citadel of Italy's Emilia-Romagna region. He bought an already established but undistinguished restaurant in 1975. It has welcomed prominent visitors (including visits from both Benny Goodman and the president of Italy) ever since. The venue suggests the inside of a chalet so effectively that you might get a sense that snow is falling outside, regardless of the season. The menu changes daily, but is likely to include such time-tested staples as homemade pasta and fresh fish. We always like to start with *antipasti de verdura,* going on to the tender, roast duck. Meat eaters, mainly Italian expats, praise the veal here, and claim you'd have to go to Venice to get calf's liver as good. The Italian province of Abruzzi is noted for its herb-flavored lamb, and Claudio does a version to make the province proud.

Zum-Jungen-Strasse 10. ℂ **069/56-54-71.** Reservations recommended. Main courses 18€–26€. AE, DC, MC, V. Mon–Fri noon–3pm; Sun–Fri 6pm–midnight. Closed mid-July to mid-Aug. U-Bahn: Marbachweg.

MODERATE

Exil ⏣ CONTINENTAL   Once a closely guarded secret, this restaurant now draws diners from across the city. The decor is minimalist, with cream walls and wooden tables relieved with pottery, pictures, and mirrors. A small garden is inviting on a lovely summer night. Well-executed dishes include a cream-of-spinach soup and a fresh spinach salad with turkey strips and herb-flavored feta cheese; no one handles spinach in Frankfurt better than the chefs here. A delightful dish is spaghetti with scampi and arugula, flavored with a Pernod sauce. Our party gravitated with glee to two main courses— roast chicken breast flavored with tarragon and served on a bed of field greens, and roast filet of lamb with rosemary sauce, accompanied by a gratin of potatoes. The dessert temptation is panacotta, rich and creamy, and filled with fresh, sweet-tasting strawberries.

Mercatorstrasse 26. (© **069/44-72-00.** Reservations necessary 3 days in advance. Main courses 8€–20€; 3-course set dinner 30€. V. Sun–Thurs 6pm–1am; Fri–Sat 6pm–2am. Bus: 30 to Hessendenkmal.

Grössenwahn ⊛ CONTINENTAL   Although it's been around only since the 1980s, there's something about this place that might make you think it's at least 50 years older. That's partly because of its location behind an ornate 19th-century facade overlooking a park, and because of the cheerfully battered dark wood paneling that sheathes the inside. Most residents of Frankfurt know Grössenwahn for its role as a catalyst to the arts, the Greenpeace movement, and some kind of political activism. Whether those themes dominate your conversation here or not, you can at least pretend to be a member of the Nordend's intelligentsia as you sip wine or beer, and order from a menu of generously portioned items. These are likely to include field greens with chunks of smoked salmon; grilled chicken breast with basil stuffing, served with morels and homemade fettuccine; or a Lombard-style ragout of venison with gnocchi and broccoli. Roasted knuckle of lamb with a rosemary-flavored sauce and white beans proves that the kitchen staff are pros. Roasted saddle of lamb—an unusual main dish that doesn't often appear in other restaurants—comes with a mushroom-studded red-wine sauce and herb-flavored *spätzle* (dumplings). Dessert might be a heavenly sabayon mousse. During clement weather, the number of seats within this restaurant is doubled when tables and chairs are set out on the pavement.

Lenaustrasse 97. (© **069/59-93-56.** Reservations required. Main courses 7€–15€. AE, MC, V. Restaurant Mon–Sat 6–11pm. Bar Mon–Thurs 4pm–2am; Fri–Sat 4pm–3am. U-Bahn: Glauburgstrasse.

King Creole ⊛ CAJUN   Jambalaya, gumbo, and Cajun spices aren't what you associate with Frankfurt. But *Der Feinschmecker,* the German gastronomy magazine, continues to cite this as one of the 200 best restaurants in the country. There's a New Orleans chic to the place with jazz music in the background and arty prints on the walls. Louisiana flavor may have lost something crossing the ocean, but the cuisine is pretty good. The lamb Creole was excellent, as was its accompanying tangy tomato sauce. The grilled red filet of red snapper arrived in a zesty orange sauce resting on a bed of green peppermint rice. Americans come here for the Cajun steak or the stuffed chicken breast with crabmeat. We always go for one of the jambalayas, which include everything from seafood to vegetable jambalaya. There's even a pumpkin soup with rabbit—an offering rarely found outside of the back roads of the deep South.

Eckenheimer Landstrasse 346. 🕐 **069/54-21-72.** Reservations recommended. Main courses 14€–17€. AE, MC, V. Mon–Sat 6–11pm. Bus: 34 or 39.

Nibelungenschaenke GREEK For those venturing into the Nordend, this is the only Greek restaurant worthy of Exedra in Stadtmitte. At this tavernlike restaurant, the Greek waiter welcomes you as if you've just come home, even if it's a first visit. The portions are large and generous, and the cuisine worthy, evoking memories of some of the finest fare you've had in the Aegean. The food is always nicely cooked, especially the braised eggplant strips and the medallions of sole served with an olive purée. For something heartier, pork filets are baked in cheese, and a beef filet comes with a béarnaise sauce. For appetizers, we suggest the meze platter with such delights as pink taramasalata and a splendid rendition of rice-filled grape leaves. For dessert, we suggest the pastry filled with walnuts and topped with vanilla ice cream. Our greatest compliment? It made us homesick for Greece.

Nibelungena Lee 55. 🕐 **069/55-42-44.** Reservations recommended. Main courses 15€–20€. No credit cards. Mon–Fri 11:30am–2:30pm and 5pm–2am; Sat 5pm–2am; Sun 11:30am–2am. Bus: 32.

INEXPENSIVE

Fisch-Brenner 🕏 *Value* SEAFOOD Established in 1894, this fish store in the Nordend is one of the most famous seafood emporiums in the province of Hesse. It occupies a not-very-large storefront that's modern, clean, blue-and-white, and loaded with on-ice inventories of every imaginable kind of fish living in Atlantic, North Sea, or Baltic waters. But despite the state-of-the-art displays, there's a strong sense that this is a neighborhood store that sold seafood to the grandparents of today's clients. Most of the inventory is hauled away by local residents for transformation into an evening's dinner, but a lunchtime crowd, many of them conscious of the health benefits of a low-cholesterol diet, ask to have their fish grilled, sauced, and served in plastic or Styrofoam containers. The contents of these can be consumed at small stand-up tables, accompanied with bread, butter, and glasses of wine or beer. Every platter is accompanied with bread, potatoes, and vegetables, and the food is both inexpensive and delicious. Joachim Schutz and family have owned and operated this place since 1985.

Spohrgasse 17A. ℰ **069/59-08-19.** Platters 4.50€–8€. No credit cards. Tues–Thurs 9am–6pm; Fri 8:30am–6pm; Sat 8:30am–1pm. U-Bahn: Eschenheimer Landstrasse. Tram 12. Bus: 30.

Harvey's ℛ *Finds* INTERNATIONAL   In the early 1990s, this bar and restaurant focused on a clientele of gay men and, to a lesser degree, women. (It was named in honor of Harvey Milk, San Francisco's martyred gay city-supervisor.) Today, the restaurant is one of the entrepreneurial success stories of Frankfurt, thanks to its ability to attract a crossover crowd of straights and gays; the result is a walloping good time. The setting is one of the few antique buildings in Frankfurt that was never damaged by the bombs of World War II. Its high-ceilinged interior sports the most amusing frescoes in the city. It's a Renaissance and pre-Raphaelite fantasy that includes clusters of pink roses against a Bordeaux-colored background, cherubs who cavort amorously on the ceiling, artfully undressed muses, and something that looks like Venus emerging from the restraints of S&M bondage. The whimsical decor changes with whatever holiday or festival happens to intrigue the staff at the time. You can order German, English, French, Norwegian, American, or vegetarian versions of breakfast in this place every day till 4pm, just in case you've had a hard time recovering from last night's binge. Menu items include one of the best club sandwiches in Frankfurt, as well as a changing array of soups (at least two new ones every day), salads, fish, pastas, and savory meat dishes. The percentage of gay clients tends to be higher here in winter than in summer, when the size of the place is quadrupled with the addition of an outdoor garden strewn with tables.

Bornheimer Landstrasse 54. ℰ **069/599-356.** Reservations recommended only for dinner on Fri–Sat. Main courses 6.50€–12€. Breakfast 8€–10€. No credit cards. Sun–Thurs 10am–1am; Fri–Sat 10am–2am. U-Bahn: Merianplatz. Tram: 12.

Wolkenbruch VEGETARIAN   For those who wouldn't even set foot in a restaurant that serves those monstrous pork shanks, Wolkenbruch is the way to go. This little macramé-filled eatery in the Nordend seems more likely to attract Greenpeacers than the average business traveler. Wholesome and tasty food is served in this eco-friendly, PC restaurant. Daily specials are served with whole-grain pitas. Everything's washed down with an organic dark beer from Bavaria, although you can opt for juice instead. The salads are very fresh and wholesome, and the kitchen is known for a vegetarian pizza piled high with fresh spinach, Gorgonzola, onions, garlic, herbs, and fresh tomatoes. Watch for the ever-changing dessert specials of the day, and leave those cigarettes back in your room.

Rotlinstrasse 47. ℂ 069/43-18-59. Main courses 7€–9€. No credit cards. Mon–Fri 6pm–midnight; Sat–Sun 10am–midnight. U-Bahn: Musterschule.

7 On the Outskirts

Some of the best and most intriguing restaurants lie on the periphery of Frankfurt but are easily reached.

HEILIGENSTOCK
MODERATE

Altes Zollhaus GERMAN/INTERNATIONAL   This restaurant is set within a half-timbered structure that was originally built in 1750 as a tollhouse. Within its timbered and nostalgically antique-looking premises, you can enjoy relatively formal meals whose ingredients change with the seasons. Between October and February, expect a rich assortment of game dishes, especially venison and pheasant, usually cooked with wine sauce and herbs. In spring, look for different combinations of asparagus dishes, including an "asparagus cocktail" garnished with strips of ham and vinaigrette sauce. During warm weather, additional seating is set up within the garden. It's a longtime family favorite and gives you a chance to escape from the commercialized heart of Frankfurt for a few hours.

Friedberger Landstrasse 531, in Heiligenstock (7km/4½ miles north of Frankfurt). ℂ 069/472-707. Reservations recommended. Main courses 12€–16€; fixed-price menus 15€. AE, DC, MC, V. Daily 6pm–midnight; Sat–Sun noon–3pm. Bus: 30 to Heiligenstock.

RÖDELHEIM
VERY EXPENSIVE

Osteria Enoteca ★★★ ITALIAN   For some of the city's finest haute cuisine, you need to venture into the Rödelheim district northwest of the inner core. It stands alone as the finest Italian dining room in the greater city area. Chef Carmelo Greco pushes the button on Italian cuisine, trying to reach its more sublime limits; his partner, Roland Brzenski, is an expert on the wines of sunny Italy and offers great advice. We could fill up on the freshly baked breads served here. Instead of butter, you smear the slices with olive paste.

An *amuse-gueule* of quail meat and egg—served with a medley of beans and peas—whetted our appetite for the filet of tuna, which was pan-seared, leaving it sushi-raw in its pink interior. It arrived on a bed of white polenta rimmed with deep-fried sausage strips. The tasting menu of six courses is highly recommended. It's always a surprise and a delight. Surely there is no chef in town who makes a better zabaglione than Carmelo.

Arnoldshainer Strasse 2. ℂ **069/78-92-16.** Reservations required. Main courses 18€–29€; fixed-price 50€–60€. AE, MC, V. Mon–Fri noon–2:30pm; Mon–Sat 7pm–1am. Bus: 34, 55, or 60.

6 Exploring Frankfurt

When bombs rained on Frankfurt in 1944, nearly all the old half-timbered buildings were leveled. In what might have been a record reconstruction, however, residents of Frankfurt rebuilt their city into a fine mélange of modern and traditional architecture, and faithfully restored some of their most prized old buildings as well.

Although Frankfurt doesn't have the monuments or museums to equal München or Berlin, its museums and exhibition halls lure some two million annual visitors.

As the cultural director of the city of Frankfurt, Dr. Hans Bernhard Nordhoff, told us, "We offer you everything from Goethe to Andy Warhol, from *Tyrannosaurus Rex* to the female ideal of Botticelli."

Many of the grandest museums lie along the Main on the south bank—often called "Museum Embankment," which in and of itself a dazzling array of contemporary architecture before you even go inside to look at the exhibits.

SUGGESTED ITINERARIES

If You Have 1 Day

Far too short, but you'll have to make do. Wander the Altstadt in the morning and pay your respects to Goethe at his restored house and museum. Lunch in one of the modern Stadtmitte cafes to capture the spirit and vitality of the city. In the afternoon, try to see at least some of the treasures of the Liebieghaus and Städel Gallery. For an authentic Frankfurt evening, go to one of the apple-wine taverns on the south bank of the Main.

If You Have 2 Days

On your second day, allow a full morning (more if you have time) to explore the treasures of the Liebieghaus and Städel Gallery that you missed on day 1. These galleries house some of the most important art and sculpture in Europe, and a visitor rushing through them in one day can't possibly absorb their treasure trove of artistic goodies. Spend as much time as you can in either gallery, perhaps having lunch at the Main Tower for the most panoramic view of Frankfurt. If time remains, head for the Palmengarten for a relaxing stroll through the historic greenhouses and conservatories, a nice break from seeing so much art in 1 day.

If You Have 3 Days

Spend your third day devoted to esoteric attractions such as the Deutsches Filmmuseum and the Museum for Kunsthandwerk, which contains one of Germany's greatest collections of applied art. Head for the zoo—one of the most important in Germany—in the afternoon. In the evening, if opera is your thing, try to attend a performance at the Alte Oper. Not into opera? Frankfurt is filled with nightclubs and bars catering to all persuasions.

If You Have 4 Days

Take a side trip. There is no better place to go nearby than to the old city of Wiesbaden, lying 40km (25 miles) west of Frankfurt. A spa since Roman times, the city is sheltered between the Rhine and the Taunus Mountains. It competes with Baden-Baden as Germany's most fashionable resort. A major cultural center filled with amusements, attractions, and fine dining, it may entice you to hang out for even a fifth day.

1 The Top Attractions

ALTSTADT 🏵🏵

Allow about half a day to explore the attractions of the old town, which was once one of the greatest and most historic in Germany before World War II bombing raids turned it to dust. It has been sensitively restored. Its specific attractions include **Goethehaus,** where Germany's greatest writer was born in 1749. He spent his early life wandering around the Altstadt, and you can follow in his footsteps. Perhaps he was dreaming of such future works as *The Sorrows of Young Werther* or contemplating the beginnings of *Faust.*

Among the more intriguing sights (detailed below) is the Dom, which was consecrated in 1239. This cathedral was chosen to serve as the electoral site for the kings of the Holy Roman Empire in 1356. Ten imperial coronations took place here between 1562 and 1792.

Among other attractions are the **Römer,** an interconnected trio of medieval patricians' houses, which functioned as the city hall of Frankfurt as early as 1405. Today it is still the official seat of Frankfurt's Lord Mayor. The Römerberg is the historic core of the old Altstadt, famous for its magnificent half-timbered houses that were reconstructed according to original plans.

At the northern edge of the Altstadt is **An der Hauptwache,** named for the old *Hauptwache* (guardhouse), which stands upon it.

Frankfurt Attractions

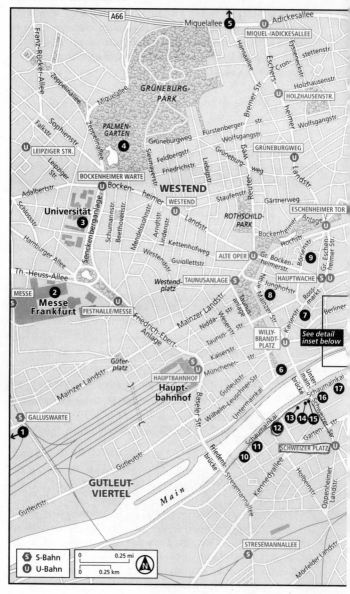

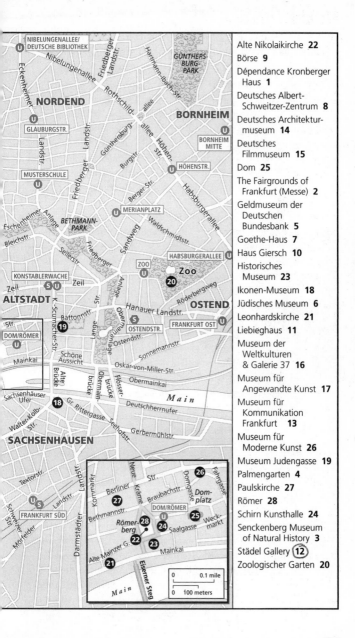

This square is the heart of modern Frankfurt. Underneath is the Hauptwache U-Bahn station with a modern shopping promenade.

Goethehaus 🅐   This house, where Johann Wolfgang von Goethe (1749–1832) was born, has been a shrine for Goethe enthusiasts since it opened to the public in 1863. One observer wrote that the postwar restoration was carried out "with loving care and damn-the-expense craftsmanship." The house is decorated in various styles, all reflecting the fashion trends of the 18th century: neoclassical, baroque, and rococo. You can view the library, where Goethe's father worked and often watched the street for the return of his son. A portrait of the severe-looking gentleman hangs behind the door of his wife's room.

On the second floor is an unusual astronomical clock built around 1749 and repaired in 1949 to enable it to run for another 200 years. One room contains a picture gallery with paintings collected by Goethe's father. These works, mainly by contemporary Frankfurt artists, influenced Goethe's artistic views for a great part of his life. One of the poet's rooms contains one of his most important childhood possessions: a puppet theater, which played a significant role in his novel *Wilhelm Meister.*

Annexed to the house is the **Frankfurter Goethe-Museum.** This museum contains a library of 120,000 volumes and a collection of about 30,000 manuscripts, as well as 16,000 graphic artworks and 400 paintings associated with Goethe and his works.

Grosser Hirschgraben 23–25. 🅒 **069/13-88-00.** Admission 5€ adults, 2.50€ students, 1.50€ children, free for children 6 and under. Apr–Sept Mon–Fri 9am–6pm; Sat, Sun, and holidays 10am–4pm. Oct–Mar Mon–Fri 9am–4pm; Sat, Sun, and holidays 10am–4pm. U-Bahn/S-Bahn: Hauptwache.

Liebieghaus 🅐🅐🅐   This sculpture museum stands alongside the Bargello in Florence as one of the most important in Europe. The building is an 1896 villa. Its collection includes objects from ancient Egypt, classical Greece and Rome, and medieval and renaissance Europe. Highlights include a small 8th-century B.C. bronze horse, and Roman copies of the *Torso* of Polycletus, Praxiteles's *Satyr,* and Myron's *Athena.* Although the most ancient artifacts generate the most excitement, the medieval section is also fascinating. Look for the *Virgin and Child* created in Trier in the 11th century; the head of Barbel von Ottenheim (attributed to van Leyden in 1462); the Riemenschneider *Madonna;* Andrea della Robbia's altarpiece of the Assumption, and the 16th-century *Black Venus with Mirror.*

Schaumainkai 71. ℭ **069/212-8617.** Admission 4€ adults and 2.50€ seniors, students, and children. Tues and Thurs–Sun 10am–5pm; Wed 10am–8pm (last entrance is at 4:30pm even on Wed). Tram: 15 or 16 to Otto-Hahn-Platz.

Städel Gallery 𝕽𝕽𝕽

This is Frankfurt's most important art gallery, containing a fine collection of most European schools of painting. The first floor features French Impressionists such as Renoir and Monet, along with German painters of the 19th and 20th centuries. Note in particular Kirchner's *Nude Woman with Hat.* Also on the first floor is Tischbein's *Portrait of Goethe in the Campagna in Italy.* But if you're short on time, go directly to the second floor to view the outstanding collection of Flemish primitives, 17th-century Dutch artists, and 16th-century German masters such as Dürer, Grünewald, Memling, Elsheimer, and many others. One of the most impressive paintings is Jan van Eyck's *Madonna* (1433). Lucas Cranach is represented by a large winged altarpiece and his rather impish, nude Venus. Recent acquisitions include Jean Antoine Watteau's *L'Île de Cythère* (1709). In the Department of Modern Art are works by Bacon, Dubuffet, Tapies, and Yves Klein.

Schaumainkai 63 (on the south bank of the Main). ℭ **069/60-50-98-0.** Admission 6€ adults, 5€ children 12 and older, free for children under 12. Wed–Thurs 10am–10pm; Tues and Fri–Sun 10am–8pm. U-Bahn: Schweizer Platz.

RÖMERBERG 𝕽

The Altstadt (U-Bahn/S-Bahn: Hauptwache) centers around three Gothic buildings with stepped gables, known collectively as the **Römer,** Römerberg (ℭ **069/21-23-48-14**). These houses were originally built between 1288 and 1305 and bought by the city a century later for use as the Rathaus (city hall). The second floor of the center house is the **Kaisersaal** (Imperial Hall), lined with the romanticized 19th-century portraits of 52 emperors; 13 of them celebrated their coronation banquets here. If the hall isn't being otherwise used (and keep in mind that this building functions mainly as a busy municipal nerve center, and not as a museum, per se), you can visit the Kaisersaal as part of a guided tour that's priced at 3€ per person (no discount for students; free for children under 12). In theory, the Kaisersaal is open for visits daily from 10am to 1pm and from 2 to 5pm. But depending on a complicated series of factors (such as the frequent use of the Kaisersaal for municipal functions), the interior of the building might not be accessible to casual visitors during either the morning or the afternoon session. Be prepared for a rather brusque staff (even the Frankfurters complain about it) and some very erratic closings.

The elaborate facade of the Römer, with its ornate balcony and statues of four emperors, overlooks **Römerberg Square.** On festive occasions in days gone by, the square was the scene of oxen roasts that featured flowing wine. Today, unfortunately, the Fountain of Justitia pours forth only water, but oxen are still roasted on special occasions.

DOMPLATZ ⍟

The dominant feature of the Altstadt is the 15th-century red-sandstone tower of the **Dom-St. Bartholomäus,** in whose chapels the emperors of the Holy Roman Empire were elected and crowned for nearly 300 years. The church was constructed between the 13th and 15th centuries on the site of a Carolingian building. It is most noted for its towering **Westturm** (west tower) ⍟⍟, which is greatly ornamented and crowned by a polygonal gable. It's topped by both a lantern and a dome. Surprisingly, the cathedral was not completed until 1877, but it was based on plans created by the Dom's original architect, Madern Gerthener. Destroyed by Allied bombs in 1944, it was rebuilt in 1953. One of its chief treasures is its mid-14th-century **choir stalls** ⍟, which represent brilliant Upper Rhine craftsmanship. In a north chancel chapter, look for *Maria Schlaf*, the Altar of Mary Sleeping, dating from 1434. It is the only altar remaining from the church's original interior. The Domplatz is open daily from 9am to noon and 2 to 6pm, and admission is free.

In the cloister of the church is the **Dom Museum** (✆ **069/29-70-32-36**), which exhibits robes of the imperial electors, among other exhibits. These robes, which are still quite sumptuous, were worn at coronation ceremonies. The oldest vestments date from the 1400s. If you walk west of the cathedral, you'll discover the Historischer Garten, or archaeological garden, with ruins of both Roman and Carolingian fortifications. The Dom Museum is open Tuesday to Friday from 10am to 5pm and Saturday and Sunday from 11am to 5pm. Admission is 2€ for adults and 1€ for children.

2 Other Top Museums

Dépendance Kronberger Haus   Set in Höchst, a suburb of Frankfurt that's the site of one of Germany's most famous porcelain manufacturers, this is an annex of the also-recommended Historical Museum. It contains more than 1,000 pieces of faience and porcelain (many of them much-sought-after antiques), paintings, a textile collection, and a battery of utilitarian objects that trace the development of industry in Germany during the 19th century. There's also a library that's of interest mainly to specialized scholars. A series of special exhibitions detail the patterns of migration in and out of Germany since the end of World War II.

Höchster-Porzellan, Bolongarostrasse 152, 65929 Frankfurt-Höchst. ⓒ **069/212-367-12.** Admission 4€ adults, 2€ for students and children 6–15, free for children under 6. Sat–Sun 11am–6pm. Take a train from Bahnhof Frankfurt to Bahnhof Höchst.

Deutsches Architekturmuseum ⓐ *(Finds)* When it opened in
1979, it was the first museum of its kind in Europe. The angular-looking building that contains it was designed by Oswald Mathias Ungers as a thought-provoking catalyst for explorations of how humankind has sheltered itself from the elements, beginning with the mud-brick structures of the Sumerians to present-day high-rises. Scholars especially appreciate its vast archives—blueprints, sketches, drawings, and descriptions by important contributors of their eras—that reflect every major architectural movement of the 20th century.

Schaumainkai 43. ⓒ **069/212-38-844.** Admission 4€ adults, 2€ students and ages 6–15, free for children under 6. Tues, Thurs–Sun 10am–5pm; Wed 10am–8pm (free admission Wed). U-Bahn: Schweizer Platz.

Deutsches Filmmuseum ⓐ This is the finest film museum in
Germany. Old films from the collection are shown continuously on the second floor. The rooms downstairs chronicle the history of the filmmaking industry. Exhibits include Emile Reynaud's 1882 Praxinoscope, Edison's Kinetoscope from 1889, and a copy of the Lumière brothers' Cinematograph from 1895. There are also models illustrating how special effects were shot, including those in *King Kong.*

Schaumainkai 41, at the corner of Schweizer Strasse. ⓒ **069/212-388-30.** Admission 2.50€ adults, 1.30€ students and children 6–14; film screenings 5.50€ adults, 4.50€ students, 2.30€ children 6–14. Tues, Thurs, and Sun 10am–5pm; Wed and Fri 10am–8pm; Sat 2–8pm. U-Bahn: Schweizer Platz.

Geldmuseum der Deutschen Bundesbank (Money Museum)
In the eyes of many visitors, Frankfurt symbolizes money, so it seems appropriate that the city has a museum devoted to coin and banknote collections. The museum displays historical collections of money, but also documents European monetary policy, and that of the European System of Central Banks. To show the story of money, the Geldmuseum also uses films, computer games, and teaching programs.

Wilhelm-Epstein-Strasse 14. ⓒ **069/95-66-30-73.** Free admission. Thurs–Tues 10am–5pm; Wed 1–9pm. Bus: 34.

Haus Giersch (Museum of Regional Art) The goal of this
museum, a former patrician mansion on the south bank of the Main, is to research and publicly showcase the art produced in and

around Frankfurt from the Middle Ages until today. Expect every-thing from medieval triptychs to blazingly contemporary acrylics painted by local artists.

Schaumainkai 83. ℂ **069/633-04-128.** Admission 4€ adults, 2€ for students and children 6–14, free for children under 6. Tues–Fri noon–7pm; Sat–Sun 11am–5pm. U-Bahn: Schweizer Platz.

Historisches Museum (Historical Museum) ✪ Since it was established in a stately building near town hall in 1878, curators of this dignified museum have systematically added exhibits that show-case the history and culture of Frankfurt. Collections include exam-ples of pottery and porcelain, paintings and lithographs, photographs, and scaled-down models of the Altstadt at various periods of its development.

Saalgasse 19. ℂ **069/212-355-99.** Admission 4€ adults, 2€ for children 6–18, free for children under 6. Tues, Thurs, Fri, Sun 10am–5pm; Wed 4pm–8pm; Sat 1–5pm. U-Bahn: Römer.

Ikonen-Museum (Icon Museum) *(Finds* Set within what was originally built as a monastery, this museum contains one of the largest collections of Greek and Russian Orthodox icons—more than 800—in Germany. They were originally part of the private col-lection of a doctor who donated them to Frankfurt in 1988. Since then, the collection has nearly doubled in size, thanks to donations, gifts, and loans from at least two state-owned museums in Berlin. Only the lushly ornate facade of the monastery remains intact; inside, architect Oswald Mathias Ungers created a rectilinear and spartan-looking decor that's in direct contrast to the lush colors and subtleties of icons loaded with silver, gilt, and polychrome.

Brückenstrasse 3–7. ℂ **069/212-362-62.** Admission 4€ adults, 2€ for children 6–15, free for children under 6. Tues and Thurs–Sun 10am–5pm; Wed 10am–8pm. Bus: 30 or 36 to Elisabethenstrasse.

Jüdisches Museum (Jewish Museum) ✪ Set within what used to be the palatial private home of the Rothschilds, this museum traces the social and religious life of Frankfurt's Jews from the 12th to the 20th century. Special emphasis is placed on the struggle for emanci-pation and integration of Jews into German life during the 19th and early 20th century, the destruction of Frankfurt's Jewish ghetto in the 1940s, and the return of Jewish life in the aftermath of Nazi atroci-ties. A permanent collection of Judaica, including a collection of menorahs made in Frankfurt during the late 1600s, is supplemented with photos, archives, and letters documenting the Holocaust.

A Jewish Cemetery

Although it's not widely publicized, you can also visit Alter Judischer Friedhof, the Old Jewish Cemetery of Frankfurt at Kurt-Schumacher Strasse and Battonnstrasse (no phone), which is open daily from 10am to 5pm and charges no admission. Near Börneplatz, a short walk east of the Römer U-Bahn, the cemetery dates from the 13th century. It was in active use until the advent of the Nazis who desecrated it. You need to produce identification such as a passport to enter.

Jewish Museum, in the Rothschildpalais, Untermainkai 14/15. ℂ 069/212-350-00. Admission 2.60€ adults, 1.30€ children 6–16, free for children under 6. Tues and Thurs–Sun 10am–5pm; Wed 10am–8pm. U-Bahn: Willy-Brandt-Platz.

Museum der Weltkulturen & Galerie 37 (Museum of World Cultures)   Formerly known as the Ethnological Museum, this museum is based on the premise that those who encounter many different world views tend to develop a more lenient attitude about the basic facts of human existence. Its exhibits confront questions posed by cultures around the world about sex and age, the meaning of ancestry, status and power relationships, and about an individual's search for finding his or her place within society. Adjoining the museum is Galerie 37, a space devoted to exhibiting the sculpture and artwork of Native American, African, Oceanian, and Indonesian artists whose works are still mostly unknown in Europe.

Schaumainkai 29–37. ℂ 069/212-35391. Admission 3.60€ adults, 2€ students 7–15, free for children 6 and under. Tues, Thurs, Fri and Sun 10am–5pm; Wed 10am–8pm; Sat 2–8pm. U-Bahn: Schweizer Platz or Train 15, 16.

Museum für Angewandte Kunst ⟨⟩   More than 30,000 objects from Europe and Asia are exhibited at the Museum of Applied Arts. Two buildings house the collection: a 19th-century villa, and a 1985 structure designed by New York architect Richard Meier. The museum has an outstanding collection of *Mainzer Meistermobel* (German rococo furnishings) created in Mainz. The glassware is a highlight, with some Venetian pieces from the 15th century. On the second floor, the Far East and Islamic department has a rich collection of Persian carpets and faience dating from the 9th century. One of Germany's finest porcelain collections is here as well.

Schaumainkai 17. ℂ 069/21-23-40-37. Admission 5€ adults, 2.50€ students and children 6–14, free for children under 6. Tues and Thurs–Sun 10am–5pm; Wed 10am–8pm. U-Bahn: Schweizer Platz.

Museum für Kommunikation Frankfurt (Museum of Communications) Originally established in 1958 as the Federal Postal Museum, and massively expanded in 1990 with a shiny, hyper-modern new building, this museum celebrates the devices that humankind has used to talk with one other. On display are what were once radically new forms of technology, ranging from antique telephones and mail-delivery buggies to some of the first computers ever built—massive boxy-looking structures from the 1950s. The art collection includes works by Joseph Beuys, Salvador Dali, and Max Ernst.

Schaumainkai 53. ℂ **069/60-60-0.** Free admission. Tues–Fri 11am–5pm; Sat–Sun 9am–7pm. U-Bahn: Schweizer Platz.

Museum für Moderne Kunst *(Finds* This museum opened in 1991 in a building created by Hans Hollein, the Viennese architect. The structure is designed like a boat, but in spite of its somewhat bizarre shape, the gallery has a bright, spacious air. (Some unkind critics have claimed that the dazzling architecture is more interesting than the exhibits). Major artists since the 1950s are displayed here, including Andy Warhol, Roy Liechtenstein (see his *Brushstroke*), and George Segal with his *Jazz Combo.*

Domstrasse 10 (in the center of the Innenstadt, near Römerberg). ℂ **069/21-23-04-47.** Admission 5€ adults, 2.50€ for students, free for children under 6. Free admission Wed. Tues and Thurs–Sun 10am–5pm; Wed 10am–8pm. U-Bahn: Römer. Tram: 11 to Domstrasse.

Museum Judengasse This is an annex of the also-recommended Jewish Museum (see above), in the heart of medieval Frankfurt. It displays archaeological remnants of synagogues and private homes, most of them now destroyed, in the Judengasse, the focal point of Jewish life in the city for a period of more than 350 years.

Börneplatz, Kurt-Schumacher-Strasse 10. ℂ **069/297-7419.** Admission 1.50€ adults, .70€ for students and children 6–16, free for children under 6. Same hours as the Jewish Museum (see above). Tram: 11 or 12 to Börneplatz.

Schirn Kunsthalle One of the many surprising things about this long and narrow gallery, which opened in 1986, is the way it managed to eke a suitable building plot out of some of the most valuable real estate in Frankfurt; a long and narrow tract between the Römer and the Dom. Today, other than within the Fairgrounds, it's the largest exhibition hall in Frankfurt, with vast inner spaces devoted to a changing array of temporary exhibitions. You might be surprised at whatever's in store while you're in town, since exhibitions often include worthy collections of both antique and contemporary paintings on loan from such other galleries as Paris's Musée d'Orsay, St. Petersburg's Hermitage, and New York's Guggenheim.

Römerberg. (𝄫 **069/29-98-82-0**. Admission 7€ adults, 5€ students and children 8–15, free for children under 8. Tues and Fri–Sun 10am–7pm; Wed–Thurs 10am–10pm. U-Bahn: Römer.

3 The Leading Churches

Alte Nikolaikirche (Old Nicholas Church)   This is a historic church across from the Rathaus. Originally it was a court chapel, but after the 15th century, it served as the church for the city fathers. Today, it's home to the Lutheran St. Paul's congregation. Inside are ancient gravestones as well as a copy of a medieval sculpture, called *Schmerzensmann* ("Man of Sorrow"), dating from 1370. Outside are Gothic sandstone sculptures portraying St. Nicholas. The 40-bell Glockenspiel plays at 9:05am, 12:05pm, and 5:05pm. A number of materials in English, including a church guide and a free walking map, are available at the information table in the church. A musical vespers service (English-German) is held each Wednesday in summer from 5:30 to 6:30pm, with tea, cookies, and conversation afterward to the accompaniment of the organ. An American pastor on staff is available to answer questions and give free tours, including a trip to the roof gallery, and to help travelers needing advice or those in emergency situations. Contact the church office across from the church.

Römerberg (South Side). (𝄫 **069/29-24-49**. Free admission. Daily 10am–8pm. U-Bahn: Römer.

Leonhardskirche (St. Leonard Church)   This church was begun in the Romanesque style but wasn't completed until the late Gothic style of architecture came into bloom. Today it is a 15th-century Gothic church with Romanesque touches. Its most distinctive feature is a set of octagonal towers at its eastern end. Inside look for the fine carvings of Master Engelbert's *Doorway* (viewed from the north aisle). The square central nave is enveloped on three sides by a gallery. There are five naves in all, supported by two 13th-century Romanesque arches. The church is also noted for its stained glass, the oldest dating from the 1400s. Left of the chancel is one of the church's artistic treasures, a painting of *The Last Supper* by Holbein the Elder.

Liebfrauenberg 3. No phone. Free admission. Wed, Fri, and Sat 10am–noon and 3–6pm; Tues and Thurs 10am–noon and 3–6:30pm; Sun 9am–1pm, and 3–6pm. U-Bahn: Römer.

Paulskirche (St. Paul's Church)   Reconstructed in a dignified but streamlined style after its devastation in 1944, this brick church evokes some of the most poignant memories of 19th-century German history. In 1848 it was selected as the meeting point for an all-German parliament, a doomed political entity that survived for only a year, but which was instrumental in defining Germany's sense of nationhood. The church was long ago secularized, and is often used as the site for various ceremonies, including the Peace Prize award from the German Book Dealer's Association. A monument to victims of the Third Reich is displayed on the northern wall, and on the premises is an exhibition that spotlights the history of the German democratic movement, and a controversial mural that satirizes the events that surrounded the 1848 parliament.

Paulsplatz. No phone. Free admission. Daily 11am–3pm. U-Bahn: Römer.

4 Additional Sights

Börse (Stock Exchange)   The reason many visitors come to Frankfurt in the first place revolves around one of the world's leading financial markets. Originally founded by city merchants in 1558, the present Stock Exchange building was constructed in the 1870s. The Börse no longer has the exciting floor activity of its pre-computer days, but it's still fun to watch the moving and shaking from the visitors gallery.

Börsenplatz 7-11. © **069/210-10**. Free admission. Visitors gallery Mon–Fri 10am–5:30pm. Guided tours free Mon–Fri at 10am, 11am, and noon; 100€ for parties of 4 at 2pm and 4pm. U-Bahn: Hauptwache.

Deutsches Albert-Schweitzer-Zentrum   The Albert Schweitzer Center honors this world-famous man; information on his humanitarian efforts represents the core of this exhibition. The center pays tribute to his work as a theologian, doctor, musician, and champion of peace. The center serves both as a museum of Schweitzer memorabilia and an archival center.

Neue Schlesingergasse 22–24. © **069/28-49-51**. Free admission. Mon–Fri 9am–4pm. U-Bahn: Hauptwache.

Zoologischer Garten 🛪   This zoo is intent on education as well as entertainment, and thus proves interesting for both young and old. Most animals are in enclosures that resemble their native habitats. One of the best examples is the African Veldt Enclosure, landscaped with hills and bushes—antelopes and ostriches roam freely. In the Exotarium, fish and various reptiles live under special climatic conditions. Penguins swim and dive in an artificially cooled polar landscape. There's also an aviary where you can watch birds preparing unusual nests. The building for small mammals, with its nocturnal section, is one of the largest and most diverse in the world.

Alfred-Brehm-Platz 16. (C) **069/213-36-039.** Admission 7€ adults, 3€ children 6–17, free for children under 6; 16€ for family ticket. Oct–Mar daily 9am–5pm; Apr–Sept daily 9am–7pm. U-Bahn: Zoologischer Garten (Zoo).

5 Messe (The Fairgrounds of Frankfurt)

The business of doing business in Frankfurt has been a tradition here for more than 750 years, when cloth and grain merchants gathered to trade in what is now the Römerplatz. In the aftermath of World War II's devastating bombings, Frankfurt has emerged as the commercial leader of a country that sets enormous emphasis on conventions and trade fairs, with about 40 huge annual fairs that attract in excess of 2.5 million visitors.

Part of Frankfurt's convention-and-trade-fair success derives from having the biggest airport, and one of the most significant rail and highway hubs, in Europe. The rest derives from a complex of exhibition halls, known collectively as Messe Frankfurt. Owned by the City of Frankfurt and the State of Hesse, it's an awesomely huge complex that occupies 365,760 sq. m (1,200,000 ft.) of flatlands, and more than 265,176 sq. m (870,000 ft.) of covered exhibition space, with more being built even as this is being written.

There's the distinct possibility that you'll get lost at least once during your time here (there's a joke that the complex's press and PR office sends out search parties for newcomers who get lost while maneuvering through the labyrinth of corridors). At the very least, you'll walk several kilometers every day while navigating your way around the anonymous-looking sprawl. Each of the complex's 10 individual exhibition halls is linked by covered walkways, the longest of which is a 2km (1¼-mile) marathon that's flanked with a mechanized airport-style walkway. The oldest and most stately looking of the buildings, used as a congregating point for thousands of people at a time, is the Congress Hall, rebuilt into its original 19th-century design after the wartime bombings. Ironically, the Congress Hall seems to trigger reactions that are both agoraphobic and claustrophobic at the same time, sometimes sending its occupants to the nearest window for glimpses of the world outside its borders.

How do you sustain life during several days of self-imposed incarceration in this glass-and-concrete jungle? Depending on the expected capacity within the convention halls, up to 20 restaurants and up to 60 snack bars, with a combined capacity of up to 5,500 diners at a time, can be counted on to churn out vast amounts of institutionalized food. Each has a price structure and menu that's dictated by a single catering company, and each adheres to a rigidly controlled internal management code that ensures acceptable quality, if not brilliantly idiosyncratic cuisine. They're configured more like short-term catering gigs than bona-fide workaday restaurants, and since none of them remains open on a constant basis, we have deliberately avoided recommending any of them. In almost every instance, each is locked up drum-tight after the close of trade-fair business every day, and then shuts down completely for several weeks at a time between jobs.

Many visitors arrive without their cars, but if you're driving, you can use any of up to 10,000 parking spaces (they're positioned underground near the Messeturm, and on tiered parking platforms on the complex's periphery as well). The cost is a very reasonable 8€ per day.

Two landmark buildings in the complex are the Messeturm and the Torhaus. The Messeturm is a reddish-toned sandstone skyscraper soaring a needlelike 29 stories above the complex's eastern edge, beside the Ludwig-Erhard Anlage. In distinct contrast, the Torhaus is a five-story blandly bureaucratic-looking administrative center for the complex, farther to the west, smack in the middle of the Fairgrounds complex.

If at any point you get confused about venues, locations, or any other detail about your trade fair, a battalion of multilingual staff members is posted every day at strategic intervals throughout the complex. Within the Torhaus, at least two floors of clearly marked rooms provide most of the service functions an exhibitor would need. These include registration services for your particular industry, a post office, a full-service travel agency, a division of the city tourist office, a kindergarten, shops, a press center, and an ecumenical chapel.

You'll navigate this sprawling mass a lot easier if you understand which of the two main entrances (and if you're unloading material from a truck, which service entrance) is closest to your particular exhibition space. The most modern and best-accessorized public entrance is the City Entrance, site of a U-Bahn station, banks, and a Lufthansa check-in desk. You can access it from the Ludwig-Erhard Anlage, midway between the soaring, reddish-colored Messeturm and the curved glass facade of the Maritim Hotel.

Older and less modern is the Torhaus entrance, which is mostly used by pedestrians getting off any of the S-Bahns of Frankfurt. Since each of the nine components of this massive complex is linked with covered passages, you can navigate your way around in any weather, albeit with something approaching exhaustion by the end of a long day at the exhibitions.

Messe Frankfurt

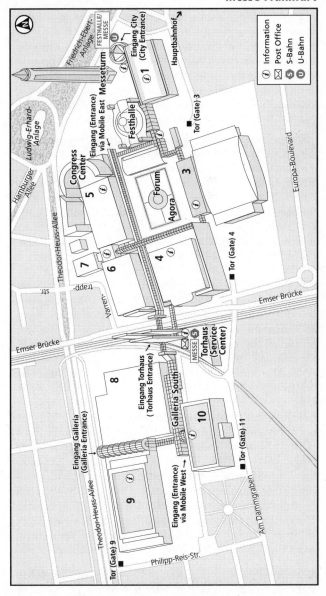

How are samples, displays, and merchandise hauled up into each of the exhibition spaces? The complex was designed so that huge delivery trucks could drive into parking bays beneath each of the exhibition halls, then unload their contents onto one of many freight elevators that haul them up to points very close to their eventual display.

For more information about Frankfurt's fairgrounds, contact Messe Frankfurt GmbH, Ludwig-Erhard-Anlage 1, 60327 Frankfurt/Main (© **069/75-75-0;** fax 069/75-75-64-33; www.messefrankfurt.com).

6 Especially for Kids

Children love the **Palmengarten** (see below). Take along a picnic—**Hertie,** at An der Zeil 390, has a good deli—and then rent a rowboat and take the kids on an excursion. Another option is the **Senckenberg Museum of Natural History,** Senckenberg-Anlage 25 (© **069/7-54-20;** U-Bahn: Bockenheimerwarte), which has an interesting collection of fossils, including dinosaur bones. Admission is 5€ for adults, 2€ for students and children over 3, and free for children 2 and under. Open daily from 9am to 5pm. Children will also enjoy the circus performances at the **Tiger Palast,** Heiligkreuzgasse 16–20 (© **069/9200-2250;** U-Bahn: Konstablerwache), which include jugglers, acrobats, and magic acts. Shows are Tuesday through Thursday at 7 and 10pm, Friday and Saturday at 7:30 and 10:30pm, and Sunday at 5 and 9pm. Admission is 45€ for adults and 23€ for children.

Another interesting possibility is **Struwwelpeter Museum,** Schirm am Römerberg (© **069/28-13-33;** U-Bahn: Römer), which is dedicated to memorabilia associated with one of Germany's most famous children's books, *Struwwelpeter* ("Slovenly Peter"). The story was written and illustrated by a local doctor, Heinrich Hoffman (1798–1874), who opened the first hospital for neurology in Frankfurt. His Slovenly Peter character gained popularity in the United States after Mark Twain translated Hoffman's work. On the premises is a museum shop selling posters, postcards, and actual copies of the Struwwelpeter books translated into many different languages. The museum is open Tuesday through Sunday from 11am to 5pm; in July and August it remains open on Wednesday till 8pm. Admission is free. The kindly staff members are strictly volunteers.

7 Parks

The Palmengarten 𝕽, Siesmayerstrasse 61 (© **069/21-23-39-39;** U-Bahn: Westend; bus: 36), is a park and a botanical garden.

During the last decade, the gardens have been renewed and the conservatories and historic greenhouses completely reconstructed. You can admire a perennial garden, an expanded rock garden, and a beautiful rose garden. The 1869 palm house is now surrounded by a huge gallery that serves as an exhibition hall for flower shows and other botanical exhibitions. In recent years, new conservatories have been added: The Tropicarium is a complex for tropical vegetation; the Sub-Antarctic House displays plants from southern Chile, Argentina, and New Zealand; and the Entrance Conservatory houses insectivorous plants and bromeliads. Collections of orchids, palms, succulents, water lilies, and many other plants are also on display.

Admission to the botanical garden is 3.50€ for adults and 1.50€ for children, or 7.50€ for a family ticket. It's open daily March to September from 9am to 8pm, October and February from 9am to 6pm, and November to January from 9am to 4pm. In the park area there's a small lake where people can row boats. In summer, concerts are given in the band shell; evening events include open-air dancing, jazz, and fountain illumination. There are some facilities for food.

Frankfurt has a lot of parkland. Locals like to point out that the city has no Central Park as in New York—the city is a central park in itself, they say. The enclosing city walls of old Frankfurt have been replaced by a botanic city ring. Along the Main is a park landscape where you'll see bankers taking their lunch break beneath statues of heroes from the past.

Bethmann Park, with its Chinese gardens, is one of the most interesting. It lies immediately to the northeast of Stadtmitte, and is reached by bus no. 30 or tram no. 12.

8 Organized Tours

THE APPLEWINE EXPRESS

Every weekend, a private tour operator commandeers a circular stretch of Frankfurt's tram tracks, extending onto both sides of the River Main, so that merrymakers can view a wide cross section of the city in a festive context. Decorated with red and blue depictions of the pottery pitchers that traditionally hold the apple wine, the *Ebbelwei* Express begins its route every Saturday, Sunday, and local holidays at 1:30pm, and makes its last stop around 6:30pm the same day. Passengers can get on or off the tram anywhere they choose, explore any of the neighborhoods the tram passes through, then reboard the next tram that passes; they come every 25 minutes. Neighborhoods include the city's medieval core, its financial district,

the apple-wine district of Sachsenhausen, and residential neighborhoods that extend as far eastward as Bornheim. The cost of 3.50€
per person includes a bottle of apple wine or mineral water and a
bag of pretzels. Tickets can be purchased on the tram, although it's
a good idea to pick up a brochure (it contains a timetable and a
route map) in advance, so you'll understand the points and times
you can get on and off and the tram. Two of the most convenient
starting points include the Main Railway Station (at Münchener
Strasse) and the Römer/Paulskirche. Brochures are available from
any branch of Frankfurt's tourist office, including the glassed-in
kiosk on the Zeil, near the Hauptwache, or from Stadtwerke
Verkehrsgesellschaft, Kundenzentrum, Kurt-Schumacher-Strasse 10
(© 069/213-22425).

CITY & RHINE TOURS

Gray Lines, Wiesenhüttenplatz 39 (© 069/27-10-10), offers the
widest range of tours, not only in Frankfurt but along the Rhine as
well. Their city tour leaves four times daily; it lasts 2 hours and costs
29€. Sights include St. Paul's Church, the Dom, Goethehaus, the
apple-wine district, and Zeil, an all-pedestrian thoroughfare with
Frankfurt's densest concentration of shops and department stores.

From March 15 to November 15, daily tours feature not only the
highlights of Frankfurt but major scenery along the Rhine, taking in
castles and vineyards. Cost is 108€ for adults and 89€ for children.
Part of this trip is by boat. Departures are daily at 1pm with a return
around 8pm.

9 Sports & Outdoor Pursuits

FITNESS CENTERS & HEALTH CLUBS

Many major hotels in Frankfurt maintain health clubs, but if yours
doesn't, consider a day ticket to one of the semiprivate health clubs
such as **Sport Fabrik,** Ginnheimerstrasse 47 (© 069/970-7210;
U-Bahn/S-Bahn: Ginnheim), or **Sportschule Petrescu,** Bleichstrasse
55–57 (© 069/29-59-06; U-Bahn/S-Bahn: Hauptwache). Both
offer roughly equivalent arrays of exercise machines, free weights,
and saunas. A day pass is around 10€ depending on what facilities
you want to use.

Only the exercise areas offered by some of the major hotels of
Frankfurt will satisfy a genuine sports buff, and even such much-
vaunted palaces as the Steigenberger Frankfurter Hof has only a
miniscule exercise area with very limited equipment. If you really

want to exercise, and also meet residents of Frankfurt, consider a visit to **The Business Health Club/The Fitness Gallery,** Kaiserstrasse 5A (© **069/96-373-200;** U-Bahn: Konstabler Hauptwache). The cost is 35€ but you'll have a huge choice of Stairmasters, treadmills, and weight resistance machines, a bar serving health drinks and vitamin shakes, and a comprehensive (co-ed) sauna area.

GOLF

Golf Anlage im Frankfurter Waldstadion, Morfelder Landstrasse 362, 60528 Frankfurt (© **069/67-80-4114**), located within the city limits, is open to all. This course has nine holes, plus a floodlit driving range. Greens fees are 13€ for 18 holes. Open daily from 10am to 9pm.

ICE-SKATING

Between November and April, you can skate at the **Eissporthalle,** am Bornheimer Hang 4, Ratsweg (© **069/21-23-08-25;** U-Bahn/S-Bahn: Eissporthalle). Open Saturday from 9am to 10:30pm and Sunday from 10am to 8pm. Admission is 5€ for adults and 4€ for children.

JOGGING

A good jogging route is along the quays of the Main River, using both sides of the river and the bridges to create a loop. Another choice is the centrally located Grünebeug Park, whose walkways are suitable for jogging.

TENNIS

Few of the tennis courts in Frankfurt allow nonmembers to play. A noteworthy exception is the **Tennisplatz Eissporthall,** Am Bornheimer Hang, 60486 Frankfurt (© **069/21-23-08-25** or 069/212-39-30-81; U-Bahn/S-Bahn: Eissporthalle), which has a half-dozen courts. They're open May to October daily from 8am to sundown. The cost is 10€ per hour.

7

Walking Tours of Frankfurt

You can cover all of the Stadtmitte or Altstadt (Old Town) on foot. In fact, this is virtually the only way to explore it, as traffic is banned on certain streets.

Nearly all the sights lie within the boundaries of the once-fortified walls, which have been turned into parkland, forming a semicircle around the old city.

After a tour of the Altstadt, you can cross the Main River to Sachsenhausen, site of the major museums and the apple-wine district.

WALKING TOUR 1	FROM HAUPTWACHE TO SACHSENHAUSEN

Start:	Hauptwache
Finish:	Apple-Wine District
Time:	3 hours
Best Time:	Daylight hours. Try to begin after 10am, and finish before rush hour of 4pm.

Your tour begins in the very historic core of Frankfurt at the:

❶ Hauptwache

This is the hub of Frankfurt. Its centerpiece is a beautifully reconstructed building, the Hauptwache, originally a baroque structure from 1730 that served as a sentry house. To fortify yourself for the walk, you might stop in at the famous Hauptwache Café on the square for a coffee and cake. Tables are placed outside in summer, and this is the best place to enjoy a panoramic view of the square itself. You can visit Katharinenkirche (St. Katherine's Church), which was originally a convent when it was constructed in 1343. Since that time, it has been destroyed and rebuilt over the centuries. It was at this church that Goethe was christened and confirmed. A vast shopping mall, reached by escalator, lies below the square. You can visit it now or continue with the walking tour itself.

Walking Tour 1: From Hauptwache to Sachsenhausen

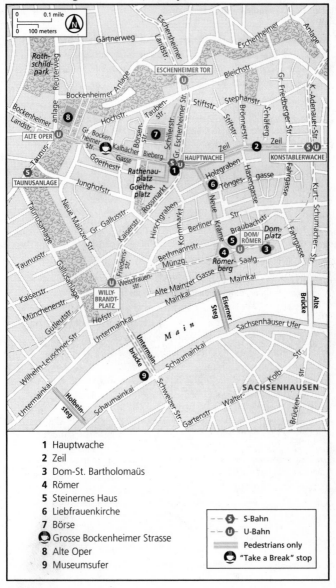

1 Hauptwache
2 Zeil
3 Dom-St. Bartholomäus
4 Römer
5 Steinernes Haus
6 Liebfrauenkirche
7 Börse
   Grosse Bockenheimer Strasse
8 Alte Oper
9 Museumsufer

- - 🟢 S-Bahn
- - 🔵 U-Bahn
   Pedestrians only
   🔵 "Take a Break" stop

From the Hauptwache, continue east along:

❷ Zeil

This is the city's largest pedestrian area and its main shopping street. It is called "the Golden Mile." Here the wealth of a capitalist society is displayed in all its opulence, and the street is flanked with department stores and specialty shops of all kinds. This area is a consumer's fantasy.

Walk east to the U-Bahn and S-Bahn hub, Konstablerwache, then cut south along Kurt-Schumacher-Strasse. Continue along this street until you come to Battonnstrasse, then head west until you reach Dom Strasse. Follow this street south into Domplatz and the site of:

❸ Dom-St. Bartholomäus

From the 16th to the 18th century, Holy Roman emperors were chosen and crowned at this former imperial college church. The church, dating from the 13th century, is sometimes called the Kaiserdom (Imperial Cathedral). Today it is a parish church, not a cathedral, although it was once the coronation church of the German Kaisers. Destroyed in 1944 air raids, the present Dom was reconstructed in 1953.

After seeing the Dom, continue directly west into the:

❹ Römer

This broad square, with the statue of Justice and a trio of adjoining burgers' houses, has, since the Middle Ages, been the site of municipal Frankfurt. Look for the gabled facades and a row of seven reconstructed medieval houses across the square. You'll see statues of four German Kaisers, including Friedrich Barbarossa, and a sculpture of an eagle, the symbol of Frankfurt. The Kaisersaal (Imperial Hall) on this square was the site of major functions during the city's imperial heyday. Nikolaikirche and the Historisches Museum are also found here.

From the Römerberg you can walk north along a traffic-free street called Neue Kräme. At Markt 44 you'll pass:

❺ Steinernes Haus

The Steinernes Haus (Stone House) dates from 1464. Like nearly all buildings in the area, it was destroyed in 1944, although at the time it dated from 1464. Reconstructed in the Gothic style in the late 1950s, it is today the venue for changing art exhibitions, and is open to the public Tuesday through Saturday from noon to 7pm. You can visit it now or come back later if the current exhibition should interest you.

Continue north along Neue Kräme, crossing Biedenstrasse and, while still going north, entering the beginning of Liebfrauenstrasse. On your right rises:

6 Liebfrauenkirche

This late Gothic church dates from the end of the 14th century. Destroyed in 1944, it was rebuilt 10 years later. Today the church is a Capuchin monastery and its interior was remodeled in the rococo style.

At the end of Liebfrauenstrasse, you're back on the Golden Mile, or the Zeil.

At this point, you have returned to the Hauptwache where the tour began, and you will have made a complete circle of the inner core of the Altstadt. If time is limited, this is a good place to end your walk as you're at an S-Bahn and U-Bahn transportation hub where connections can be made to all parts of Frankfurt. However, if you have more time, you can extend the tour to include some sights in the western sector of Stadtmitte or the Altstadt. If you've got the endurance, you can eventually head south across the Main to visit Frankfurt's concentration of museums and its apple-wine district.

If you wish to continue the tour at this point, cross the Hauptwache to Rathenauplatz at the far western extremity, and continue north along Börsenstrasse to the:

7 Börse

This is Frankfurt's leading stock exchange. Dating from 1558, this is now one of the leading stock exchanges of the world, and Germany's leading money market. There's a visitors gallery for those who'd like to look inside at some of the wheelings and dealings. The building opens onto Börsenplatz.

At this point you should backtrack slightly, heading south again to Rathenauplatz. Continue west along Grosse Bockenheimer Strasse.

TAKE A BREAK
Frankfurters refer to Grosse Bockenheimer Strasse as *Fressgasse* or "pig-out alley." It's one of the liveliest streets in Frankfurt, and the home to delis, cafes, restaurants, wine merchants, and more food than you'll see anywhere else in the city. Yes, they even sell frankfurters by the truckload. If it's a summer day, you can sit and eat at the sidewalk tables of your choice for some people-watching.

At the end of Grosse Bockenheimer Strasse, you will have arrived at Opernplatz and the site of:

8 Alte Oper

This old opera house was built in the 1870s. Destroyed in the war, it has been handsomely restored. Even Kaiser Wilhelm I, who journeyed here from Berlin for its original opening night in 1880, would surely be pleased. The new opera house was built along the same classical lines as the original.

Although we've been concentrating on old (or at least reconstructed) Frankfurt, at Opernplatz you're at a good vantage point to observe new Frankfurt, especially its avant-garde architecture. Immediately to the north lies Rothschild Park. A look south toward Taunusanlage reveals the twin towers of the Deutsche Bank. Frankfurters jokingly call these towers *zoll und haben* or "debit and credit." To your left, crowned by antenna, is the 255m (850-ft.) Commerzbank, currently the tallest building in Europe.

From the Opernplatz you can head south into a "green lung" of Frankfurt, moving toward the Taunusanlage. This parkland forms the western boundary of the Altstadt. When Frankfurt's fortified city walls were torn down, the land mass was beautified with parkland. If you keep walking through this green belt, you come to Willy-Brandt-Platz. From here you can take Mainzer Strasse to the Untermainbrücke, which upon crossing you'll be at:

⑨ Museumsufer

This area contains Frankfurt's greatest concentration of museums, opening onto Schaumainkai along the south bank. We've previewed all of these museums in chapter 6. If your time is limited, the two most important museums here are **Städel** and **Liebieghaus.** In fair-weather months you get not only museums, but the city's weekly flea market on Saturdays from 9am to 2pm.

After visiting some of the museums, or at least walking past them to admire their facades, continue east along Sachsenhäuser Ufer, passing the Alte Brücke across the Main on your left. This street becomes Deutschtern-ufer. Follow it until you come to Grosse Rittergasse, then head southeast into the heart of the apple-wine district. If it's a summer evening, this district becomes a virtual outdoor festival, and you can end your tour by visiting any number of taverns for food, drink, and good times.

WALKING TOUR 2   SACHSENHAUSEN

Start:	**Baseler Platz**
Finish:	**Zum Gemalten Haus**
Time:	**2 hours**
Best Time:	**Daylight hours. Try to begin after 10am, and finish before rush hour of 4pm.**

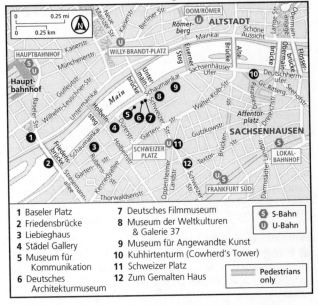

1 Baseler Platz
2 Friedensbrücke
3 Liebieghaus
4 Städel Gallery
5 Museum für
   Kommunikation
6 Deutsches
   Architekturmuseum
7 Deutsches Filmmuseum
8 Museum der Weltkulturen
   & Galerie 37
9 Museum für Angewandte Kunst
10 Kuhhirtenturm (Cowherd's Tower)
11 Schweizer Platz
12 Zum Gemalten Haus

S S-Bahn
U U-Bahn

Pedestrians only

For those with more time, this tour picks up at Museumsufer (see above) where the last tour left off. For your exploration of the scenic highlights of the Left Bank of Frankfurt, you can actually begin on the Right Bank at:

❶ Baseler Platz

This is one of the main squares of the Right Bank, located directly south of the Hauptbahnhof, the rail station. Although of no great interest itself, the square is convenient to reach and a good starting point for your tour.

From this square you can head immediately south along the:

❷ Friedensbrücke

After crossing the bridge, head immediately to your left (or east) along what Frankfurters call Museumsufer (Museum Riverbank). Actually, the river-bordering street is labeled Schaumainkai.

One of the most important museums appears on your right as you walk east along the Schaumainkai:

❸ Liebieghaus

This is one of Germany's most important museums of sculpture. Liebieghaus is in a building that evokes a castle; the structure was built in 1896 by Baron Heinrich Liebieg, the Czech industrialist.

The artistic output of some 5,000 years of civilization is displayed inside, and you'll want to return later for a more thorough inspection of this treasure trove.

After leaving Liebieghaus, the next museum that you'll approach as you walk northeast is:

❹ Städel Gallery

This is one of Frankfurt's most important museums, devoted to a world-class art collection. This gallery is one of the most comprehensive in Europe and, unlike the galleries of Berlin and München, isn't rooted in a royal collection, but grew from the collection of a local banker who launched it as an art college in the early 19th century. Walk on by (at least for a moment), because you could spend an entire day here and not even begin to take in its wealth of offerings. The wealth of paintings from the early Netherlandish School could easily occupy 2 or even 3 hours of your time.

Continue to walk northeast. The next museum is:

❺ Musuem für Kommunikation

Frankfurt's Museum of Communication exists in a reconstructed post office from the 1800s. Among other things, this museum is big on telephones. Regardless of the claims made by fans of Alexander Graham Bell, Frankfurt bills itself "as the birthplace of the telephone." Not all phones are antique. At some exhibits visitors can talk to each other on picture phones.

The next museum you pass as you continue northeast is:

❻ Deutches Architekturmuseum

Opened in 1979, this avant-garde building was designed by the famous architect, Oswald Mathias Ungers. The building is actually a restyling of a 19th-century villa that once stood here. The structure was completely gutted and painted a dazzling white, its center a sort of "house within a house," which dominates the building like an oversized doll's house. The effect is very claustrophobic, and even though a museum devoted to architecture, many local architects protest the design.

Close at hand on our northeastward trek is the:

❼ Deutsches Filmmuseum

If you go inside and wander into the on-site theater, you might never finish the walking tour, as you'll get caught up in the old and often forgotten films still shown here. One of the highlights is a reconstruction of the Grand Café in Paris where the Lumiere brothers showed the first ever public film. A Frankfurt cinema from 1912 is also reproduced.

The next museum after the bridge, Untermainbrucke, is:

8 Museum der Weltkulturen & Galerie 37

This museum is sometimes known as Museum für Volkerkunde (Museum of Ethnology). If such things interest you, its vast collection of masks and totems from all over the world will enchant you. Many of the exhibits here, such as those in Galerie 37, are rotating. If you have the time you can explore rare collections from Africa, the Americas, Indonesia, and the vast nations of the Pacific.

Next into view (as you march northeast) is the:

9 Museum für Angewandte Kunst

Frankfurt's Museum of Applied Arts is housed in two different buildings, displaying some 30,000 objects from Asia and Europe. The architect, Richard Meier, took the 17th-century Villa Metzler and attached a striking modern building to it to display the collections.

After bypassing the museum, continue your eastward trek along the Main, the river-bordering street, Schaumainkai changing its name to Sachsenhäuser Ufer. You will pass (on your left) one of the Main's most important bridges, Alte Brücke (old bridge) leading to the Römer and the heart of medieval Frankfurt. If you can't continue the walking tour, this is a good point at which to break from it. But if you have more time and energy, continue east along the river. As you near the junction with Grosser Rittergasse, turn to the southeast until you come to:

10 Kuhhirtenturm or Cowherds' Tower

This site, the last of the nine towers constructed in the 1400s, is clearly visible. Once this tower and its extended walls formed part of the fortifications that defended Sachsenhausen against attack. Paul Hindemith, the famous composer, lived in the tower from 1923 to 1927 while employed by the Frankfurt Opera House.

After viewing the tower, continue to walk southeast to the junction with Dreie-ichstrasse. Head south on Dreieichstrasse until you come to the junction with Glutzkowstrasse. Head west along this street until you reach:

11 Schweizer Platz

This is the heart of the apple-wine district of Sachsenhausen, and also the hub of the most important U-Bahn stops south of the Main. From here you can end the tour and catch a U-Bahn to virtually anywhere you're going in Frankfurt. But if you stick around to explore the district, this is the time for a break.

Directly north of Schweizer Platz, at Schweizer Strasse 67, you can visit the most famous apple-wine tavern of the district:

12 Zum Gemalten Haus

Normally we take time out for a break in the middle of a walking tour, but in this case our refueling stop comes at the end, out of fear that once you enter one of these apple-wine dives, you'll probably be in no condition to continue the tour. Generation upon generation of cider drinkers have treated their bellies to this home brew, which is more potent that it appears. Along with the wine, you can fill up on *wurst* and sauerkraut and sit outdoors in the *Gartenlokal* (garden area) if the weather's fair. If there are three in your party, order the plate of deli meats, *frankfurter platte*. It will certainly finish off your appetite for the day.

8

Shopping

When it comes to shopping, Frankfurt has just about everything. The specialty shops here are so much like those back in the States that most visitors from America will feel right at home. Shops in the central area are open Monday through Friday from 9am to 6:30pm, and Saturday from 9am to 2pm (to 4 or 6pm on the 1st Sat of the month).

1 The Top Shopping Streets

In Frankfurt, the shopping scene is divided into different regions. On the **Zeil,** or "the Golden Mile," a pedestrian zone between the Hauptwache and Konstablerwache, you'll find department stores, clothing shops, shoe stores, and furniture outlets. Once one of the most famous shopping streets on the Continent, the Zeil was destroyed in World War II and hasn't regained all of its former prestige, though it still has the highest sales of any shopping area in Germany. In the 14th century, it was a cattle-round-up market. Nearby is the **Kleinmarkthalle,** a covered market with international grocery products.

The **Hauptwache,** in the center of Frankfurt, has two shopping areas, one above and one below ground. Groceries, books, flowers, clothing, tobacco, photo supplies, recordings, and sporting equipment abound. In the Hauptwache-Passage are restaurants, travel agencies, and banks.

Schillerstrasse, another pedestrian zone, lies between Hauptwache and Eschenheimer Turm, near the stock exchange. Walking from Schillerstrasse northeast toward Eschenheimer Tor, you'll pass many elegant boutiques and specialty shops.

Southwest of the Hauptwache is the Alte Oper. You can reach it by taking either the **Goethestrasse,** with its exclusive stores evocative of Paris or Milan, or the parallel **Grosse Bockenheimer Strasse,** traditionally nicknamed *Fressgasse* or "Pig-Out Alley." Most wine dealers, delis, and butcher shops here look back on a long and venerable past. At **Opernplatz** you'll find a variety of restaurants and cafes.

Tips **Value-Added Tax**

As a member of the European Union, Germany imposes a tax on most goods and services known as a **value-added tax (VAT)**, or, in German, *Mehrwertsteuer.* Nearly everything is taxed at 15%. Note that goods for sale already have the 15% tax factored into the price, but that the listed prices of services, such as getting a mechanic to fix your car, don't include VAT, so an extra 15% will be tacked on to the bill.

The good news is that visitors to Germany—if they shop at the right places, and if they're not EU residents themselves—can get refunds on VAT. Stores that display a "Tax Free" sticker will give you a Tax-Free Shopping Check at the time of purchase. Upon leaving Germany for home, take the check to the appropriate counter at the airport (many large train stations and even ferry terminals also have these counters), and your money will be refunded at once. If you're going to another EU country instead of going directly home, make sure you get a Customs official to stamp your check to prove legal export, and afterwards mail the check to the following address: Tax-Free Shopping Service, Mengstrasse 19, 23552 Lübeck, Germany. If you want the payment to be credited to your bank card or your bank account, mention this. Your money will then be refunded.

West of the Hauptwache is Rossmarkt, leading to **Kaiserstrasse.** It passes the BFG skyscraper, which has three floors of exclusive retail stores, boutiques, and restaurants, and directly connects the downtown area to the Hauptbahnhof. Kaiserstrasse is also known for its large selection of stores selling clothing, audio and photography equipment, and stainless-steel ware. The heart of the fur trade in Frankfurt is **Düsseldorfer Strasse,** opposite the Hauptbahnhof. Most book dealers are located around the Hauptwache and **Goethe-platz.** Antiques, old books, etchings, and paintings can be found on **Braubachstrasse** (near the Römer), at the Dom, and on Fahrgasse.

Art and antiques are the domain of **Alt-Sachsenhausen,** an appealing and original neighborhood. The famous **Frankfurt Flea Market** takes place here every Saturday from 8am to 2pm along the

Main River on the Sachsenhausen side. To get there, walk from the Römer toward the river and cross the Eisener Steg bridge.

2 Department Stores

Hertie   A Frankfurt shopping tradition along the Golden Mile, this vast store offers clothes and shoes for every mood. It also caters to a wide range of budgets. Families with small children may want to check out the selection of toys, and foodies will delight in the food hall with tidbits from all over the globe. On the ground floor is a selection of jewelry and cosmetics, among other items. Zeil 90. ℰ 069/92-90-50. U-Bahn: Konstablerwache.

Kaufhof   Hertie's main competitor, this department store accurately touts itself as the place for one-stop shopping. It's got about everything for sale on its seven floors, including a food hall in the basement (although we think Hertie excels in this area). Nonetheless, Kaufhof has enough merchandise to dazzle—porcelain, accessories, clothes, jewelry, and glassware. Tired of shopping? Retreat to the top-floor restaurant, which has one of the most panoramic views of Frankfurt. Zeil 116–125. ℰ 069/21910. U-Bahn: Hauptwache.

3 Goods A to Z

ART

America Haus   The U.S. Information Research Center can be counted on for a constantly changing display of art with a Stateside slant. Paintings, sculptures, crafts, and photography are frequently exhibited. The center does not sell art, but if you're interested in a particular piece, you'll be directed to galleries selling that artist's work. Expect a security check when entering. Staufenstrasse 1. ℰ 069/ 971-4480. U-Bahn: Westend.

Frankfurter Kunstkabinett Hanna Bekker vom Rath   This is the grand doyenne of the city's art galleries and has been for more than half a century. The focus is on German artists who create "classical" modern works. Braubachstrasse 14–16. ℰ 069/28-10-85. U-Bahn: Römer.

BOOKSHOPS

The British Bookshop   Loaded to the ceiling with English-language books "that are selected and stocked by people who genuinely love books," this is the premier outlet in Frankfurt for the kind of esoteric tomes that you might only expect in Boston, New York, Edinburgh, or London. If they don't have it in stock, they can order it. Börsenstrasse 17. ℰ 069/28-04-92. U-Bahn: Eschenheimer Tor.

Oscar Wilde   This is the most highbrow of the several gay book-stores of Frankfurt, alternating intellectual tomes on Germany's gay history and culture with a collection of (mostly German-language) erotica and photography books. Alte Gasse 51. ℂ **069/28-12-60.** U-Bahn: Konstablerwache.

FASHION

For routine wear, check out the vast array of clothing at the department stores recommended above. The following stores focus mainly on women's clothing, but do have some clothing for men as well.

Caos 2   For funky shopping, Caos is the place to go. Cluttered and a bit messy, the shop often has hidden gems, but you'll have to fight your way through the stacks of clothing, which include evening wear and accessories. Adalbertsrasse 27. ℂ **069/77-44-36.** U-Bahn: Bockenheimer Warte.

Chris Bittong   The shop of this designer is classic, elegant, and filled with opulent luxury. In addition to the perfectly tailored look, Chris Bittong also stocks an array of matching accessories. The clothing is created in-house. Oppenheimer Landstrasse 19. ℂ **069/62-84-64.** U-Bahn: Schweizer Platz.

Kleidoskop   You won't really feel like Secondhand Rose here, even though the shop specializes in secondhand clothing. In spite of that, it has designer fashion in the medium-price range, and much of the clothing appears to be new. For those who like designer labels, there is an array of Gucci, Armani, Prada, and other big names—all up for grabs at cut-rate prices. Oeder Weg 56. ℂ **069/55-08-37.** U-Bahn: Eschenheimer Tor.

GIFTS

Mercedes Benz Giftshop   This is the only store of its kind in Germany, selling memorabilia associated with one of Germany's most famous auto manufacturers. Inside, in a more upscale version of what you might expect from a Harley-Davidson store, you'll find jackets, vests, baseball caps, and key rings commemorating the Mercedes lore and mystique. There's even luggage, one piece of which was specifically designed to fit snugly into the trunk of one of Mercedes's most experimental, and most expensive, limited-edition sports cars. Kaiser-strasse 19–21. ℂ **069/973-55-490.** U-Bahn: Willy-Brandt-Platz.

JEWELRY

Christ Juweliere & Ohrmacher   This is the largest jewelry-and-watch retail store in Europe. On two floors there is an array of almost any goodie you'd like to adorn yourself with, including sparkling studs, rings, and bracelets, along with necklaces and even dashing wrist and pocket watches. All items can be altered to fit. Check out the top-quality selection of pearls from the South Pacific. Kaiserstrasse 1. ✆ 069/13-88-20. U-Bahn: Hauptwache.

Friedrich This exquisite store is the product of Cristoph and Stephan Friedrich, two of Germany's best designers. The brothers work with gold, platinum, silver, and assorted gemstones. Goethestrasse 9. ✆ 069/28-43-53. U-Bahn: Alte Oper.

House of Silver *(Finds)* This little shop set in the midst of the apple-wine taverns of Sachsenhausen is a discovery. Savvy Frankfurter collectors go here to indulge their taste in silver jewelry. The store is small but the range is wide, going from classic motifs to jewelry along more modern lines, with some showing ethnic influences. Schweizer Strasse 73. ✆ 069/62-76-81. U-Bahn: Schweizer Platz.

PORCELAIN

Höchster Porzellan Manufacture GmbH This gilt and blue–painted showroom contains one of Germany's largest inventories of Höchst porcelain, which has been created for more than 150 years. The quality of the "white gold" is almost flawless, and the prestige level of virtually anything associated with this outfit is about as good as it gets in Frankfurt today. (Even Goethe's mother collected the stuff, praising its virtues to her impressionable and articulate young son.) Unless the object of your desire lies on the sale table, where items might be marked down as much as 40% off retail prices, expect to pay high prices—around 153€ for a teacup, for example. But as a member of the sales staff will tell you, you can request particular color schemes for whatever object you select, as long as it's within the historical/aesthetic framework of the era when the original item was produced. Look, in particular, for illustrated platters inspired by the Struwwelpeter legends, beloved by German children for generations. Am Kornmarkt/Berliner Strasse 60. ✆ 069/29-52-99. U-Bahn: Römer.

Mitsukoshi The more frequently visited half of this shop is devoted to one of the most complete inventories of Meissen porcelain in Frankfurt. The other half contains a relentlessly upscale assortment of luxury goods made by, among others, Gucci. Widely publicized by journalists in Tokyo and Osaka, this shop is an essential stop in Frankfurt for most of the Japanese travelers visiting Frankfurt. As such, most of the staff members speak fluent Japanese, and when tour buses arrive, there's likely to be mobs of Asian clients eager to order from one of Europe's oldest porcelain manufacturers. Part of the second floor contains a "museum" with copies of antique Meissen candelabra and tureens, any of which can be duplicated if you have enough money and the time to wait for their eventual delivery. Kaiserstrasse 13. ℂ **069/92-18-87-0.** U-Bahn: Willy-Brandt-Platz.

TEDDY BEARS

Teddy-Paradies Set a few steps from the Römer (town hall), this shop acts as a magnet for teddy-bear collectors, aficionados, and fetishists from around the world. It claims to have a larger inventory than any other store in the province—2,500 different items from artisans throughout Germany.

These toys have been grabbed up by bear-lovers such as Whitney Houston, the chairman and CEO of the J.P. Morgan Bank, and other luminaries, some of whom have bought dozens of bears at a time. Ask the owner, Volker Bredhauer, for bears with specific identities: Options include, among others, dentist bears, doctor bears, and biker bears in full S&M drag. The top-of-the-line items are by well-known artisans who include Diedrich Drobney and Wolfgang Pyschny, both of whom are among the patron saints of the bear-making world. Some bears sell for as little as 3€, while one-of-a-kind bears sell for as much as 1,990€. Römerberg 11. ℂ **069/133-77-000.** U-Bahn: Römer.

TOBACCO

Havanna Lounge Small, upscale, and choice, this hideaway shop sells many of the cigars you've learned to recognize from Nicaragua, the Dominican Republic, and Jamaica, as well as lots of them (especially obscure brands from Cuba) that you might never have seen before. There's a walk-in humidor with more than 150 types of cigars. Friedensstrasse 12. ℂ **069/13-37-82315.** U-Bahn: Kaiserplatz.

9

Frankfurt After Dark

For details of what's happening in Frankfurt, you can pick up copies of *Journal Frankfurt* at newsstands throughout the city. Also listing events are *Fritz* and *Strandgut,* both free and available at the tourist office.

To purchase tickets for many major cultural events, go to the tourist office at the Hauptbahnhof. The department store **Hertie,** Zeil 90 (*©* **069/294848**), also has a theater-ticket office, which is open during regular store hours.

Of course, one of the greatest ways to spend an evening in Frankfurt is at one of the *Apfelwein* (apple-wine) taverns across the south bank of the Main, in the district of Sachsenhausen. For a selection of our favorites, refer to section 4 in chapter 5.

1 The Performing Arts

Alte Oper   The old opera house is still the pride of Frankfurt, even though opera is no longer presented here. This building was reopened in 1981, following its reconstruction after World War II bombings. The original structure had been officially opened in 1880 by Kaiser Wilhelm I. At that time, it was hailed as one of the most beautiful theaters in Europe. Today the Alte Oper is the site of frequent symphonic and choral concerts. Opernplatz. *©* 069/1-34-04-00. www.alteoper.de. Tickets 35€–72€. Box office Mon–Fri 8:30am–8:30pm; Sat 9:30am–2pm. U-Bahn: Alte Oper.

English Theater   This English-language theater was founded by the actress Judith Rosenbauer, who is still its artistic director. It began in a Sachsenhausen backyard, but was later moved to this location, compliments of the city of Frankfurt. The Art Deco auditorium, which seats 230, has an adjoining cafe. Musicals, comedies, dramas, and thrillers are produced. During the season (Sept–July), performances are Tuesday through Saturday at 7:30pm and Sunday and Wednesday at 6pm. Kaiserstrasse 52 (near the Hauptbahnhof). *©* 069/ 24-23-16-20. Plays 19€–28€, reduced student price 14€; musicals 29€–39€, reduced student price 20€; Sat prices are 8€ less. Box office daily 11am–6:30pm. S-Bahn: Hauptbahnhof.

Kunstlerhaus Mouson Turm This variety theater hosts plays, classical-music concerts, and dance programs almost every night of the week. Waldschmidtstrasse 4. ✆ 069/4058-9520. Admission 12€–20€. Box office Tues–Fri 11am–7pm; Sat–Sun 3–7pm. U-Bahn/S-Bahn: Merianplatz.

Oper Frankfurt/Ballet Frankfurt This is Frankfurt's premier showcase for world-class opera and ballet. Acclaimed for its dramatic artistry, the **Frankfurt Opera** is under the baton of Sylvain Cambreling. The world-renowned **Frankfurt Ballet** is directed by William Forsythe. Willy-Brandt-Platz (between the Hauptbahnhof and the Innenstadt). ✆ 069/134-04-00. Admission 12€–80€. Box office Mon–Fri 8am–8pm; Sat 8am–6pm. U-Bahn: Willy-Brandt-Platz.

Theater der Stadt Frankfurt There are three stages at the Frankfurt Theater. One belongs to the **Frankfurt Municipal Opera,** whose productions have received worldwide recognition in recent years. Two stages are devoted to drama. If your German is adequate, you might want to see a performance of **Städtische Bühnen/Schauspiel,** a forum for classic German plays as well as modern drama. (The 3rd stage is the **Stadtische Kammerspiel.**) Untermainanlage 11. ✆ 069/13-40-400. Admission 10€–40€. Box office Mon–Fri 10am–6pm; Sat 10am–2pm. U-Bahn: Willy-Brandt-Platz.

2 The Club & Music Scene
CABARET

King Kamehameha Club This is the hottest, most popular, and most interesting nightclub in Frankfurt, with a mystique that has become almost legendary. It occupies what was built around 1900 as a brewery; a soaring brick smokestack marks the entrance for the long lines that form outside every night. Inside, you'll find several distinct and sprawling subdivisions, including an area with a stage for live acts that appear between sets of recorded dance music. Other hangout sites include a glassed-in *biergarten* with a long, skinny reflecting pool. There's also a VIP cigar lounge that you can enter by invitation only—it's reserved for VIPs and members of whatever musical group (often from Detroit and Los Angeles) is appearing at the time. Expect attractive crowds of hipsters from every nation in Europe, elbow-to-elbow dancers, and lots of flirting. The Romanian-born manager, Rådu, advises that the real energy of this place begins after 10:30pm. The establishment's name, incidentally, was the result of a tongue-in-cheek search for something royal, something Polynesian, something fun, and something memorable. Open Wednesday through Sunday from 8:30pm to 4am. Hanauer Landstrasse 192. ℭ 069/48-00-370. Cover Thurs–Fri 8€, Sat 10€. Tram: 11 or 14.

Tiger Palast This is the most famous and popular cabaret in Frankfurt. It was named after co-founder Johnny Klinke's Chinese zodiac birth year (the Tiger). Klinke founded the club with Margarita Dillinger in the late 1980s. Shows are presented in a not very large blue and black theater, where guests, which have included Joan Collins, sit at tiny tables to see about eight different artists per show. The acts may include four Italian acrobats, three Russians who jump into one another's arms from dizzying heights, an East Indian shadow puppeteer who imitates the likenesses of famous German and U.S. politicians, a Mexican juggler, or a Ukrainian ballet artist who dances to the melodies of Edith Piaf. A tiger, a panther, and a sea lion all make carefully choreographed appearances as well. The shows are family-style and suitable for children. Each performance lasts 2 hours with breaks for drinks and snacks. Two restaurants, Tiger Restaurant and Palastbar & Tigerbistrot, are associated with this cabaret (see section 2 in chapter 5). Shows Tuesday through Thursday at 7pm and 10pm, Friday and Saturday at 8:30pm and 10:30pm, and Sunday at 5pm and 9pm. Heiligkreuzgasse 16–20. ℭ 069/92-00-22-50. Tickets 45€; half price for children under 12. Drinks from 10€.

DANCE CLUBS

In a 16-square-block area in front of the Hauptbahnhof, you'll find a rowdy kind of entertainment: the Germans call *erotische spiele* ("erotic games"). Doormen will practically pull you inside to view porno movies, sex shows, sex shops, even discos teeming with prostitutes. *Warning:* This area can be dangerous—don't come here alone.

For less lurid activities in a safer environment, head to the live-music clubs, discos, bars, and cafes across the Main River in the Sachsenhausen district. Most gay bars and clubs are located in a small area between Bleichstrasse and Zeil.

Batschkapp Frankfurt music venues come and go but Batschkapp has been going strong since the 80s. In the north of Frankfurt, it is often the scene of rock and pop concerts. Indie, crossover, hip-hop, and heavy metal music are frequently featured. Various evenings are often designated as club nights—"Idiot Ballroom" on Friday, for example, or "Bubbilicious" on Saturday. Open Friday and Saturday 10pm to 2am. Maybachstrasse 24. ℭ 069/9521-8410. U-Bahn: Konstablerwache.

Cooky's Tuesday through Sunday, DJs at Cooky's mix a dance soundtrack of hip-hop and house music. Hours are Tuesday, Thursday, and Sunday from 11pm to 4am, Friday and Saturday from 10pm to 6am. Am Salzhaus 4. ℂ **069/28-76-62.** Cover Sun and Tues–Thurs 6€, Fri–Sat 7€. U-Bahn/S-Bahn: Hauptwache.

Das 21 Jahrhundert Although this is a stylish dining venue, there's a bar on three different floors, all with a fashionable glass and steel decor. A DJ spins the tunes, mostly hip-hop and house music, starting at 9pm. The place can get very crowded on weekends. When you get hungry, you can ask for one of the small candlelit tables in the dining area. Open Sunday through Thursday 10am to 2am, Friday and Saturday 9am to 3am. Öder Weg 21. ℂ **069/55-67-46.** U-Bahn: Eschenheimer Tor.

Galerie Management here encourages patrons to arrive in a jacket and necktie, but if that doesn't bother you, you might find this place relatively glamorous, and even a bit chic. Its venue changes radically from an after-office bar, when local office workers unwind after a day in Frankfurt's high-pressure business climate, to a late-night dance club and pickup joint. Some of the paintings that decorate the walls of this place are for sale—that's the policy that inspired this nightclub's name. Open Thursday through Saturday from 9pm to 3am. Düsseldorferstrasse 1–7. ℂ **069/230-171.** Cover Thurs 8€, Fri–Sat 10€. U-Bahn: Hauptbahnhof.

Helium The DJ is known for playing some of the hippest, hottest house and techno music in town for a trendy crowd in their 20s and early 30s who call this place home. No one seems dying of thirst as the party scene unfolds here until the early morning hours when the danced-out patrons stagger out to catch 2 hours sleep before reporting to work in one of Frankfurt's skyscrapers. In summer the action spills onto the street. Open daily 11am to 4am. Bleidenstrasse 7. ℂ **069/287035.** U-Bahn: Hauptbahnhof.

Living XXL *(Finds* If you opt for a visit to this cafe-style restaurant and nightclub, don't be intimidated by the XXL-size magnitude of the corporate headquarters around you. Glass-fronted and minimalist, and soaring over the financial district that surrounds it, it has won many architectural awards, and as a symbol of Western capitalism it hardly has any equal in Germany. Set on the building's street level, and ringed with windows that present the interior as a kind of voyeuristic theater for passersby on the street, you'll find it incongruously positioned within a building that's otherwise devoted exclusively to banking and finance.

During the day it functions as a breezy, cosmopolitan restaurant-cum-cafe. Decorated in tones of metallic gray with touches of scarlet, it's an artful but rather stark departure from the *gemütlichkeit* (coziness) that many restaurants nearby take pains to provide. The cuisine leans toward the savory, light fare that appeals to the rail thin models who are often seen escorted by powerful financiers. Expect a menu of salads, wok-cooked Asian food, sliced Beijing duck with soy-flavored sesame sauce, chicken satay with salad and chili sauce, and goat-cheese salads layered with strips of sliced duck breast. Soups that might help revive your flagging spirits on a chilly Frankfurt evening include fresh tomato flavored with basil. And there's usually a grilled filet steak with peppercorn sauce, or braised seabass, on the menu. Set menus cost from 15€ to 19€ and main courses go from 8€ to 15€.

After midnight the place is transformed into a subdued and not terribly raucous dance club. Clients tend to be rather stylish, and many happen to be gay, thanks to the many special events that are announced in advance within the gay and mainstream press. Live music is presented here about once a month. The club is open Tuesday and Wednesday until 1am, and Thursday through Saturday until 3 or 4am. In the Headquarters of the European Central Bank, Kaiserstrasse 29. ℂ 069/242-9370. Cover Thurs–Sat after 11pm 6€–16€. U-Bahn: Willy-Brandt-Platz.

Nacht Leben   This club has a cafe-bar on its street level and a dance club in the cellar. Here you can either have drinks and conversation, or dance to the throbbing beat of hip-hop, funk, soul, and house. The club occasionally books a live band. Open Monday through Thursday from 11am to 2am, Thursday through Saturday from 11am to 4am. Kurt-Schumacher-Strasse 45. ℂ 069/2-06-50. Cover Fri–Sat 5€–7€. U-Bahn/S-Bahn: Konstablerwache.

Ostparkstrasse 25   Don't let the facade fool you: This "dive" opens onto an interior with a couple of mammoth, vaulted rooms. In the first vault is a bar with a DJ deck. As you go deeper, the rear has an even larger DJ deck and stage. What kind of music? Hip-hop, indie, you name it. On Saturday live bands are often brought in and the dance floor really gets active as the evening wears on. Open Thursday 8pm to midnight, Friday and Saturday 8pm to 8am. Ostparkstrasse 25. ℂ 069/4908-5820. Cover 8€. U-Bahn: Ostend.

LIVE MUSIC

An Sibin   This Irish cellar pub is decorated with pushcarts, wagons, and antique instruments. There's a band on most nights; the music is Irish-only on Tuesday. You'll find Guinness on tap, English and Irish pub grub, and a friendly barkeep who'll teach you a few phrases in Gaelic. Open Monday through Thursday from 7pm to 2am, Friday and Saturday from 7pm to 4am. Wallstrasse 9. ✆ 069/6-03-21-59. U-Bahn/S-Bahn: Hauptwache.

Der Jazzkeller This basement club, established in 1952, is one of the most famous and atmospheric jazz clubs in Germany. Its reputation is as solid as the 200-year-old redbrick walls that surround it. The place has played host to such jazz luminaries as Louis Armstrong, Dizzy Gillespie, and Gerry Mulligan. Thursday and Saturday, live music is presented usually beginning at 9pm. On nights when there is no live music, the club becomes a late-night pub. Open Tuesday through Sunday from 9pm to 3am. Kleine Bockenheimer 18A, near Goethestrasse. ✆ 069/28-85-37. Concerts 6€–21€. U-Bahn/S-Bahn: Alte Oper.

One Ninety East *(Finds* Of the many nightclubs in Frankfurt, this one pays more homage to New York City–style house music than any other in town. Part of this derives from its ownership by a German-American team of DJs, one of whom makes frequent pilgrimages to New York and L.A., returning with suitcases full of whatever recordings are hot at the time. Originally conceived as a pair of underground storage rooms for a brewery, it contains two bars, an industrial-looking decor of blue lights and brushed steel, and a clientele that's about 30% gay, 60% straight, and 10% unidentifiable. Don't be surprised if you don't see the entrance to this place from the busy Hanauer Landstrasse: You'll have to navigate your way into a 19th-century brick courtyard (the *Uniongelände* complex) that's the headquarters of a local labor union. The club is open Wednesday through Saturday from 10pm to 4am. Hanauer Landstrasse 190. ✆ 069/5060-17-180. Cover 8€ Fri–Sat only. Tram: 11 or 14.

Sinkkasten At this live-music institution, regulars show up regardless of who's playing. Rock, reggae, blues, pop, jazz, and African music might be found here, except on Thursday, late Friday, and Saturday, when the club turns dance club. Come early to beat the crowd or risk being turned away. Open Sunday through Thursday from 9pm to 2am, Friday and Saturday from 9pm to 3am. Bronnerstrasse 5–9. ✆ 069/28-03-85. Dance club 5€, concerts 7€–18€. U-Bahn/S-Bahn: Konstablerwache.

3 Gay & Lesbian Frankfurt

Blue Angel This club was named after gay icon Marlene Dietrich's first movie hit. The DJs keep you guessing by mixing dance styles. The revelry often picks up steam late in the night, so hours generally extend into the early morning. Bronnerstrasse 17. ✆ **069/28-27-72**. Cover 5€–8€. U-Bahn/S-Bahn: Konstablerwache.

Harvey's Cafe Bar The Harvey in the name is from Harvey Milk, the martyred gay official in San Francisco who is today a legend in the gay world. Frankfurt gays and straights mingle here democratically in a fun-loving, pre–World War II setting (it escaped the bombing raids). The whimsical decor is as gay as the crowd. In summer, tables overflow into an outdoor garden filled with revelers and beer drinkers. Harvey's is open Sunday to Thursday from 10am to 1am, Friday and Saturday until 2am. Bornheimer Landstrasse 64. ✆ **069/ 49-73-03**. U-Bahn/S-Bahn: Hauptwache.

La Gata This is the most crowded, most visible, most proud, and most notorious lesbian bar in Frankfurt, with a frequently reinforced reputation for refusing entrance to men, especially if they're heterosexual. The decor evokes a somewhat macho-looking English pub, with white walls, lots of dark-stained bar fixtures, and bulletin boards plastered with photos of some of the bar's regular clients. Soups and snacks are available for between 2€ and 5€ each. The bar is open nightly from 8pm to 1am. Seehofstrasse 3. ✆ **069/614-581**. U-Bahn: Südbahnhof.

Lucky's Manhattan Best described as a gay cafe and bar wrapped into one, Lucky's also has aspects of a conservative tearoom. Most folks come here to drink beer or apple wine, or perhaps to nibble on the limited array of toasts and crepes. It's a worthwhile place to begin an evening on the town. Lucky's operates Sunday through Thursday from noon to 1am, and Friday and Saturday from noon to 2am. Schäfergasse 27. ✆ **069/28-49-19**. U-Bahn/S-Bahn: Konstablerwache.

Mr. Dorian's Club New management, as of early 2001, breathed new life into a gay bar where men in their 40s and 50s meet somewhat provocative younger partners (some of whom expect to be paid for their company). There's dancing to recorded house and garage music Friday and Saturday nights after 10pm, but usually the place just functions as a bar where even the most unlikely looking patron can find male companionship. Alte Gasse 34. ✆ **069/92-88-29-66**. U-Bahn: Konstablerwache.

Pulse This is a cafe with an active bar trade; a clientele that's mostly fashionable, male, and gay; and a throbbing Valentine-colored decor of red, black, and gray. Come here for breakfast after a late night out; there are salads, sandwiches, and late-night platters that include mini-quiches. Menu items cost from 2€ to 14€. Some nights, house and garage music begins after 10pm, transforming the place into a dance club with food service. The club is open Monday through Friday from 11am to 1am, Saturday until 3am or 4am, and Sunday from 9:30am to 1am. Bleichstrasse 38A. ℂ 069/13-88-68-02. U-Bahn: Konstablerwache.

Stall This is the premier leather bar of Frankfurt, attracting a close-knit group of local men who are willing to welcome like-minded newcomers into their midst. Descend a steep staircase to reach its cellar-level premises, where the drinks you consume are noted as you order them on a white card. This is the raunchiest of Frankfurt's gay bars, but in the words of many of its patrons, "we're relatively conservative compared to what's going on in Berlin and Köln." Open nightly from 10pm to 4am. Stiftstrasse 22. ℂ 069/29-18-80. U-Bahn: Hauptwache.

4 Bars & Cafes

Balalaika For one of your most charming evenings in Frankfurt, head across the Main to Sachsenhausen—not for an *Apfelwein* tavern, but to visit this shoe box–size club. It is the domain of Anita Honis, an American from Harlem who imbues the club with her personal charm and her music. Several times a night she'll bring out her guitar and entertain guests while perched on a wooden bar stool. It's open Sunday through Thursday from 8pm to 2am and Friday and Saturday until 3am. Dreikönigstrasse 30. ℂ 069/61-22-26. Bus: 30 or 36.

Bar Oppenheimer This is a hidden away little bar on the Left Bank in Sachsenhausen, the setting of many apple wine taverns. With its minimalist decor, it attracts a wide rang of clients in their 20s to their 40s. Many are office workers from nearby skyscrapers; others are students. The bartenders have a number of cocktail specialties, including Jamaican nights with drinks beginning at 7€. For the whisky drinker, there are nearly two dozen brands from which to choose. Open Sunday through Thursday 8pm to 1am, Friday and Saturday 8pm to 2am. Oppenheimer Strasse 41. ℂ 069/62-66-74. U-Bahn: Schweizer Platz.

Café Laumer This classic German *Kaffeehaus* with a large garden attracts a middle-aged crowd. Back in the old days, it was known as the favorite retreat of Frankfurt philosophers. Today it serves some of the best pastries in town. It's open Monday through Saturday from 7:30am to 7pm and Sunday from 9am to 7pm. Bockenheimer Landstrasse 67. ℂ 069/72-79-12. U-Bahn: Westend.

Café Karin   The mayor of Frankfurt first steered us to this place. He claimed that "the real Frankfurter" patronizes this cafe. "Come here for a preview of German culture," His Honor told us. With its art-filled walls, old wooden tables, and daily newspapers (which some patrons read for hours), it's a place to relax and linger. Perhaps every hour or so a waiter might come over, but don't count on it. We like to hit this place for breakfast, and then later stop off for a nightcap around midnight. The cafe is open Monday through Thursday from 9am to 1am, Friday and Saturday until 2am, and Sunday from 10am to 7pm. Grosser Hirschgraben 28. *C* 069/29-52-17. U-Bahn: Hauptwache.

Café Studio Bar   The staff still hasn't recovered from the night Mick Jagger walked in and casually ordered two drinks at this top-floor round bar. In fair weather, guests take their cocktails and sit out on the terrace enjoying the night air, with views of the Katharinenkirche. The bar attracts a well-dressed crowd in their 20s to 40s who must pass the test of getting by the doorman's eagle eye. He's hired to keep out "undesirables" and those "not wearing proper attire." Open Monday through Saturday 6pm to 3am. Katharinenforte 6. *C* 069/1337-9225. U-Bahn: Hauptwache.

Champion's Bar   In its way, it's the most gregarious and cosmopolitan sports bar in Frankfurt, uniting (at least for a moment) salespeople from around the world into a fraternity of revelers enjoying burgers or steaks, french fries, salads, beer, and televised sporting events. Its walls are lined with the kinds of sporting memorabilia that you might expect in Milwaukee or Pittsburgh, and the furniture is the kind of woodsy, indestructible stuff you might remember from your favorite boozers bar in college. All of it combines into a busy bar and nightlife spot that can be surprisingly personable despite the huge proportions of the bustling commercially minded hotel that contains it. The TV remains tuned to sporting events—at least half of which are U.S.-derived—throughout the day and evening. On tap you'll find four kinds of reasonably priced beer. Open Sunday through Thursday from noon to 2am, Friday and Saturday from noon to 3am. On the lobby level of the Marriott Hotel, Hamburger Allee 2–10, directly across the boulevard from the Fairgrounds. *C* 069/7955-2540. U-Bahn: Messe.

die rote bar   The Red Bar (its name in English) tries to live up to its namesake with red silicon "nipples" on the bar. Young people in their 20s and early 30s flock here for the recorded music and great drinks which begin at 6.50€ per libation. On certain nights the atmosphere can be electric. Only those who scored it big in the stock market that day come in here and order a bottle of Black Bowmore for 1,000€. The latest music is played, and a small menu offers mainly sandwiches. If you get tired of the crowds, you can always retreat to one of the toilets where you'll hear (recorded, of course) the sound of the sea. Open Monday through Friday 9pm to 1am, Saturday and Sunday 9am to 2am. Mainkal 7. ✆ 069/29-35-33. U-Bahn: Römer.

Felix   A great place for young singles to meet their counterparts, this bar features a smart, dressy crowd who sip cocktails at the 17m-long (55 ft.) wooden bar. The setting is smart and trendy with wallpaper the color of autumn pumpkins and red leather chairs. As one young man told us, rather enigmatically, "Young Frankfurt comes here nightly to get silly and serious." Open Sunday through Thursday noon to 2am, Friday and Saturday noon to 3am. Rahmhofstrasse 2–4. ✆ 069/28-21-00. U-Bahn: Hauptwache.

Fox and Fiddle   Configured like a British pub, this place focuses more on dancing, drinking, and karaoke than any other pub in Frankfurt. There's a beer garden in back (it's open only when the weather is clement), a spacious and woodsy-looking bar area near the front, a dining area that serves reasonably priced burgers, pastas, and steaks, and a dance area where no one will care how raffishly you're dressed. (This is in deliberate contrast to clubs where the dress code might be a bit more spiffy.) A favorite pasta served here comes with bacon, sun-dried tomatoes, and mushrooms; steak-and-kidney pie is always available too. The dancing begins every night in the cellar at 9pm till closing. And if it all gets a bit too animated for you, you can hang out upstairs at the pub or restaurant anytime during operating hours, and choose among the variety of beers deriving from both Germany and England. Hours are Sunday through Wednesday from 11am to 1am and Thursday through Saturday until 4am. Bleich Strasse 46. ✆ 069/2165-5833. Cover 2€ for dance club and karaoke patrons; no cover for dining guests. U-Bahn: Eschenheimer Tor.

Fox and Grapes   Set on the street level of a building in the apple-wine district (Sachsenhausen), this is an amiably battered English-style pub that specializes in beers, whiskies, and glasses of "new world" wines. Most of these derive from South Africa and Australia. Small and cozy (there are just 40 seats), it broadcasts sporting events from cricket, rugby, soccer, and American football fields around the world, and will, at rare intervals and if there's a call for it, haul out a karaoke machine. Menu items focus on small, snack-style items such as club sandwiches, pastas, burgers, cheese platters and a full

English breakfast that's served at any hour you ask for it. Open Monday through Friday from 5pm to 3am, Saturday 11am to 3am, and Sunday 11am to 1am. Garden Strasse 17. ✆ 069/6032-9801. U-Bahn: Schweizer Platz.

Fox and Hound   Woodsy-looking and paneled in the battered, faux-Victorian style that you might associate with British pubs, this bar and restaurant was established in the mid-1990s, and has ever since staunchly defended its right to be British within an otherwise Teutonic sea. Don't expect tea, scones, or excessive emphasis on fussy manners—it's the kind of blunt and bustling place where rugby, cricket, and soccer emanates from TV screens, and where food runs the gamut from pub-grub snacks to full-fledged "real food." Catering to a clientele of financial-district workers, its bar includes more than 30 types of whiskeys; four kinds of beer on tap, including brands from Germany, England, and Australia; dart-throwing contests every Friday night; a Sunday-night "stump the stars" quiz; and a huge emphasis on major sporting events, when ardent fans of whatever happens to be broadcast that night will make their opinions widely known. Open Monday through Thursday from 11am to 1am, Friday and Saturday 11am to 2am, and Sunday 6pm to 2am. Niedenau 2, in the West End. ✆ 069/9720-2009. S-Bahn: Taumusanlage.

Fünftes Element   This restaurant and bar takes its name from *The Fifth Element,* a sci-fi movie. Patrons have compared a visit here to a ride in a time machine. The interior is futuristic, with lots of steel, glass and wood. Glass walls separate the restaurant and bar. A DJ plays music ranging from the golden oldies of various decades of the 20th century to hip-hop. Open Monday through Saturday 11:30 am to 3am, Sunday 5pm to 3am. Grosse Eschenheimer Strasse 20. ✆ 069/2199-6441. U-Bahn: Eschenheimer Tor.

Havanna Bar   This place starts to fill up after 5pm when the offices close for the day. At one of the longest bars in Frankfurt, you'll see some of the most fashionably dressed young people, drawn to the ambience provided by dark wooden chairs and tables and a small conservatory with big windows and benches. As the hours pass the club gets more and more crowded. Some fruity, tropical inspired nonalcoholic drinks are served, although there is plenty of hard liquor. Want something new? Try a Cuban beer called Hatuey (it's forbidden to import it into the United States). Open Sunday through Thursday 6pm to 2am, Friday and Saturday 6pm to 3am. Schwanenstrasse 2. ✆ 069/49-56-33. U-Bahn: Ostend.

Jimmy's Bar   To impress that really big client, take him or her to Frankfurt's most elegant bar in the Hessischer Hof, its most elegant hotel. Against a backdrop of gentle piano music, you can drink your Tom Collins in style and enjoy the city's smoothest service. The Cuban *mojito,* so beloved by Hemingway, has made it to Frankfurt and is the drink of the hour. The bartenders know how to fill all requests, no matter how unusual. Open nightly from 8pm to 4am. Hessischer Hof, Friedrich-Ebert-Anlage 40. © **069/75-400.** Bus: 32 or 33. S-Bahn: Platz der Republik.

Joe Pena's   This watering hole was seemingly inspired by a cantina you might encounter driving down from California to Tijuana. Lit by candles, it attracts a young crowd in their 20s and early 30s. In summer the action overflows onto an outdoor terrace. You can come here to drink from the large selection of tequilas, among other drinks, or else dig into some South of the Border fare. Happy hour with reduced drink prices ends by 8pm nightly. On occasion, Mexican musicians perform for your entertainment. Open daily 6pm to 1am. Robert-Mayer-Strasse 18. © **069/70-751-56.** U-Bahn: Bockenheim Warte.

Luna   This hip bar is always packed. With cool jazz playing in the background, Luna attracts the young professionals of Frankfurt who come here for cocktails. The bartenders perform gymnastics (reminiscent of Tom Cruise's in the flop movie *Cocktail*) while making such drinks as Grasshoppers, juleps, champagne fizzes, and tropical coladas. The place is packed on weekends. It's open Sunday through Thursday from 7pm to 2am and Friday through Saturday until 3am. Stiftstrasse 6. © **069/29-47-74.** U-Bahn: Hauptwache.

Strandperle   One of the smallest but most charming bars of Frankfurt lies in the south pier of the Eiserner Steg. Only about 20 savvy guests at a time can squeeze into a cramped place. The aura is cozy, convivial, hip, and cool. Try for a seat in the alcove whose walls are lined with Turkish carpets. Open Sunday through Thursday from 5pm to 2am, Friday until 3am, and Saturday from 6pm to 3am. Schaumainkai 17. © **069/60-32-56-67.** Bus: 46.

Studio Bar   Eclectic, fun, and funky, this bar attracts young professional men and women, often in their Versace outfits, and many who work nearby at the Börse (stock exchange). International beers, an array of cocktails, and an American-themed snack menu await you. This is a penthouse bar, which in summer opens onto a rooftop terrace. The bar is open Monday through Saturday from 5pm to 1am. Katharinenpforte 6. © **069/13-37-92-25.** U-Bahn/S-Bahn: Hauptwache.

Triebhaus This is one of the oldest and most traditional of Frankfurt's pubs, drawing a crowd ranging in age from their 20s to their 40s. Plenty of antique bric-a-brac hangs from the walls, and it has a mellow atmosphere. Many young office managers and executives come here, and the word has gotten out to some local hustlers, many from Eastern Europe who often come here to negotiate "terms" with a prospective client—and we're not talking stock market tips. Open daily 6pm to 2am. Elephantengasse 11. ✆ 069/29-12-31. U-Bahn: Konstablerwache.

Wäldches Frankfurt doesn't even try to compete with München in terms of the number of beer gardens it has, but there are still quite a few. A local favorite is also the busiest brewpub. It's located in the Ginnheimer Woods, but is easily reached by public transportation. Come here in the summer and enjoy the atmosphere provided by huge barrel tops, wooden tables, and a brass drum in which the Wäldches beers are home-brewed. There's also a *biergarten* cuisine served, with authentic German dishes. From mid-April to mid-September, it's open Monday through Saturday from noon to 12:30am and Sunday until 11pm. Off season the hours are Monday through Saturday from 4pm to 12:30am and Sunday from noon to 11pm. Am Ginnheimer Wäldchen 8. ✆ 069/52-05-22. U-Bahn: Niddapark.

Yours Sports Bar This American-style sports bar is one of Frankfurt's most frequented venues at night. The interior is in a traditional wooden style, but the electronics are modern, including a quarter of giant TVs where patrons avidly watch sporting events. Several nights are theme oriented—for example, the all-you-can-eat-of-spare-rib night on Monday costing 9€. Some of the patrons here seem to survive on nothing but chicken wings. There's a wide list of specialty cocktails beginning at 7.50€. Open Monday through Thursday noon to 1am, Friday and Saturday noon to 2am, and Sunday 5pm to 1am. Berger Strasse 111. ✆ 069/4059-0052. U-Bahn: Höhenstrasse.

10

Side Trips from Frankfurt

The best day trip from Frankfurt is to the old spa town of Wiesbaden. The transportation link (see below) is so speedy that many visitors to Frankfurt attending one of its many fairs prefer to stay at one of the hotels at the spa, then commute to Stadtmitte in Frankfurt. In fact, many Frankfurters do the same every morning, preferring to work in Frankfurt, but live in the more relaxed environment of Wiesbaden.

Another day trip, for those who have the time, is a visit to the Taunus Hills, lying northwest and west of the city of Frankfurt.

Spa lovers also flock to the traditional old resorts of Bad Homburg and Bad Neuheim.

1 Wiesbaden

40km (25 miles) W of Frankfurt, 151km (94 miles) SE of Bonn

This sheltered valley, between the Rhine and the Taunus Mountains, has held a spa since Roman times. Today, Wiesbaden competes with Baden-Baden for the title of Germany's most fashionable resort. Its success is based partly on its 26 hot springs, with temperatures of 47°C to 66°C (117°–150°F), and partly on its proximity to Frankfurt's transportation centers, which gives the spa a distinctly international flavor.

Wiesbaden is also a major cultural center. Every spring it plays host to the International May Festival of music, dance, and drama. The major concert halls are in the **Kurhaus,** a lively, multiroomed structure centered around a cupola-crowned hall. In addition to concerts, the complex hosts plays and ballets, plus a variety of social gatherings, such as international conferences, congresses, exhibitions, and trade fairs. It also holds a casino, a lively restaurant, and an outdoor cafe.

For active visitors, Wiesbaden offers horseback riding, a golf course, swimming, tennis, and hiking. The streets of the city are enjoyable for

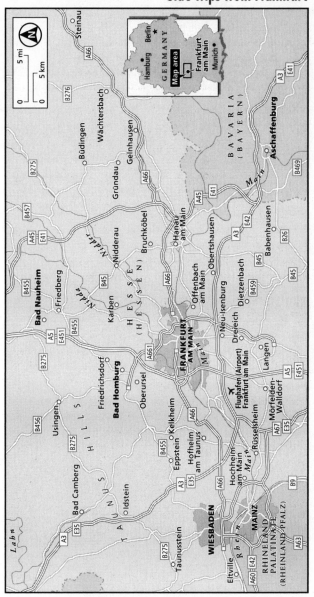

strolling, as is the **Kurpark,** which has a lake surrounded by old shade trees. It's especially beautiful at night, when the lights of the spa are reflected in the water and the huge fountains are lit. The park stretches for about a kilometer (½ mile) northward along the Kuranlagen, ending in a fancy residential quarter, the Sonnenberg. People-watching on the **Wilhelmstrasse** is another favorite pastime.

ESSENTIALS
GETTING THERE
BY TRAIN Trains run between Frankfurt airport and Wiesbaden about every hour, leaving from the airport's lower level (trip time: 30 min.). Tickets can be purchased at machines in the station area or at the airport's railway ticket counter. There's also frequent train service from the center of Frankfurt on S-Bahn S-1 and S-9 (trip time: 30–40 min.). For information, call ℭ **01805/996633.**

BY BUS **Deutsche Touring GmbH** operates frequent service between Wiesbaden and other cities in Europe (including Frankfurt) both in and outside of Germany. For information within Frankfurt, call ℭ **069/23-07-35.** For information in Wiesbaden, call ℭ **0611/780-2173.**

BY CAR Wiesbaden lies at a major crossroads, with access via the A3 Autobahn from the north and south, connecting with the A66 Autobahn from the west and east. Travel time by car from Frankfurt (Route 66) is about 20 to 30 minutes, depending on traffic. From the Frankfurt airport to Wiesbaden by car is about 20 minutes.

VISITOR INFORMATION
The **Verkehrsbüro,** Marktstrasse 6 (ℭ **0611/1-72-97-80;** www.wiesbaden.de), is open Monday through Friday from 9am to 6pm and Saturday from 9am to 3pm. Closed on Sunday.

GETTING AROUND
The Hauptbahnhof is the junction point for most of the city's bus lines. Buses are blue-sided, and charge, depending on the distance within the city limits you travel, between 1.90€ and 3.90€ for rides to most points in town. City buses operate daily between 5am and midnight, at intervals of between 10 and 15 minutes Monday through Friday, with less frequent service on Saturday and Sunday. Kirchgasse and Langgasse are two of the most prominent streets in the pedestrian zone, but the closest point to catch a bus to either of them is in front of the Stadtteater.

Wiesbaden

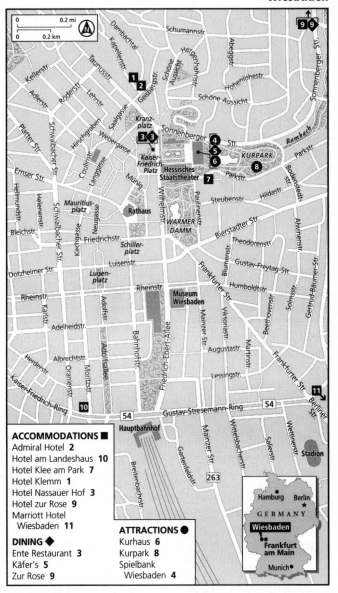

0   0.2 mi
0   0.2 km

ACCOMMODATIONS ■
Admiral Hotel **2**
Hotel am Landeshaus **10**
Hotel Klee am Park **7**
Hotel Klemm **1**
Hotel Nassauer Hof **3**
Hotel zur Rose **9**
Marriott Hotel
  Wiesbaden **11**

DINING ◆
Ente Restaurant **3**
Käfer's **5**
Zur Rose **9**

ATTRACTIONS ●
Kurhaus **6**
Kurpark **8**
Spielbank
  Wiesbaden **4**

GERMANY
Hamburg   Berlin ★
Wiesbaden
Frankfurt
am Main
Munich ●

SHOPPING

The shopping scene here is prosperous, squeaky-clean, and in the eyes of some, a bit smug. The resort's major shopping artery is **Wilhelmstrasse** (especially for clothing and upscale housewares, jewelry, and gift items). Wiesbaden is also a center for antiques, although we find them too pricey. **Taunusstrasse** is lined with antique shops.

WHERE TO STAY
VERY EXPENSIVE

Hotel Nassauer Hof 𝆺𝅥𝆺𝅥𝆺𝅥   The super-luxurious Nassauer Hof, often referred to as the "grande dame" of Wiesbaden, is among the most appealing hotels in town. It's an old favorite with up-to-date conveniences. The spacious rooms feature soundproof windows, elegant furnishings, and comfortable mattresses; some have air-conditioning. Bathrooms contain deluxe beauty products and robes. The hotel stands in the city center, within walking distance of the Kurhaus, Spielbank, theaters, and the shopping area.

Kaiser-Friedrich-Platz 3–4, 65183 Wiesbaden. ✆ **800/223-6800** in the U.S., or 0611/13-30. Fax 0611/13-36-32. www.nassauer-hof.de. 169 units. 305€ double; 470€ suite. AE, DC, MC, V. Parking 17€. Bus: 5, 18, or 25. **Amenities:** 2 restaurants; bar; 24-hr. room service; beauty spa; pool; sauna/solarium; fitness center; baby-sitting; laundry. *In room:* A/C, TV, minibar, hair dryer.

EXPENSIVE

Hotel Klee am Park 𝆺𝅥𝆺𝅥 *(Finds)*   This hotel is highly recommended for those who might find the older, more luxurious Nassauer Hof a bit too monumental. Klee am Park is a modern hotel in a tranquil setting, surrounded by its own informal gardens. The theater, casino, and shopping area are nearby. Rooms have French doors opening onto balconies; some have sitting areas large enough for entertaining.

Parkstrasse 4, 65189 Wiesbaden. ✆ **0611/9-00-10.** Fax 0611/9-00-1310. www.klee-am-park.de. 54 units. 138€–158€ double. Rates include breakfast. AE, DC, MC, V. Free parking. Bus: 8. **Amenities:** Cafe/restaurant; bar; terrace; limited room service; laundry/dry cleaning. *In room:* TV, minibar, hair dryer.

Marriott Hotel Wiesbaden 𝆺𝅥   Lots of businesspeople stay at the Marriott instead of staying in Frankfurt, as it's only 20 minutes from the Frankfurt airport. Rooms are modern and comfortably furnished. The small bathrooms are well maintained, each with a tub and shower. Because of its location outside of the center, the hotel is more suited for motorists who don't want to face the traffic of Wiesbaden. Think of it as a good roadside motel, one that is almost equally convenient for visiting Wiesbaden or Frankfurt. If you want the old spa ambience of Wiesbaden, then opt for one of our better choices such as Klee am Park.

Abraham-Lincoln-Strasse 17, 65189 Wiesbaden. ℭ **800/854-7854** in the U.S. and Canada, or 0611/79-70. Fax 0611/76-13-72. www.marriott.com. 205 units. Mon–Thurs 125€ double, Fri–Sun 95€ double (rate includes breakfast); 165€ suite. AE, DC, MC, V. Free parking. Bus: 5, 18, or 25. **Amenities:** Restaurant; bar; pool; sauna; fitness center; solarium; baby-sitting; laundry/dry cleaning. *In room:* A/C, TV, minibar, hair dryer.

MODERATE

Admiral Hotel *(Value* The centrally located Admiral is a favorite of traditionalists and one of the best values in Wiesbaden. Our readers constantly praise the owners for their hospitality. Rooms are furnished in a charmingly old-fashioned way, often with brass beds. Bathrooms are small yet clean and contain showers. The hotel offers health food. The owners are a retired U.S. Army officer and his German-born wife.

Geisbergstrasse 8, 65193 Wiesbaden (a 5-min. walk from the Kurhaus). ℭ **0611/ 5-86-60.** Fax 0611/52-10-53. www.admiral-hotel.de. 28 units. 125€ double. Rates include buffet breakfast. AE, DC, MC, V. Parking 9€. Bus: 1 or 8. *In room:* TV, hair dryer.

Hotel am Landeshaus This hotel in central Wiesbaden is one of the spa's best reasonably priced hotels. It's completely modern, but also warm, cozy, and inviting. Rooms are well kept, with small, shower-only bathrooms. Guests can enjoy drinks in a rustic ale tavern.

Mortitzstrasse 51, 65185 Wiesbaden (within walking distance of the railroad station). ℭ **0611/99-66-60.** Fax 0611/99-66-66. 20 units (with shower only). 92€ double. Rates include buffet breakfast. AE, MC, V. Parking 6€. Closed Dec 22–Jan 5. Bus: 10, 14, or 16.

INEXPENSIVE

Hotel Klemm *(Finds* This hotel occupies a late-19th-century Jugendstil villa with solid stone walls. Although the setting is well scrubbed and respectable, it has touches of genteel shabbiness that seem to go well with the nostalgia that permeates this part of Wiesbaden. This place enjoys many repeat visitors. Rooms are simple but comfortable and well kept, with shower-only bathrooms. They only serve breakfast.

Kapellenstrasse 9, 65193 Wiesbaden (near the Kurhaus). ℭ **0611/58-20.** Fax 0611/58-22-22. www.info-wiesbaden.de/hotel-hlemm. 64 units (with shower only). 100€–120€ double. Rates include breakfast. AE, DC, MC, V. Bus: 1, 2, or 8. *In room:* TV, minibar, hair dryer.

Hotel Zur Rose More modern, less impressive, and a bit more impersonal than the old-fashioned restaurant with which it's associated (see below under "Where to Dine"), this is a small-scale, family-run establishment where most members of the somewhat uncooperative staff speak absolutely nothing other than dialectical German. Bedrooms are within a two-story, relatively modern annex of the restaurant, and are outfitted in tones of pale pink, with furnishings in a style that the owners describe as modern *landhaus* (contemporary "country house" style). Three of the seven units are small singles, often occupied by salesmen or clients of the restaurant too drunk to drive home after an evening meal. Each of the units has a tile-trimmed bathroom with shower/tub combination.

Bremthaler Strasse 1 (20-min. bus ride east of the center of Wiesbaden), 65207 Naurod. ℂ 06127/40-06-06. Fax 06127/4007. 7 units. 79€ double. Rate includes breakfast. AE, MC, V. Bus 21. **Amenities:** Restaurant; limited room service; laundry/dry cleaning. *In room:* TV.

WHERE TO DINE

Ente Restaurant ★★★ CONTINENTAL/MEDITERRANEAN This restaurant serves the best food in town. The innovative chef makes sure the meals are as pleasing to the eye as they are to the palate. Cuisine is light and modern. Specialties change from week to week. Typical offerings include parfait of duck livers, a whole roast duck for two, roast medallions of venison with chanterelles, and clams in puff pastry. Desserts alone are reason to visit, especially the lemon soufflé with strawberries and the mountain-honey ice cream. Ente also has one of the best wine lists in Europe, including many moderately priced bottles. A boutique, delicatessen, wine cellar, and bistro are attached.

In the Hotel Nassauer Hof, Kaiser-Friedrich-Platz 3–4. ℂ **0611/133666.** Reservations required. Main courses 25€–32€; fixed-price dinner 59€–90€. AE, DC, MC, V. Restaurant and bistro daily noon–2:30pm and 6–10pm. Bus: 5, 18, or 25.

Käfer's INTERNATIONAL Käfer's directs two restaurants within one at the stately and prestigious Kurhaus. The more appealing of the two is Käfer's Bistro, a replica of the kind of bustling, upscale, well-run bistro you might find in Lyon or Paris. In an adjoining room is the airier, quieter, and more self-consciously formal Casino Restaurant. The menu and prices are the same as in the bistro, but the atmosphere is calmer and, frankly, a bit more stuffy. Men are required to wear a jacket and tie. Menu items change every 4 weeks. Examples might include smoked salmon served with a *Rösti* pancake, crème fraîche, and chives; Canadian lobster with yogurt-flavored cocktail sauce and lemon; penne pasta with pesto sauce and grilled giant prawns; vegetarian dishes; and in springtime, asparagus with filet mignon, bacon, or salmon steak. Dessert might be a mousse flavored with three kinds of chocolate.

In the Kurhaus, Kurhausplatz 1, 65189. ℭ **0611/53-62-00.** Reservations recommended. Main courses 13€–25€. AE, MC, V. Daily 11:30am–2am. Bus: 1, 2, or 8.

Zur Rose *Finds* FRENCH/GERMAN   This nearly 200-year-old restaurant, located in a half-timbered building, offers cozy, nostalgic decor, with a ceramic-tile oven, rose-colored lace tablecloths, and candlelight. You can enjoy freshly baked rolls as you peruse the menu. Begin with cucumber-cream soup with dill-flavored shrimp, then try the Barbarie duck breast with goose-liver sauce. Smoked salmon, trout, and other fresh fish and shrimp are also regularly featured. For dessert, try puff pastry filled with fresh fruits or poppy-seed mousse with rum-marinated fruits.

Zur Rose also rents 10 rooms, each with shower, TV, and phone. The charge for a double is 70€, including breakfast.

Bremthaler Strasse 1 (east of the town center), 65207 Naurod. ℭ **06127/40-06-06.** www.hotelzurrose.de. Reservations recommended. Main courses 6€–60€. AE, DC, MC, V. Tues–Sun 7am–2am. Bus: 21, 22, or 23.

WIESBADEN AFTER DARK

"Rien ne va plus" is the call when the ball starts to roll on the gaming tables at the **Spielbank Wiesbaden,** Im Kurhaus, Kurhausplatz 1 (ℭ **0611/53-61-00;** bus: 1, 8, or 16). The casino is open daily from 3pm to 3am and admission is 2.50€. Roulette, blackjack, and poker are the featured games. It's located at the end of Wilhelmstrasse, one of the most famous streets in Wiesbaden. To enter, you must present a passport or an identification card. Men must wear jackets and ties.

Music and **theater** flourish in Wiesbaden throughout the year. For information on performances during your visit, check at the Wiesbaden tourist office (see "Visitor Information," above). For information about any of the conference and cultural facilities in the **Kurhaus** compound, Kurhaus Platz 1, including the casino and theater, call ℭ **0611/17290.**

Hessisches Staatstheater, Christian-Zais-Strasse (ℭ **0611/13-23-25;** bus: 1), built in 1894 by Emperor Wilhelm II, is one of the most beautiful theaters in Germany. It presents a program of operettas, musicals, ballets, and plays. The season lasts from September 15 to June 30; tickets are 6.50€ to 38€.

An important event is the **International May Festival.** The festival features concerts, classical in-house drama productions, and a wide selection of guest performances by internationally renowned theater companies. For information and tickets, call ✆ **0611/132325.**

The **Park Café,** Wilhelmstrasse 36 (✆ **0611/3-93-21;** bus: 1), incorporates a cafe, brasserie, and mostly, a dance club. It's sprawling and often very busy. The cover ranges from 5€ to 8€, and it's open daily from 9pm to 4am. You might also check out the **Ratstube,** Matstrasse 8 (✆ **0611/37-25-08;** bus: 4, 5, 14, or 15). Open daily from 7pm to midnight (until 1am Fri–Sat).

2 The Taunus Hills

32km (20 miles) NW of Frankfurt

The low mountains of the Taunus region have always been known for their cool and invigorating microclimate and—during the Middle Ages—their easy defensibility from hostile armies. During the 19th century, some of the most prestigious citizens of Hesse (including the Rothschilds) built palatial villas there, and after the unification of Germany, both Kaiser Wilhelm I and his English-born mother selected the region for the construction of private homes, charities, and social clubs.

Today, the twin villages of Kronberg and Königstein, along with Königstein's high-altitude suburb of Falkenstein, harbor what German economists classify as one of the wealthiest (some sources say *the* wealthiest) enclaves in Germany. Some members of these communities commute every day to the soaring towers of Frankfurt, and then retreat at night to the jealously guarded, stately looking precincts of this lofty hideaway.

In terms of strolls, the most interesting and scenic of the three villages is Königstein, whose entrance onto the world stage really began around 1880 when it became a rather visible theater for the spectacularly dysfunctional relationship between the curmudgeonly Kaiser Wilhelm I and his strong-willed mother, Princess Victoria of England. If you opt for a visit to Königstein, you can stroll among half-timbered buildings and through medieval streets, soaking up old-fashioned Teutonic charm.

Attractions include a ruined **medieval fortress** on the highest promontory of the town, **Burg Königstein,** Burgweg (no phone). Call the tourist information office for information. Evocative of a set for a Wagnerian opera, with a view that stretches out over the town and the Taunus hills, it was presented as a gift from Kaiser

Wilhelm to his mother, who promptly spent large sums of her own money to partially restore it. Despite her efforts, don't expect anything more than a picturesque ruin, and an entrance price of 1.50€. Visiting hours are as follows: October to March daily 9:30am to 3pm; April to September daily 9am to 7pm.

The village's most visible and proudest religious edifice is an 18th-century baroque church, the **Sankt Marian Kirche,** Kirchstrasse. For information about these attractions, contact **Königstein's Tourist Office,** Kurparkpassage, Hauptstrasse 21 ((© **06174/ 202251**). It's open Monday, Tuesday, Thursday, and Friday from 9am to 6pm, and Wednesday and Saturday from 9am to 1pm.

The entire Taunus region, incidentally, became famous during the Industrial Revolution as a place whose pure air could help cure respiratory, arthritic, and stress-related illnesses. The local spa, **Kurbad,** contains a modern swimming pool that at times is packed with locals and day-trippers alike. A full day's use of the pool costs 8.50€. Massage therapy costs about 25€ for a 25-minute session, and a full array of other "cures" and treatments are available for additional fees. For more information, contact Kurbad Königstein, Le Cannet-Rocheville Strasse 1 (© **01674-92650**).

The neighboring village of **Kronberg** also offers visual doses of old-fashioned Teutonic atmosphere, albeit in forms that are a bit less charming. For information about the city core of Kronberg (which should be avoided in favor of other venues if you're rushing on to more pressing business at the trade fairs), contact **Kronberg's Tourist Office** at Rathaus, Katharinenstrasse 7 (© **01673/703221**).

Frankly, the average short-term visitor to Frankfurt would probably never set foot in either Kronberg or Königstein/Falkenstein except for the presence here of three monumental buildings (now hotels) with extraordinary histories that relate to World War II. All three offer genuinely intriguing alternatives to a stay at more commercialized and urban hotels in central Frankfurt, and as such, might appeal to you. Recommendations of those three hotels follow below.

GETTING THERE

To reach Königstein, take Train K-12 from the Hauptbahnhof to the Bahnhof in Königstein. Trains depart every 30 minutes Monday through Friday, every 60 minutes Saturday and Sunday, for a one-way fare of about 4€. To reach Kronberg, take U-Bahn S-4 (departures are about every 20–25 min. all week long) for a 35-minute ride to the line's final terminus. One-way fares cost about 3.50€. To reach Falkenstein, take either of the above-mentioned routes, then hire a taxi (they line up at both stations) to haul you away to your final destination.

WHERE TO STAY & DINE

Kempinski Hotel Falkenstein-Königstein Frankfurt ✿✿✿ Of the three hotels we recommend in Kronberg and Königstein-Falkenstein, this is the most whimsical, most elegantly informal, most hip, and most fun. It was commissioned in 1876 as a sanatorium, and designed by one of the most important German-born architects of his day, Heinrich Siesmayer (1817–1900). In 1909, his original design evolved into seven separate buildings, each conceived as a recuperation site and holiday home for Wilhelm II's high-ranking officers, most of whom he considered his personal friends. Each is a gracefully restored stone structure built in the English farmhouse style, and arranged in a half-moon shape overlooking an English garden and the faraway city lights of Frankfurt. During World War II, the site functioned as a military hospital, and until the arrival of the Kempinski chain, it devolved into a psychiatric hospital. After 5 years of extensive restoration, it reopened to feature opulent, restful, plush bedrooms flooded with sunlight from floor-to-ceiling windows. Bathrooms are very large and trimmed with stone and tile.

Debusyweg 4, D-61462 Königstein-Falkenstein am Taunus. ⓒ **06174/900.** Fax 06174/90-90-90. www.kempinski-falkenstein.com. 62 units. 200€–279€ double; 339€–489€ suite. Rates include breakfast. AE, DC, MC, V. Take S-Bahn S-4 to the end of the line at Kronberg, then hire a taxi. **Amenities:** Restaurant; bar; health club; outdoor pool; room service. *In room:* TV, minibar, hair dryer.

Schlosshotel Kronberg ✿✿✿ This is one of the most spectacular hotels in Europe. It was built by Princess Victoria, daughter of Britain's Queen Victoria, who later ruled with her husband, Emperor Frederick III, for 99 days over a united Germany. After the death of her husband and the ascent of her son (Wilhelm II) to the throne of Germany, she built this massive Anglo-German castle between 1894 and her death in 1904, and began accumulating art treasures. No other hotel in Frankfurt (and perhaps in all of Germany, for that matter) is as lavishly furnished with the antiques of its original builder, despite the fact that dozens of valuable objects were pilfered from the site by the American occupying forces after World War II. Bedrooms are furnished with antiques, more or less as they might have been during the building's heyday, and public areas include, among others, portraits by Sir Joshua Reynolds and medieval triptychs. Gardens—including an Italian-style, terraced rose garden—are absolutely spectacular. Don't expect a jolly good time in this hotel—a stay here is akin to an overnight in an awe-inspiring museum.

Hainstrasse 25, 61476 Kronberg/Taunus. (Ⓒ) **800/223-6800** in the U.S., or 06173/ 70101. Fax 06173/701-267. 58 units. 285€–420€ double; 605€–1,485€. AE, DC, MC, V. Free parking. Directions: S-Bahn line 4 from Frankfurt to the end of the line (Kronberg). From there, hire a taxi. **Amenities:** Restaurant; tennis court; 18-hole golf course; piano bar; room service; laundry/dry cleaning. *In room:* TV, minibar, hair dryer.

Sonnenhof Königstein ☆☆ *(Finds)*   Staid, secure, restrained, and less expensive than you might think, this hotel was built between 1888 and 1894 for the banker Wilhelm Carl von Rothschild (1828–1901) and his wife, Hanna Mathilde, as their summer home. When it was finished, the housewarming was attended by Empress Victoria (wife of Emperor Frederick III), and the Prince of Wales. In 1938 the builder's grandson was forced to cede the building to the Nazi regime before he emigrated from Germany. In 1955 the building was transformed into a hotel, and expanded in 1964 with an additional, rather anonymous-looking modern wing. Today you'll discover a combination of a historic monument and a hotel, all surrounded by a verdant park. Bedrooms include 14 high-ceilinged, stately, and just a wee bit dowdy rooms in the building's historic core, and 31 modern and comfortable, but relatively undramatic, accommodations in the new wing. Note that despite the spectacular history of this hotel, it isn't as hip and vibrant as the Kempinski, in nearby Falkenstein, or as staggeringly opulent as the Schlosshotel Kronberg in nearby Kronberg.

Falkensteiner Strasse 9, 61462 Königstein/Ts. (Ⓒ) **06174/2908-0.** Fax 06174/29-08-75. www.sonnenhof-koenigstein.de. 43 units. 140€–168€ double. Half-board supplement costs 25€ per person per day. AE, DC, MC, V. Take S-Bahn S-4 to the end of the line at Kronberg, or from the Hauptbahnhof in Frankfurt, take train K-12 to Königstein, then hire a taxi. **Amenities:** Restaurant; bar; pool; sauna; solarium; fitness equipment; tennis court; room service; laundry/dry cleaning. *In room:* TV, hair dryer.

3 Aschaffenburg

40km (25 miles) SE of Frankfurt, 77km (48 miles) NW of Würzburg

Aschaffenburg was originally a Roman settlement on the right bank of the Main River and became an important town in the Middle Ages. In recent years it's grown industrially, but even with 250 garment manufacturers, the town has remained peaceful and provincial.

Its many parks and shady lanes make it a fitting gateway to the streams and woodlands of the Spessart Hills. Weekly fairs are held on the square, where fishers along the banks of the Main sell seafood straight from their buckets. Many traditional shops are in a pedestrian zone, with lamps, fountains, and flowers.

ESSENTIALS
GETTING THERE
BY TRAIN The **Aschaffenburg Bahnhof** is on the major Nürnberg-Würzburg-Frankfurt line and on the regional Maintal Aschaffenburg–Mittenburg-Wertheim line, with frequent connections in all directions. From Frankfurt, 45 trains arrive daily (trip time: 30–45 min.). For information, call ℭ **01805/99-66-33.**

BY BUS There is no direct bus service between Frankfurt and Aschaffenburg.

BY CAR Access by car is via the A3 Autobahn east and west.

VISITOR INFORMATION
Contact **Tourist-Information,** Schlossplatz 1 (ℭ **06021/39-58-00;** www.info-aschaffenburg.de). It's open Monday through Friday from 9am to 5pm and Saturday from 10am to 1pm.

GETTING AROUND
Aschaffenburg and the region immediately around it are served by a network of green-painted buses whose junction point is the Hauptbahnhof, the city's main railway station. Because many of the streets within the city's historic core are reserved for pedestrians, many sightseers take bus no. 1, 4, 5, or 8 between the Hauptbahnhof and the Stadthalle (town hall), immediately adjacent to the Altstadt (old town). Buses run daily from 5:30am to 9pm. Rides within the central zone cost 1.50€ per person each way. An all-day ticket goes for 2.50€. For information, call the city tourist office at ℭ **06021/39-58-00.**

SEEING THE SIGHTS
The best park in Aschaffenburg is **Schönbusch Park,** Kleine Schönbuschallee 1 (ℭ **06021/873-08;** bus: 4), located 3km (2 miles) across the Main. It's a marvel of planning, using the natural surroundings as a setting for formal 18th-century gardens, shady lanes, temples, and gazebos. At the edge of the mirror-smooth lake is a small neoclassical castle (really a country house) once used by the electors of Mainz. The house is open April to October, Tuesday

through Sunday from 9am to 6pm. Admission is 3.50€ for adults, 2.50€ for students, and free for children under 15. In summer it's possible to rent a small boat to go on the lake. There's also a cafe-restaurant that's open daily from 8am to 8pm.

The most impressive castle in Aschaffenburg is the huge Renaissance **Schloss Johannisburg** ✻, Schlossplatz 4 (✆ **06021/386-570;** bus: 1, 2, or 8), reflected in the waters of the Main. Erected from 1605 to 1614, it became the residence of the rulers of the town, the prince-electors of Mainz. The red-sandstone castle is almost perfectly symmetrical, with four massive lantern towers surrounding an inner courtyard. From April to October Tuesday through Sunday, the castle is open from 10am to noon and 1 to 6pm; off season, Tuesday through Sunday from 10am to 4pm. Admission is 2.50€ for adults and 2€ for children 14 and under. While here you might visit the Schlossweinstuben (see "Where to Dine," below). From the castle gardens you can reach the **Pompeianum,** built by Bavaria's King Ludwig I as a replica of the Castor and Pollux palace discovered among the ruins of Pompeii. The Pompeianum is open mid-March to mid-October Tuesday through Sunday from 10am to noon and 2:30 to 6pm. Admission is 2€ for adults, 1.50€ for students, and free for children.

Stiftskirche St. Peter and St. Alexander, Stiftsgasse 5 (✆ **06021/2-24-20;** bus: 1, 4, or 10), has stood on its hill overlooking the town for 1,000 years. Its architecture has changed over the centuries with remodeling and reconstruction, and today it stands as a combination of Romanesque, Gothic, and baroque. Its most precious treasure is the painted retable *The Lamentation of Christ,* by Mathias Grünewald. The interior is decorated with several paintings of the school of Lucas Cranach, as well as a marble-alabaster pulpit by Hans Juncker. One of the oldest pieces is a Roman-style crucifix from A.D. 980. Adjacent to the north side of the church is a Romanesque cloister from the 13th century. The church is open Wednesday through Monday from 10am to 1pm and 2 to 5pm. Admission is free, but a tour costs 2€ adults and 1.50€ for children and students.

WHERE TO STAY

Aschaffenburger Hof   This establishment is housed in a tall yellow building with a single balcony on each floor. The small rooms, although no style-setters, are pleasantly furnished. Try for one overlooking the courtyard. Each accommodation is equipped with a small, tiled bathroom with shower. The restaurant is locally popular for its fresh, modern cuisine that includes some vegetarian dishes.

Frohsinnstrasse 11, 63739 Aschaffenburg. ⓒ **06021/386810.** Fax 06021/2-72-98. 62 units. 76€–96€ double. Rates include breakfast. AE, DC, MC, V. Parking 4€. Bus: 1, 3, 4, 6, or 10. **Amenities:** Restaurant; room service; laundry/dry cleaning. *In room:* TV.

Hotel Dalberg   Newly built in 1994, this hotel occupies a prominent site that's within a 5-minute walk from Aschaffenburg's historic core and its pedestrian zone. With an all-white, four-story facade, it offers cozy, well-designed rooms, each with a tiled shower. On the premises you'll find a rustic-looking *Weinstube* (wine room) serving regional cuisine and drinks from a bar.

Pfaffengasse 12–14, D-63739 Aschaffenburg. ⓒ **06021/3560.** Fax 06021/21-98-94. 26 units. 89€–125€ double. Rates include breakfast. AE, MC, V. Bus: 1 or 4. **Amenities:** Restaurant; bar. *In room:* TV, minibar.

Hotel Post   This is the town's premier hotel, offering greater comfort than its rivals. Close to the heart of town, it was built in 1919 and completely renovated in 2000. Rooms are well maintained and decorated in traditional style. Some units come with a tub and shower, others only a shower. The dining room is a stylized version of an old posting inn; it includes an original mail coach, timbered walls and ceiling, and lead-glass windows. Reasonably priced and very good Franconian meals are served here.

Goldbacherstrasse 19-21, 63739 Aschaffenburg. ⓒ **06021/33-40.** Fax 06021/1-34-83. www.post-ab.de. 69 units. 102€–134€ double. Rates include breakfast. AE, DC, MC, V. Parking 4€. Bus: 1, 3, 4, 6, or 10. **Amenities:** Restaurant; indoor swimming pool; sauna; solarium; laundry. *In room:* TV, minibar.

Syndikus   An unpretentious three-story facade greets visitors to this hotel. The bar area is rustically decorated with timbered ceilings and wheel chandeliers. All rooms are well maintained and have up-to-date furnishings, and each has a shower. Although the hotel is open year-round, its restaurant is closed in August.

Löherstrasse 35, 63739 Aschaffenburg (a few blocks from the cathedral). ⓒ **06021/44-9990.** Fax 06021/44-99944. 20 units. 73€–83€ double; 93€–145€ suite. Rates include breakfast. MC, V. Parking 3.50€. Bus: 3 or 6. **Amenities:** Restaurant. *In room:* TV.

WHERE TO DINE

Schlossweinstuben FRANCONIAN/BAVARIAN   One of the most alluring corners of this historic castle is its popular wine cellar. Here you'll find a wide variety of German wines to complement the conservative but well-prepared menu items. A meal might begin with liver-dumpling soup, followed with a game specialty (depending on the season). The selection of very fresh fish is likely to include trout and pike. There is no pretension to this cuisine—it's just good, hearty, rib-sticking fare.

Schloss Johannisburg. *©* **06021/1-24-40.** Reservations recommended. Main courses 12€–32€. No credit cards. Tues–Sun 10am–midnight. Bus: 1, 3, or 4.

ASCHAFFENBURG AFTER DARK

No one in Aschaffenburg ever claimed that its citizenry didn't like to drink, so if you're trying to let the good times roll, you'll often find yourself in hard-drinking company. The two densest concentrations of bars lie within the Dahlburg neighborhood, specifically around the Rossmarkt, in the heart of Aschaffenburg's Old Town.

You'll find within a few paces of one another three hot and hopping choices, each at the edge of the Rossmarkt. They include the **Einstein Bar,** Rossmarkt 36 (*©* **02061/27777**), where clients nibble on Mexican-inspired tacos, tortillas, quesadillas, and drink sometimes prodigious amounts of party-colored cocktails, especially margaritas. Nearby is one of the oldest and most folksy small-scale pubs in the city, **Engelsburg,** Dahlburg 66 (*©* **02061/13292**). Charming and unfailingly Teutonic, it's a good choice for suds and old-world charm. Also nearby is **Schlappes-Eppl,** Schlossgasse 28 (*©* **06021/25531**), a simple and straightforward cultural monument where both light and dark beer are brewed and consumed (and often spilled!) on-site. An all-ages crowd seems to enjoy the rollicking old-fashioned setting.

Hipper and trendier nightlife choices include **Domus,** Sandgasse 41 (*©* **06021/28777**), where a hyper-modern decor was gracefully fitted into the shell of an antique building, and where both a restaurant and a singles bar await your pleasure. Its most visible competitor for the trend-conscious crowd is **Marquesas,** Pfaffengasse 12 (*©* **06021/3560**), which functions as both a restaurant and a pub. Exotic within this very German town is **The Irish Pub,** at Weissenburgerstrasse 56 (*©* **06021/80142**), providing all the nostalgia and jocularity of Eire. A mixture of recorded and (less frequently) live Irish music improves the sociability factor.

If you're looking to go dancing, consider **Aladin's,** at Hauptstrasse 10, in the nearby hamlet of Goldbach (*©* **02061/56625**). The club is frequented by an under 30 crowd. The more staid (and a bit dowdier) **Tanzpalast,** Luitpoldstrasse 15 (*©* **02061/22766**), lies in the heart of the Dahlburg section of Aschaffenburg's old town. Here the clientele tends to be between 30 and 50, and the music tends toward hits fashionable during the 1970s and 1980s.

4 Bad Homburg ⊛

16km (10 miles) N of Frankfurt, 45km (28 miles) NE of Wiesbaden

Bad Homburg is one of Germany's most attractive spas, still basking in the grandeur left over from 19th-century Europe. The spa's saline springs are used to treat various disorders, especially heart and circulatory diseases. The town has been a popular watering spot since Roman times. Royalty from all over the world have visited. King Chulalongkorn of Siam (Thailand) was so impressed that he built a Buddhist temple in the Kurpark. Czar Nicholas I erected an onion-domed Russian chapel nearby. The name of the town was popularized by England's Edward VII when, as Prince of Wales, he visited the spa and introduced a new hat style, which he called the "homburg." The town became the gaming capital of Europe when the Blanc brothers opened their casino in 1841.

The **Spa Park** ⊛ is a verdant, carefully landscaped oasis in the middle of an otherwise rather commercial-looking town. The actual spa facilities are in the **Kaiser Wilhelms Bad,** Im Kurpark (© **0611/1729660**). They're open Monday from 10am to 10pm, Tuesday through Friday from 7:30am to 10pm, and Saturday from 10am to noon. Tuesdays are reserved for women only. It costs 18€ for use of the sauna and pool. The immaculately tended gardens in the surrounding Kurpark are filled with brooks, ponds, arbors, and seasonal flowers. The town center has a sprawling pedestrian-only district that offers many shops, restaurants, and cafes.

ESSENTIALS
GETTING THERE

BY TRAIN Visitors from Frankfurt usually opt to take the S-5 train, which runs from Frankfurt's main railway station to Bad Homburg for a cost of 3.50€ each way. The trip takes about 20 minutes. Call © **01805/99-66-33** for information.

BY BUS The **Alpina-Airport-Express** is Bad Homburg's hourly, nonstop shuttle service to and from the Frankfurt airport (trip time: 30 min.).

BY CAR Access by car from the north or south is via the A5 Autobahn, exiting at Bad Homburg.

VISITOR INFORMATION

For information, go to the **Verkehrsamt im Kurhaus,** Louisenstrasse 58 (© **06172/1780;** www.bad-homburg.de). It's open Monday through Friday from 8:30am to 6:30pm and Saturday from 10am to 2pm.

GETTING AROUND

Public transport in Bad Homburg is provided by a network of green-and-white buses whose main junction points are the Hauptbahnhof (a 10-min. walk southwest of the city center) and in front of the Kurhaus, in the city center. Buses, which run daily from 5am to midnight, charge 1.25€ per ride.

SIGHTS & ACTIVITIES

Bad Homburg Palace   This palace was the residence of the landgraves of Hesse-Homburg from its construction in 1680 until the mid–19th century. Its builder, Prince Frederick II von Homburg, preserved the White Tower from the medieval castle that stood on the site. In the late 19th century, the palace became a summer residence for Prussian kings and, later, German emperors. After World War I, the state assumed ownership. The interior contains 18th-century furniture and paintings, including a bust of Prince Frederick II by Andreas Schlüter, Germany's greatest baroque sculptor. The former "telephone room of the empress" includes *Cleopatra* by Pellegrini.

Schlossverwaltung (a few blocks from the spa gardens). © **06172/178-160.** Admission 3.50€ adults, 2.50€ children under 14. Palace and formal gardens Tues–Sun 10am–4pm. Bus: 1, 4, or 11.

Taunus Therme   A large recreation area, Taunus Therme boasts several pools, a sauna, a solarium, and a health center, plus TVs, cinemas, and two restaurants.

Seedammweg. © **06172/4-06-40.** Admission Mon–Fri 14€ for 2 hr., 17€ for 4 hr., 27€ for full day; Sat–Sun and holidays 15€ for 2 hr., 19€ for full day; daily free for children 3 and under. Sun–Tues 9am–11pm; Wed and Fri–Sat 9am–midnight. Bus: 6.

WHERE TO STAY
EXPENSIVE

Maritim Kurhaus-Hotel *&*   This hotel near the spa facilities offers visitors plush rooms, many with tall bay windows. As sleek and up-to-date as this hotel is, it's still far outclassed by the Steigenberger Bad Homburg. Double rooms feature king-size beds; singles have queen-size beds. All rooms contain computer outlets. Some rooms have balconies or terraces, permitting wide views over the greenery of the surrounding park. The luxurious bathrooms contain a combination tub and shower. Both international and regional fare are served at the Bürgerstube, which is open daily.

Kurpark, Ludwigstrasse, 61348 Bad Homburg. © 06172/66-00. Fax 06172/66-01-00. www.maritim.de. 148 units. 125€–179€ double; 185€–263€ suite. AE, DC, MC, V. Parking 10€. Bus: 1, 2, 3, 4, 11, or 12. **Amenities:** Restaurant; bar; indoor pool; sauna; limited room service; babysitting; laundry/dry cleaning. *In room:* TV, dataport, minibar, hair dryer, safe.

Steigenberger Bad Homburg ✿✿✿
This is the resort's best and most prestigious hotel. Europe's high society used to stroll here in days of yore, and an ambience of luxury still prevails. Rooms are beautifully furnished and have extra-long beds. Each room offers individually adjustable air-conditioning. The spacious bathrooms contain deluxe luxury items, sumptuous robes, and combination tub and showers. The elegant Parkside Restaurant offers creative contemporary cuisine. There's also the French-style Charly's Bistro.

Kaiser-Friedrich-Promenade 69–75 (opposite the spa gardens and casino), 61348 Bad Homburg. © 800/223-5652 in the U.S. and Canada, or 06172/18-10. Fax 06172/18-16-30. www.steigenberger.de. 169 units. 124€–226€ double; 355€ suite. AE, DC, MC, V. Parking 13€. Bus: 1, 2, 3, 4, 11, or 12. **Amenities:** Restaurant; bistro; bar; sauna; solarium; steam bath; room service; babysitting; laundry/dry cleaning. *In room:* A/C, TV, minibar, hair dryer, safe.

MODERATE

Hardtwald Hotel ✿
This hotel, which resembles a chalet set in a forest, is an ideal retreat near the spa gardens. In spring, flowers overflow from its window boxes. Its rooms overlook the forest. Each is comfortably furnished and well maintained, coming with a compact tiled bathroom with tub and shower or only shower. The chef of Schellers, the excellent, flower-filled dining room, uses only the freshest of ingredients to prepare his well-known international and German dishes. In summer, tables are set on the large patio. Next to the hotel is a stable where you can rent horses.

Philosophenweg 31 (a 20-min. walk from the center of town), 61350 Bad Homburg. © 06172/82512. Fax 06172/898-560. 42 units. 80€–190€ double. Rates include buffet breakfast. AE, DC, MC, V. Bus: 3. **Amenities:** Restaurant; bar; room service; laundry. *In room:* TV, minibar.

Parkhotel Bad Homburg ✿Value
This is your best bet for a moderately priced spa vacation. This hotel has an enviable location in the middle of the Kurpark's well-maintained gardens, near the thermal springs. Although its design is modern and angular, its edges are softened with window boxes. Rooms are conservatively furnished.

Bathrooms are well kept and contain a combination tub and shower. On the premises are a bar and a sunroom. The hotel restaurant serves Chinese cuisine.

Kaiser-Friedrich-Promenade 53–55, Am Kurpark, 61348 Bad Homburg. ℂ **06172/ 80-10.** Fax 06172/80-14-00. www.parkhotel-bad-homburg.de. 123 units. 99€–145€ double; 164€–220€ suite. Rates include buffet breakfast. AE, DC, MC, V. Parking 10€. Tram: 5. **Amenities:** 2 restaurants; bar; sauna; solarium; room service; laundry. *In room:* TV, minibar.

INEXPENSIVE

Haus Daheim *Value* When you're trying to save, head here. This hotel, in a light-blue corner building, is one of the finest small hotels in the town. The comfortable rooms have good beds with firm mattresses, plus tiled bathrooms with showers. This is an admittedly modest choice after the hotels reviewed above, but for value, it's hard to beat.

Elisabethenstrasse 42 (a short walk from the Kurhaus), 61348 Bad Homburg. ℂ **06172/67-73-50.** Fax 06172/677-35-500. www.hotel-haus-daheim.de. 19 units. 107€–157€ double. Rates include buffet breakfast. AE, DC, MC, V. Parking 8€. Tram: 5. **Amenities:** Breakfast salon. *In room:* TV, minibar, hair dryer, safe.

WHERE TO DINE

Casino-Restaurant FRENCH/GERMAN At this site, you can gamble and dine at the same time. Until a few years ago, this was the only restaurant in Germany that directly adjoined the gaming tables of a casino. It's one of the finest in town, although not in the same class as Sängers. The dining room is decorated in a formal, vaguely English style. It offers attentive service and a winning combination of light French and German cuisine. The frequently changing menu features seasonal specialties with the freshest of ingredients—head chef Gunther Schwanitz begins each workday at the local markets. Lobster is a universal favorite here, attracting diners from as far away as Frankfurt. Although the main kitchen service stops at 10:30pm, there's a reduced menu until 12:30am.

Im Kurpark. ℂ **06172/1-70-170.** Reservations required. Jacket and tie required for men. Main courses 12€–24€; fixed-price menu 30€. AE, DC, V. Daily 6–10:30pm. Tram: 5.

Sängers Restaurant ✦✦✦ FRENCH Local food lovers and spa devotees crowd this restaurant to enjoy the highly personal and inventive cuisine, the best in the spa. The two elegant dining rooms are outfitted in the style of Louis XIV. Menu items might include carpaccio of turbot with Iranian caviar; goose-liver terrine served with brioche and gelatin of wild berries; a foam-capped celery soup with quail eggs; roast breast of duck on a bed of rhubarb; and a succulent array of desserts.

Kaiser-Friedrich-Promenade 85 (next to the Steigenberger Bad Homburg). ✆ 06172/92-88-39. Reservations required. Main courses 25€–30€; fixed-price dinner 55€–95€. AE, MC, V. Tues–Fri noon–2pm; Mon–Sat 7–11pm. Closed the 1st week of Jan. Bus: 1, 4, 11, or 12.

BAD HOMBURG AFTER DARK

Spielbank Im Kurpark (✆ **06172/1-70-10;** tram: 5), called the "Mother of Monte Carlo," is the spa's major attraction. This casino opened way back in 1841 and helped make Bad Homburg famous. Roulette, blackjack, and baccarat are the games here. Passports are required for entrance, and men must wear jackets and ties. Admission is 2.50€. Hours are daily from 2:30pm to 3am.

The most active dance club in town is the **Tennis Bar,** Kisseleffstrasse 20 (✆ **06172/2-60-41;** bus: 6), named for the municipal tennis courts in the nearby Kurpark. It offers both recorded and live rock music. If you thought you were too old to hang out in a dance club, think again, as this one attracts clients ages 25 and over. It's open Tuesday through Saturday from 9pm, with a varying cover. More traditional is the town's favorite beer hall and *Weinstube,* **Zum Wasser Weibehen,** Am Mühlberg 57 (✆ 06172/2-98-78; bus: 1, 4, or 11). About 1.5km (1 mile) east of the town center, you'll find another folkloric place, **Zum Ruppe Karl,** Hamburgerstrasse 6 (✆ **06172/4-24-84;** bus: 2 or 12), whose home-style cuisine is enhanced with the establishment's homemade apple wine. The **Kurhaus** also contains a handful of bars, cafes, and shops that usually stay open late.

5 Bad Nauheim

35km (22 miles) N of Frankfurt, 64km (40 miles) NE of Wiesbaden

Like many spas throughout Germany, Bad Nauheim became popular in the early part of the 20th century, when the railroad became a convenient and inexpensive means of transportation. Still going strong today, this resort at the northern edge of the Taunus Mountains is a center for golf, tennis, and ice-skating, as well as the starting point for hiking up the 236m (773 ft.) Johannisberg, which towers over the town.

The warm carbonic-acid springs of the spa are used to treat heart and circulatory disorders and rheumatic diseases. The Kurpark is attractive, well maintained, and filled with promenaders all summer long. The impressive bathhouse is the single largest complex of Jugendstil architecture in Germany. The Sprudelhof (fountain court), at the center, stretches from the Hauptbahnhof to the Kurpark and all the way to the Kurhaus. All the important sights, including the bathhouse complex, can be visited in half a day. The resort has a busy activity calendar, with concerts twice daily, along with operas, plays, dances, and fashion shows.

ESSENTIALS
GETTING THERE
BY TRAIN   Bad Nauheim can easily be reached from Frankfurt. Trains arrive at least once per hour (every 30 min. during rush hours) during the day (trip time: 30 min.). Service is on the Weatherman line between Frankfurt and Giessen. For information, call © **01805/99-66-33.**

BY CAR   Access is via the A5 Autobahn from the north and the south. Driving time from Frankfurt is about half an hour.

VISITOR INFORMATION
For information, go to the **Verkehrsverein,** Neue Kurolonnade (© **06032/92-99-22;** www.bad-nauheim.de). It's open Monday through Friday from 10am to 6pm, Saturday noon to 4pm, and Sunday 11am to 4pm.

WHERE TO STAY
Advena Hotel Rosenau   This is one of the better choices at the resort, though it's not nearly as good as the Parkhotel am Kurhaus. The Rosenau is an updated version of a German manor house, with white walls and a red-tiled hip roof. Inside, the decor is one of light-toned wood and pastel colors. Rooms are modern and attractive, with combination tub and shower. On the premises there's a good bistro and the fine Rosengarten restaurant (see "Where to Dine," below).

Steinfurther Strasse 1 (west of Grosser Teich, the town lake), 61231 Bad Nauheim. © 06032/9-64-60. Fax 06032/964-6666. 54 units. 90€–170€ double. Rates include continental breakfast. AE, DC, MC, V. Free parking. Closed Dec 27–Jan 8. **Amenities:** 2 restaurants; bar; pool; room service; laundry/dry cleaning. *In room:* A/C, TV, minibar, hair dryer.

Hotel Gaudesberger   This centrally located hotel is known mainly for its restaurant (see "Where to Dine," below). Rooms are simply furnished, each coming with a small bathroom with shower.

Fun Fact **Elvis in Bad Nauheim**

Many famous guests have visited this spa, including Otto von Bismarck (1859) and Richard Strauss (1927). Franklin D. Roosevelt spent about 2 years here with his family when he was a small child. Locals believe that Bad Nauheim was spared destruction during World War II, even though a Nazi radio transmitter was installed here, because President Roosevelt had fond memories of the place.

Real fame came to the spa when a private named Elvis Presley arrived and found a home off-base, right next to the Kurhaus. The singer was stationed in nearby Friedberg/Hessen at Ray Barracks Kaserne from October 1958 to March 1960, and his presence had an electrifying effect on the German youth scene. It was here that Elvis fell in love with Priscilla. She was 14 at the time, and when she first arrived at the plain, old-fashioned villa where he lived, the street was full of German girls, waiting by the sign AUTOGRAPHS BETWEEN 7 AND 8PM ONLY. After that first meeting, she saw him once more, and when he returned to the States, he vowed to send for her.

Elvis and FDR weren't the only famous Americans to visit. It was the habit of newspaper magnate William Randolph Hearst to come here every year with his mistress, Marion Davies, and a dozen or so of her women friends; Hearst would have the women chauffeured around the countryside in style. He firmly believed Bad Nauheim's physicians were the answer to his minor heart problem. Here he had his notorious meeting with Mussolini in 1931 ("a marvelous man"), and from here he flew to Berlin to meet Hitler in 1934. He claimed that he had done "much good" in advising Hitler to drop his persecution of the Jews, but afterwards he spent most of his life trying to live down his image as a supporter of the Nazi cause.

Except for a phone, there are no in-room amenities. The place is plain and decent, not grand in any way. The staff does not speak English.

Hauptstrasse 6, 61231 Bad Nauheim. ℂ and fax **06032/25-08.** 8 units, none with bathroom. 50€ double. Rates include continental breakfast. AE, DC, MC, V. Closed Jan 15–Feb 15. **Amenities:** Restaurant.

Parkhotel am Kurhaus 🍷🍷 This modern hotel is the finest in town, with better amenities than the Rosenau. It's located in the middle of the park that rings the resort's thermal springs. Its public areas are filled with green plants and arching windows. Rooms, with big sliding glass windows and balconies, provide calm, quiet, and conservative comfort. Bathrooms are luxurious and contain deluxe luxury items and combination tubs and showers. Special diets and vegetarian menus are offered.

Nordlicher Park 16, 61231 Bad Nauheim. ☏ 06032/30-30. Fax 06032/30-34-19. www.dolce.com. 159 units. 141€–221€ double; 271€ suite. Rates include continental breakfast. AE, DC, MC, V. Parking 5€–8.50€. **Amenities:** 2 restaurants; cafe; English pub; bar; room service; babysitting; laundry/dry cleaning. In room: TV, minibar, hair dryer, safe.

WHERE TO DINE

Restaurant Gaudesberger INTERNATIONAL A large menu of well-prepared dishes is offered here in comfortable but simple surroundings. You can stick to the tried-and-true choices, such as chateaubriand with béarnaise sauce or herring filet in dill sauce, or you can dip into the other specialties, such as pork in curry-cream sauce, ox tongue in Madeira sauce, or trout and salmon prepared in at least four different ways. Ingredients are fresh, and everything is prepared home-style. The staff is cooperative and courteous.

In the Hotel Gaudesberger, Hauptstrasse 6. ☏ 06032/25-08. Reservations recommended. Main courses 9.50€–18€. AE, DC, MC, V. Thurs–Tues 11:30am–2pm and 5:30–9pm.

Rosengarten INTERNATIONAL This restaurant is known as one of the best in town. It serves a fixed-price lunch plus a la carte evening meals. The flavorful dishes might include cream of tomato and young-vegetable soup, roast breast of young hen, and filet of salmon with fresh herbs, plus several different pork and game dishes, depending on the season. The cookery is not innovative, but we were impressed with its honesty and freshness. There are no pretensions here.

In the Hotel Rosenau, Steinfurther Strasse 1. ☏ 06032/9-64-60. Main courses 15€–18€; fixed-price buffet lunch 18€. AE, DC, MC, V. Tues–Sun noon–2pm and 6–10pm. Closed Dec 27–Jan 30.

BAD NAUHEIM AFTER DARK

Despite its small size and sedate appearance, there are lots of outlets for dining and drinking in Bad Nauheim, and although there aren't any of the hip dance clubs you expect in Frankfurt, there are at least two somewhat sedate emporiums for fox trots, waltzes, polkas, and cheek-to-cheek dancing. Both of these lie within a short walk of the *Sprudel Haus* (spa facilities).

Patronized by older citizens, and focusing on traditional dances for couples, they include the **Terrassencafé,** Parkstrasse 9 (© **06032/ 4844**), where individual telephones on each of the tables allow coy (or sometimes blatant) advances to be made among potential partners. It's slightly more recent competitor is **Tanz Café König,** Ludwigstrasse 17 (© **06032/2235**), which can be a lot of fun if you enjoy slow dancing or are nostalgic for the dance styles of your parents.

Clustered within the heart of the town you'll find such bars and bistros as the **Bistro Café,** Marktplatz 3 (© **06032/32719**), a small and intimate place where no one will mind if you remain just to drink; **Die Scheune,** Marktplatz 5 (© **06032/35581**), where a large, two-floor, wood-paneled venue greets newcomers with rustic Teutonic nostalgia and occasional them parties (a "Night in Mallorca" was a recent, palm-filled example). Persons under 35 tend to gravitate to the faux-tropical **Havana Bar,** Ritterstrasse 2 (© **06032/93-27- 67**), where piña coladas and sunset-colored drinks create a tropical illusion in the land of *wurst* and sauerkraut. **König Eck,** Hauptstrasse 15 (© **06032/35499**), is a pub that focuses on beer and wine. A popular last resort is **Willi's Pub,** Burgstrasse 10 (© **06032/2609**), where carefully oiled paneling and a congenially battered decor replete with a collection of antique tools (including some old-fashioned sewing machines) attest to the place's deeply entrenched popularity.

Index

See also Accommodations and Restaurant indexes below.

RESTAURANTS

FROMMER'S® COMPLETE TRAVEL GUIDES

Alaska
Alaska Cruises & Ports of Call
Amsterdam
Argentina & Chile
Arizona
Atlanta
Australia
Austria
Bahamas
Barcelona, Madrid & Seville
Beijing
Belgium, Holland & Luxembourg
Bermuda
Boston
Brazil
British Columbia & the Canadian
  Rockies
Budapest & the Best of Hungary
California
Canada
Cancún, Cozumel & the Yucatán
Cape Cod, Nantucket & Martha's
  Vineyard
Caribbean
Caribbean Cruises & Ports of Call
Caribbean Ports of Call
Carolinas & Georgia
Chicago
China
Colorado
Costa Rica
Denmark
Denver, Boulder & Colorado
  Springs
England
Europe
European Cruises & Ports of Call
Florida

France
Germany
Great Britain
Greece
Greek Islands
Hawaii
Hong Kong
Honolulu, Waikiki & Oahu
Ireland
Israel
Italy
Jamaica
Japan
Las Vegas
London
Los Angeles
Maryland & Delaware
Maui
Mexico
Montana & Wyoming
Montréal & Québec City
Munich & the Bavarian Alps
Nashville & Memphis
Nepal
New England
New Mexico
New Orleans
New York City
New Zealand
Northern Italy
Nova Scotia, New Brunswick &
  Prince Edward Island
Oregon
Paris
Philadelphia & the Amish Country
Portugal
Prague & the Best of the Czech
  Republic

Provence & the Riviera
Puerto Rico
Rome
San Antonio & Austin
San Diego
San Francisco
Santa Fe, Taos & Albuquerque
Scandinavia
Scotland
Seattle & Portland
Shanghai
Singapore & Malaysia
South Africa
South America
South Florida
South Pacific
Southeast Asia
Spain
Sweden
Switzerland
Texas
Thailand
Tokyo
Toronto
Tuscany & Umbria
USA
Utah
Vancouver & Victoria
Vermont, New Hampshire &
  Maine
Vienna & the Danube Valley
Virgin Islands
Virginia
Walt Disney World® & Orlando
Washington, D.C.
Washington State

FROMMER'S® DOLLAR-A-DAY GUIDES

Australia from $50 a Day
California from $70 a Day
Caribbean from $70 a Day
England from $75 a Day
Europe from $70 a Day

Florida from $70 a Day
Hawaii from $80 a Day
Ireland from $60 a Day
Italy from $70 a Day
London from $85 a Day

New York from $90 a Day
Paris from $80 a Day
San Francisco from $70 a Day
Washington, D.C. from $80 a Day

FROMMER'S® PORTABLE GUIDES

Acapulco, Ixtapa & Zihuatanejo
Amsterdam
Aruba
Australia's Great Barrier Reef
Bahamas
Berlin
Big Island of Hawaii
Boston
California Wine Country
Cancún
Charleston & Savannah
Chicago
Disneyland®
Dublin
Florence

Frankfurt
Hong Kong
Houston
Las Vegas
London
Los Angeles
Los Cabos & Baja
Maine Coast
Maui
Miami
New Orleans
New York City
Paris
Phoenix & Scottsdale

Portland
Puerto Rico
Puerto Vallarta, Manzanillo &
  Guadalajara
Rio de Janeiro
San Diego
San Francisco
Seattle
Sydney
Tampa & St. Petersburg
Vancouver
Venice
Virgin Islands
Washington, D.C.

FROMMER'S® NATIONAL PARK GUIDES

Banff & Jasper
Family Vacations in the National
  Parks
Grand Canyon

National Parks of the American
  West
Rocky Mountain

Yellowstone & Grand Teton
Yosemite & Sequoia/ Kings Canyon
Zion & Bryce Canyon

FROMMER'S® MEMORABLE WALKS

Chicago
London

New York
Paris

San Francisco
Washington, D.C.

FROMMER'S® GREAT OUTDOOR GUIDES

Arizona & New Mexico
New England

Northern California
Southern New England

Vermont & New Hampshire

SUZY GERSHMAN'S BORN TO SHOP GUIDES

Born to Shop: France
Born to Shop: Hong Kong,
  Shanghai & Beijing

Born to Shop: Italy
Born to Shop: London

Born to Shop: New York
Born to Shop: Paris

FROMMER'S® IRREVERENT GUIDES

Amsterdam
Boston
Chicago
Las Vegas
London

Los Angeles
Manhattan
New Orleans
Paris
Rome

San Francisco
Seattle & Portland
Vancouver
Walt Disney World®
Washington, D.C.

FROMMER'S® BEST-LOVED DRIVING TOURS

Britain
California
Florida
France

Germany
Ireland
Italy
New England

Northern Italy
Scotland
Spain
Tuscany & Umbria

HANGING OUT™ GUIDES

Hanging Out in England
Hanging Out in Europe

Hanging Out in France
Hanging Out in Ireland

Hanging Out in Italy
Hanging Out in Spain

THE UNOFFICIAL GUIDES®

Bed & Breakfasts and Country
  Inns in:
  California
  Great Lakes States
  Mid-Atlantic
  New England
  Northwest
  Rockies
  Southeast
  Southwest
Best RV & Tent Campgrounds in:
  California & the West
  Florida & the Southeast
  Great Lakes States
  Mid-Atlantic
  Northeast
  Northwest & Central Plains

  Southwest & South Central
    Plains
  U.S.A.
Beyond Disney
Branson, Missouri
California with Kids
Chicago
Cruises
Disneyland®
Florida with Kids
Golf Vacations in the Eastern U.S.
Great Smoky & Blue Ridge Region
Inside Disney
Hawaii
Las Vegas
London

Mid-Atlantic with Kids
Mini Las Vegas
Mini-Mickey
New England and New York with
  Kids
New Orleans
New York City
Paris
San Francisco
Skiing in the West
Southeast with Kids
Walt Disney World®
Walt Disney World® for Grown-ups
Walt Disney World® with Kids
Washington, D.C.
World's Best Diving Vacations

SPECIAL-INTEREST TITLES

Frommer's Adventure Guide to Australia &
  New Zealand
Frommer's Adventure Guide to Central America
Frommer's Adventure Guide to India & Pakistan
Frommer's Adventure Guide to South America
Frommer's Adventure Guide to Southeast Asia
Frommer's Adventure Guide to Southern Africa
Frommer's Britain's Best Bed & Breakfasts and
  Country Inns
Frommer's Caribbean Hideaways
Frommer's Exploring America by RV
Frommer's Fly Safe, Fly Smart
Frommer's France's Best Bed & Breakfasts and
  Country Inns
Frommer's Gay & Lesbian Europe

Frommer's Italy's Best Bed & Breakfasts and
  Country Inns
Frommer's New York City with Kids
Frommer's Ottawa with Kids
Frommer's Road Atlas Britain
Frommer's Road Atlas Europe
Frommer's Road Atlas France
Frommer's Toronto with Kids
Frommer's Vancouver with Kids
Frommer's Washington, D.C., with Kids
Israel Past & Present
The New York Times' Guide to Unforgettable
  Weekends
Places Rated Almanac
Retirement Places Rated